WEST ACADEMIC PUBLISHING'S EMERITUS ADVISORY BOARD

JESSE H. CHOPER
Professor of Law and Dean Emeritus
University of California, Berkeley

LARRY D. KRAMER
President, William and Flora Hewlett Foundation

GRANT S. NELSON
Professor of Law Emeritus, Pepperdine University
Professor of Law Emeritus, University of California, Los Angeles

JAMES J. WHITE
Robert A. Sullivan Emeritus Professor of Law
University of Michigan

AF711111

WEST ACADEMIC PUBLISHING'S LAW SCHOOL ADVISORY BOARD

MARK C. ALEXANDER
Arthur J. Kania Dean and Professor of Law
Villanova University Charles Widger School of Law

JOSHUA DRESSLER
Distinguished University Professor Emeritus
Michael E. Moritz College of Law, The Ohio State University

MEREDITH J. DUNCAN
Professor of Law
University of Houston Law Center

RENÉE MCDONALD HUTCHINS
Dean & Professor of Law
University of Maryland Carey School of Law

RENEE KNAKE JEFFERSON
Joanne and Larry Doherty Chair in Legal Ethics &
Professor of Law, University of Houston Law Center

ORIN S. KERR
William G. Simon Professor of Law
University of California, Berkeley

JONATHAN R. MACEY
Professor of Law,
Yale Law School

DEBORAH JONES MERRITT
Distinguished University Professor,
John Deaver Drinko/Baker & Hostetler Chair in Law Emerita
Michael E. Moritz College of Law, The Ohio State University

ARTHUR R. MILLER
University Professor and Chief Justice Warren E. Burger Professor of
Constitutional Law and the Courts, New York University

A. BENJAMIN SPENCER
Dean & Trustee Professor of Law
William & Mary Law School

THE INTERNATIONAL CRIMINAL COURT

IN A NUTSHELL®

LEILA NADYA SADAT
James Carr Professor of International Criminal Law, Washington University in St. Louis School of Law
Special Adviser on Crimes Against Humanity to the ICC Prosecutor (2013–2023)

PATRICK KEENAN
Professor of Law and Hurd Faculty Scholar, University of Illinois College of Law

MILENA STERIO
Charles R. Emrick Jr.-Calfee Halter & Griswold Professor of Law, Cleveland State University College of Law

WEST ACADEMIC

The publisher is not engaged in rendering legal or other professional advice, and this publication is not a substitute for the advice of an attorney. If you require legal or other expert advice, you should seek the services of a competent attorney or other professional.

Nutshell Series, In a Nutshell and the Nutshell Logo are trademarks registered in the U.S. Patent and Trademark Office.

© 2024 LEG, Inc. d/b/a West Academic
860 Blue Gentian Road, Suite 350
Eagan, MN 55121
1-877-888-1330

West, West Academic Publishing, and West Academic are trademarks of West Publishing Corporation, used under license.

Published in the United States of America

ISBN: 978-1-63460-532-8

PREFACE AND ACKNOWLEDGEMENTS

The purpose of this book is to provide a guide to the structure and practice of the International Criminal Court. It was written for the beginning student as well as practitioners, policymakers, and journalists who might wish to acquaint themselves with this important and complex global institution. We have endeavored to present a text that is comprehensive but does not overwhelm the reader. Hopefully we have achieved the correct balance.

This book was completed as the international community celebrated the 25th anniversary of the Rome Statute's adoption, marking an important milestone in international law and practice. While the International Criminal Court has its critics, the central importance of the institution in a world of increasing global authoritarianism and great power conflict cannot be overstated. The ten chapters of the book cover the basic features of the Court's operation and establishment, as well as its relationship with key global and national stakeholders, including the United Nations and the United States.

Chapter 1 is an essential precursor to the chapters that follow, explaining the process and purpose of the Court's establishment and some of its current and future challenges. Chapters 2, 3 and 4 describe the key jurisdictional features of the Court, how situations and cases come before it, the organs of the

Court, including the defense, and the relationship between the Court and the United Nations. Chapters 5 and 6 address the substantive law of the Court, individual criminal responsibility for the commission of ICC crimes, how such crimes are proven, and what defenses are available to the accused. Both Chapters 7 and 8 focus on the procedural law of the Court: Chapter 7 addresses preliminary examinations and investigations, while Chapter 8 discusses the pre-trial, trial, and appeals processes. Chapter 9 focuses on victims, including their participation rights, support, safety, and reparations. Perhaps the most important stakeholders of the Court are the victims for whom it seeks to provide relief, redress, and justice. It thus seemed critical to have an entire chapter focused upon them. Finally, Chapter 10 addresses the relationship between the International Criminal Court and the United States, surveying the attitude of various U.S. administrations to the ICC, as well as the possibility of complementarity with the U.S. legal system.

As scholars and researchers, we are well aware that the International Criminal Court is not the only institution addressing international and transnational crimes. Likewise, criminal law is not the only tool that policymakers can use to address conflict and criminality. This book is not intended to replace thoughtful conversations about transitional justice, the relationship between peace and justice, and the challenge of achieving universal justice in a world of power politics. Rather, the book offers the reader the opportunity to explore how the ICC works in practice; and serves as a guide to an important, and relatively poorly understood, global institution in an effort to render it more accessible.

We have written the book in what we hope is a conversational style and have included references at the end of each Chapter to both the literature supporting the Chapter and other sources that we have found helpful. These may serve as background reading, or provide the reader with a more in-depth examination of the issues addressed. The literature on the ICC is vast, and we apologize in advance for omitting many fine books and articles for the sake of brevity.

Finally, one of our objectives in writing the book is our hope that a better understanding of the institution will lead to greater acceptance of it and enthusiasm for it. The literature on the ICC can be extraordinarily complex and technical, sometimes overshadowing the fact that the purpose of the institution is to provide and to promote justice. We have each worked with the Court, or on the issues it addresses, in various capacities. All three of us believe in the central mission of the ICC: to provide a global institution that can deliver and promote justice for individuals suffering the commission of atrocity crimes around the globe.

As of this writing, 124 countries are ICC States Parties, and 129 are under the jurisdiction of the Court. Although most countries in Africa, Europe, Latin America, and North America have joined, gaps remain. Particularly problematic is the absence of three permanent members of the U.N. Security Council—China, Russia and the United States—from the Court. Our hope is that one day, all States will join the Court and commit themselves to preventing and punishing aggression, crimes against humanity, genocide, and war crimes.

Finally, we would like to thank the many individuals who made this book possible or who inspired us to write it. Washington University Law students Kelly Adams, Markus Baldermann, Olivia Brick, Kate Falconer, Jack Hueseman, and Leheng ("Tenny") Xu provided indispensable research support and citation checking, as did Washington University Law Librarians Tove Klovning and Hyla Bondareff. We are also indebted to Jennifer Allison who did a terrific job copy-editing the text, as well as to Mac Soto, our editor at West Publishing who helped us through the process. The wonderful law librarians at Cleveland State University College of Law and the University of Illinois College of Law provided valuable research support as well.

In addition to her family, and especially her husband Andrew, son Sam, and daughters Kyra and Emily, who endured many late nights while this book was being finished, Leila would particularly like to thank the late Prof. M. Cherif Bassiouni, who served as Chair of the Drafting Committee for the Rome Diplomatic Conference, and former Nuremberg Prosecutors Benjamin Ferencz and Whitney Harris for their friendship, inspiration, and leadership. They believed in the dream of global justice and a permanent international criminal court during a time when such an idea seemed impossible to imagine. Leila would also like to thank Chief

Prosecutor Fatou Bensouda, and her successor, Karim A.A. Khan, K.C., for the privilege of serving as their Special Adviser on Crimes Against Humanity.

In addition to his daughters Claire and Madeleine, who offered great patience and support while he worked on this book, Patrick would like to thank Stephen B. Bright, whose inspiration and mentorship at the Southern Center for Human Rights showed how the law can be a tool for justice for all.

Milena would like to thank her husband, Frederic, and her children, Luca, Lara, and Elena, for their patience and support during the research, drafting, and editing process related to the writing of this book.

OUTLINE

TABLE OF CASES

References are to Pages

THE INTERNATIONAL CRIMINAL COURT

IN A NUTSHELL®

CHAPTER 1

ESTABLISHMENT OF THE INTERNATIONAL CRIMINAL COURT

I. INTRODUCTION

On July 17, 1998, a Statute for a new, permanent International Criminal Court was adopted at a United Nations Diplomatic Conference. The successful outcome of the negotiations was unexpected, and when the Conference opened in Rome, Italy, on June 15, 1998, it was unclear whether it would lead to a concrete outcome. Twenty-five years later, although the ICC faces many challenges, it occupies permanent premises in The Hague and has become a key global institution, with 124 States Parties.

II. HISTORY OF THE COURT'S ESTABLISHMENT FROM WORLD WAR I–WORLD WAR II

§ 1-1 INTRODUCTION: THE TRIAL OF THE KAISER AND THE POST-WORLD WAR I EXPERIENCE

Although precedent for the trial of what are known today as war crimes and crimes against humanity can be traced back many centuries, to the 1474 trial of Peter von Hagenbach for atrocities committed serving the Duke of Burgundy, the use of established international courts and tribunals as fora to try these and other crimes is of relatively modern vintage.

In 1919, at the end of World War I, the Preliminary Peace Conference established a Commission on the Responsibility of the Authors of the War and on the Enforcement of Penalties, charged with inquiring into the "responsibility of the authors of the war." The 15-member Commission recommended that an international "high tribunal" be created by the peace treaty that would settle the conflict, and that it would provide for the trial of "all enemy persons alleged to have been guilty of offences against the laws and customs of war and the laws of humanity." Those individuals would also be excluded from any amnesties to which the warring parties agreed. The Commission's proposal excluded trial for the charge of "waging of a war of aggression," arguing that it was not yet directly contrary to positive law, although it was "conduct which the public conscience reproves and which history will condemn."

The U.S. members of the Commission objected to the references to the "laws of humanity," as well as to any trial of the Kaiser Wilhelm (William II of Hohenzollern), arguing that a head of State could not be held judicially liable for the commission of a crime, but was accountable only to the political authority of his country. The provisions of the Treaty of Versailles, entered into on June 28, 1919, represented a compromise on these points. Specifically, Article 227 of the treaty provided for the arraignment of Kaiser Wilhelm for the "supreme offence against international morality and the sanctity of treaties." He was to be judged by a tribunal guided by the "highest motives of international policy" (as opposed to international law). Kaiser Wilhelm avoided arrest, however, and lived in exile in The Netherlands, which refused his extradition, arguing that his surrender would violate Dutch neutrality.

Article 228 of the Versailles Treaty provided for war crimes trials (but not for violations of the "laws of humanity") of other Germans, and the Allies submitted an initial list of 900 accused to German authorities. The German government refused to surrender anyone, proposing instead to try a limited number of individuals in their national courts (before the *Reichsgericht*) in Leipzig. Only twelve men were tried. Of them, five were found not guilty, and the remaining seven received minimal prison sentences ranging from six months (for mistreating prisoners of war) to four years (for sinking a hospital ship and machine-gunning the survivors).

Thus ended the first modern experience with international criminal justice. Although public opinion in Germany considered the Leipzig trials excessively harsh, undoubtedly perceiving them to be a form of "victor's justice," outside Germany the trials were viewed as a disappointment. They did, however, set a precedent for what was to come. In the 1920s, expert bodies, including the Committee of Jurists of the League of Nations, the International Association of Penal Law, and the International Law Association proposed the creation of a permanent international criminal court, but these proposals did not immediately bear fruit. Likewise, an international terrorism court was proposed in a 1937 treaty that never entered into force. Some experts objected to these proposals on the grounds of state sovereignty and argued that alleged perpetrators had a right to be judged under domestic law and by their compatriots. They agreed with the U.S. view that heads of state could not be held liable by the international community and were accountable only to their own citizens. Others argued that there was no international criminal code with which potential defendants could be charged. Finally, some argued that resort to a court, rather than preventing war, might make matters worse, as the lawyers would "begin a war of accusation and counter accusation and recrimination," which could prevent soldiers and sailors from opposite sides from shaking hands and settling matters peaceably. These arguments continue to surface today.

§ 1-2 THE NUREMBERG AND TOKYO TRIALS

The failure of existing rules and institutions to prevent a second "great war" in the twentieth century undoubtedly provided the motivation for some to take a more serious look at war crimes trials following the Second World War. The Allies announced their intentions to hold trials in declarations issued at St. James in 1942 and in Moscow in 1943. However, holding a trial of Axis prisoners once the war ended was not a foregone conclusion. Winston Churchill wanted to execute the Nazi leaders, and President Roosevelt's cabinet was divided. Morgenthau, the Secretary of the Treasury, called for the execution of "German arch-criminals;" while Stimson, the Secretary of War, advocated for trials. The Soviet

Union strongly favored trials, especially for the crime of aggressive war. Stimson's view prevailed, and on August 8, 1945, the four allied powers adopted the Charter of the International Military Tribunal at Nuremberg (IMT).

The Nuremberg Charter provided for the trial of the "major war criminals of the Axis powers," and included three crimes in its jurisdiction: crimes against peace (for the waging of an aggressive war), war crimes, and crimes against humanity. Twenty-three accused were indicted, twenty-two were tried, nineteen were convicted, and three were acquitted. Twelve were sentenced to death and executed by hanging. The remainder received prison sentences ranging from ten years to life. Although the proceedings were dubbed a form of "victor's justice," their procedural fairness, together with the fact that twenty-three nations ratified the Nuremberg Charter, ensured their continued importance and legacy. Moreover, the principles established by the Charter and the International Military Tribunal itself were adopted by the newly created United Nations in 1946, and subsequently codified by the U.N. International Law Commission (ILC).

The Tokyo Tribunal has had a much different legacy. Following Japan's unconditional surrender on September 2, 1945, a tribunal like the IMT was established by proclamation of the Supreme Commander of the Allied Powers, General Douglas MacArthur, as modified by the Far Eastern Council, whose membership included, in addition to the four Allied Powers, China, Australia, Canada, the

Netherlands, the Philippines, and New Zealand. The Charter of the Tokyo Tribunal (also known as the International Military Tribunal for the Far East or the IMTFE) largely tracked the Nuremberg Tribunal. The bench was expanded to encompass eleven members (the Far Eastern Council member states, plus India), and the rules provided that the ultimate appeal in all cases was to General MacArthur. The IMTFE tried twenty-eight Japanese military and political leaders. Seven were sentenced to death, three died of natural causes or were found mentally unfit, and eighteen received prison sentences. The proceedings resulted in a lengthy judgment and a stinging dissent by Justice Radhabinod Pal, from India, who objected to the exclusion of crimes committed by the Allied Powers and to the lack of judges from the vanquished nations on the bench. These issues were compounded by the doubtful procedural fairness of the trial itself, and the fact that the proceedings were not originally made available to researchers. Thus, unlike the Nuremberg Tribunal, the Tokyo Tribunal had little positive effect on the development of international criminal law, although recent scholarship has revived interest in the proceedings.

§ 1-3 THE ROAD TO THE ROME STATUTE, 1945–1998

Following the Second World War, the United Nations embarked upon a codification and institution-building effort. The Convention on the Prevention and Punishment of the Crime of Genocide was adopted by the General Assembly in 1948, and the four Geneva Conventions relating to the conduct of war and the protection of war victims followed one year later. In a resolution accompanying the adoption of the Genocide Convention, the General Assembly invited the International Law Commission (ILC) to "study the desirability and possibility of establishing an international judicial organ for the trial of persons charged with genocide or other crimes." Thus instructed, the ILC embarked upon a fifty-year-long odyssey, voting initially in 1950 to support the desirability and feasibility of creating an international criminal court, only to have the question of the court's establishment taken away from it by the General Assembly, which handed it over to the Committee on International Criminal Jurisdiction composed of the representatives of Member States. Although this Committee and a successor committee produced drafts of a statute for a new international criminal court, their work was shelved as the Cold War made consensus impossible to achieve.

In 1989, the question of a permanent international criminal court was resurrected following the collapse of the Soviet Union and the new possibility of constructive action at the United Nations. The General Assembly instructed the International Law Commission to proceed with its work on international criminal law and the ILC adopted a new version of a Draft Code of Crimes in 1991. In 1992, it established a Working Group which produced a report that laid out the basis for the establishment of an international criminal court. The General Assembly responded positively to this proposal, and the ILC adopted a final draft statute in 1994 that served as the text upon which negotiations of the International Criminal Court Statute could proceed.

As the development of the ICC's statute was taking place, war in the former Yugoslavia and the Rwandan genocide led to the establishment of *ad hoc* international criminal tribunals to address the atrocities committed during those conflicts. Those tribunals were established by United Nations Security Council resolutions, rather than an international treaty. They exercised jurisdiction over the commission of war crimes, crimes against humanity, and genocide, but not the crime of aggression (crimes against peace). The relative success of these *ad hoc* institutions—which indicted more than 250 accused during their more than twenty-five years of existence—led to the establishment of "hybrid" international criminal tribunals to address the Sierra Leone civil war, the Cambodian genocide, and crimes committed during the conflict leading to East Timorese independence in 1999, as well as the creation of the Special Tribunal for Lebanon, which was charged with addressing the assassination of Lebanese Prime Minister Rafiq Hariri in 2005.

The ILC's 1994 draft of the ICC statute included five categories (but not definitions) of crimes: (1) genocide, (2) crimes against humanity, (3) serious violations of the laws and customs applicable in armed conflict, (4) aggression, and (5) "treaty crimes" set forth in "suppression conventions" that would be set forth in an annex. The treaty crimes category included serious offenses, such as the grave breaches regime of the 1949 Geneva Conventions and Protocol I to those Conventions, aircraft hijacking, apartheid, crimes against internationally protected persons, hostage taking, torture, offenses against the safety of maritime navigation, and narcotics trafficking. The 1994 draft was premised on a new principle: the notion of "complementarity" which meant that the proposed court would complement national criminal justice systems which would have priority over cases that might otherwise come to the court. Specifically, the 1994 draft conditioned all cases upon the consent of either the implicated State or the Security Council, except in cases of genocide, over which the jurisdiction of the proposed court was automatic. Finally, the 1994 draft suggested that the prosecutor and deputy prosecutor could be elected on a "stand-by" basis and that the judges—except for the President—would only be paid when actually sitting.

The General Assembly convened an *Ad Hoc* Committee to discuss the ILC's 1994 draft, and subsequently established a Preparatory Committee to begin the arduous process—both technical and political—of developing a statute acceptable not only to U.N. Member States, but also to civil society. Composed of State representatives, the Preparatory Committee held fifteen weeks of official and inter-sessional meetings between March 1996 and April 1998. The text that emerged from these protracted and intense negotiations, which were closely followed by a global coalition of non-governmental organizations (NGOs), was a complex document containing more than 1300 "bracketed" provisions, representing divergences of views between governments. When the Rome Diplomatic Conference convened on June 15, 1998, it faced a herculean task: to bring the 165 States in attendance to a consensus on several points, including the court's ultimate establishment, the desirability of which was far from unanimously agreed, as well as the principles under which it would operate, the crimes it would punish, the jurisdictional reach and strength of the court's statute, and its enforcement capabilities.

III. THE ROME DIPLOMATIC CONFERENCE OF PLENIPOTENTIARIES

§ 1-4 THE ORGANIZATION OF THE ROME CONFERENCE

In the summer of 1998, the text of what we now know as the Rome Statute for the International Criminal Court (Rome Statute) was negotiated and adopted. The mood of the conference alternated between anxiety and exhilaration as delegates took up the extraordinarily complex draft text submitted by the Preparatory Committee and attempted to achieve consensus on the difficult issues that needed to be addressed.

The negotiations undoubtedly would have failed but for several propitious factors. Perhaps the most important of these was the emergence of a group of approximately sixty "like-minded" States, which had started as a caucus in 1994 and emerged as a formal and powerful group of countries committed to the court's ultimate establishment based upon certain core principles. There also emerged a strong NGO coalition—the Coalition for the International Criminal Court (CICC)—which engaged in a tireless campaign in support of the Court. The CICC disseminated crucial information during the Diplomatic Conference to small delegations that could not keep abreast of all of the activities of the Conference's working groups and provided daily updates on the status of negotiations by email, in a newsletter, and on the radio.

Strong leadership played a significant role as well. Key U.N. leaders, including former Secretary General Kofi Annan and Under-Secretary General for Legal Affairs Hans Corell, championed the court. In addition, able and experienced diplomats undertook the negotiations, most of whom had also participated in the Preparatory Committee meetings and understood each other and the issues well. Finally, delegates had recent precedent on their side. The successful establishment of the *ad hoc* international criminal tribunals for the former Yugoslavia and Rwanda had demonstrated the feasibility of conducting modern international criminal proceedings.

§ 1-5 KEY FEATURES OF THE NEGOTIATIONS

Those charged with drafting what became the Rome Statute had to resolve a host of contentious legal and organizational issues. One issue that proved relatively easy was the complementarity principle: delegates agreed that the court should be complementary to domestic courts instead of taking precedence over them. Less clear, however, was the appropriate approach to the court's jurisdiction. Some argued that it should be "inherent," meaning that States joining the treaty would automatically be subject to the proposed court's jurisdiction. Others argued that States should be required to opt into each particular case before jurisdiction could attach. Drafters also disagreed with how cases should come to the court. Some argued that the Security Council should function as a filter, giving the Security Council's permanent members a veto over all future cases. This approach was rejected by most other U.N. Member States. The general issue of what the relationship between the court and the United Nations would be was also difficult, as it was determined that the court should be created as a free-standing institution rather than a U.N. organ.

Drafters also faced doctrinal issues. They had to determine whether war crimes committed in non-international armed conflicts would be included. They debated whether and how to include the crime of aggression in the statute. And they debated how to best accommodate the interests of victims and witnesses, prosecutors, and defendants, as well as how to allocate power and functions among them. Indeed, some of the debates became so fractious that NGO representatives, who were generally allowed access to meetings, were asked to leave as the Conference's leaders endeavored to achieve consensus.

§ 1-6 OUTCOME OF THE ROME CONFERENCE

On July 17, 1998, after five weeks of difficult negotiations, the Conference leaders (the "Bureau") proposed a compromise text that they hoped would accommodate the various positions represented. While there was general agreement among the delegates on the proposed court's principal features, major sticking points remained. On the final day of the negotiations, both India and the United States attempted to undo the Bureau's "package" proposal by offering amendments. These were met with "no-action" motions proposed by Norway, which carried overwhelmingly. The U.S. delegation had argued throughout the negotiations that the statute should not permit any trials of individuals without the consent of their State of nationality unless the Security Council referred the case (thereby insulating U.S. nationals from prosecution before the Court). Not willing to accept the defeat of its amendments, the United States then called for a vote on the Statute as a whole. The United States lost the vote, with 120 States voting in favor of the statute, 7 opposed, and 21 States abstaining. According to close observers of the vote, which was unrecorded, China, Iraq, Israel, Qatar, Syria, and Yemen joined the United States in opposing the Statute. Delegates supporting the Statute—and NGO representatives—erupted in cheering and crying as the tensions of the past five weeks gave way to the realization that a seventy-five yearlong effort had just borne fruit.

IV. WHY WAS THE INTERNATIONAL CRIMINAL COURT ESTABLISHED?

As the Preamble of the Rome Statute notes, the establishment of the Court was a response to the victimization of millions of children, women, and men by the commission of "unimaginable atrocities" over the course of the twentieth century. The Court's aim is to "put an end to impunity for the perpetrators" of these atrocities, which are the "most serious crimes of concern to the international community as a whole," thereby contributing to the prevention of these crimes.

Thus, like all criminal courts, the ICC aims both at the specific deterrence of particular offenders and, over time, the general deterrence of future perpetrators. Because it is a permanent court that is not just responsive to particular outbreaks of mass criminality, either during armed conflict or in peacetime, it may also play a role in atrocity prevention, as early empirical studies have suggested. Some scholars continue to maintain that the presence of international criminal courts and tribunals may cause defendants to double down on the commission of crimes for fear of being arrested, particularly with the partial foreclosure of exile as a viable option. Yet arrest warrants have generally been shown to have a positive effect (over time) in conflict situations. Like other international criminal courts and tribunals, the ICC also endeavors to enhance both national and international efforts to combat crimes, establish the truth of what took place, and provide reparations to victims, thereby making an important contribution to the maintenance of international peace and security.

V. THE ROME STATUTE SYSTEM

§ 1-7 OVERVIEW OF THE STATUTE AND ENTRY INTO FORCE

The negotiators of the treaty establishing the International Criminal Court created an institution almost breathtaking in its complexity. The Court's 128-article Statute is divided into thirteen parts, each addressing various features of the Court's establishment, jurisdiction, or operation. The Statute is supplemented by important ancillary documents negotiated following the Rome Conference (but prior to the Statute's entry into force), including the Elements of Crimes, the Court's Rules of Procedure and Evidence, a Relationship Agreement between the Court and the United Nations, an agreement on the privileges and immunities of the Court, and the rules of procedure for the Court's Assembly of States Parties (ASP) that oversees the Court's management and oversight.

The drafting of these ancillary documents was taken up by a Preparatory Commission that was composed of representatives of Member States which had signed the Final Act of the Rome Diplomatic Conference and other States which were invited to participate in the Rome Conference. Many Preparatory Commission delegates represented their governments during both the Preparatory Committee meetings that had prepared the draft

Statute taken up in Rome, and during the Diplomatic Conference. This facilitated the work of preparing the Statute's entry into force, as these delegates had worked together on the Court's Statute for years.

The Statute attained the requisite ratifications needed for entry into force with the deposit of eleven ratifications in April 2002, bringing the total number of States Parties to sixty-six. On July 1, 2002, the Rome Statute entered into force.

§ 1-8 ORGANIZATIONAL STRUCTURE

The Court's organizational structure is much more complex than those of the international tribunals that preceded it. This is addressed briefly in this Chapter and again in Chapter 3. The four organs of the Court are the Presidency, the Judiciary (composed of three divisions: Appeals, Trial, and Pre-Trial Divisions), the Office of the Prosecutor, and the Registry. In addition, the Assembly of States Parties (ASP), which was established by Part 11 of the Statute, oversees the operations of both the Court (including its budget) and the Trust Fund for Victims, which was created in accordance with a decision of the ASP under Article 79. The Trust Fund for Victims administers and distributes funds and other forms of assistance for the benefit of victims of crimes within the Court's jurisdiction. It advocates for victims and mobilizes individuals, institutions with resources, and the goodwill of those in power for the benefit of victims and their communities. As of the summer of 2023, the Court has an annual budget of approximately € 170 million and more than 900 staff members from approximately 100 States.

§ 1-9 THE JUDICIARY

The Court has eighteen judges, nominated and elected by secret ballot by the ASP. ICC elections are complex because of the requirements imposed by both the Rome Statute and the ASP procedural rules, and multiple rounds of balloting are typically required in order to complete them. Each judge must be a national of an ICC State Party (Article 36(4)(b)) and be a person of "high moral character, impartiality and integrity" who possesses the qualifications required for appointment to his or her State's highest judicial office. Article 36 of the Statute requires the Assembly to "take into account" the need for gender balance, equitable geographical representation, and the representation of the principal legal systems of the world. Each judge serves one non-renewable nine-year term, and at least nine of the judges must have established competence and experience in criminal law and procedure (known as "List A" judges); while five must have competence and experience in relevant areas of international law (known as "List B" judges). Pursuant to Article 39 of the Statute, the judges organize themselves into Divisions upon their election, and elect the members of the Presidency. Five judges sit as members of the Appeals Chamber, which decides upon a Presiding Judge for each appeal. Three judges sit in each Trial Chamber and Pre-Trial Chamber, although the functions of the Pre-Trial Chamber may be carried out by a single judge if the Statute so provides. The Pre-Trial Chamber oversees the initiation of a case until confirmation of the charges against the accused, after which time the accused is committed to a Trial Chamber for trial.

The Presidency is one of the four organs of the Court, under Article 38 of the Statute. It is composed of the President and the First and Second Vice-Presidents, who serve for a term of three years or until the end of their respective terms of office as judges, whichever is earlier. They are elected by an absolute majority of the judges and are eligible for re-election. Under Article 38(3), the President's responsibility for the administration of the Court focuses on three principal areas: (1) the Court's judicial and legal functioning, including decisions constituting and assigning cases to Chambers and judicial review of certain decisions of the Registrar; (2) administration; and (3) external relations. However, the President does not provide administrative oversight to the Court's Office of the Prosecutor.

§ 1-10 THE OFFICE OF THE PROSECUTOR

Like the judges of the Court, pursuant to Article 42 of the Statute, the ICC Prosecutor and Deputy Prosecutor(s) are elected by the Assembly of States Parties and serve one non-renewable nine-year term. Although the Prosecutor and Deputy Prosecutor(s) must be of different nationalities from one another, unlike the judges they need not be nationals of an ICC State Party. Because the ICC Prosecutor drives the Court's caseload, it is not surprising that, during the Statute's negotiation both during and prior to Rome, the discussions related to the powers of the Prosecutor were quite contentious. One innovation of the ICC Statute is that the Prosecutor can initiate cases on his or her own initiative, using the *proprio motu* powers set forth in Article 15(1), and subject, of course, to the jurisdiction and admissibility requirements of the Statute.

As a response to concerns about potential prosecutorial overreach, the Statute contains extensive checks on the Prosecutor's power, including a requirement that a Pre-Trial Chamber authorize any investigation brought on the Prosecutor's own initiative only if it independently determines that there is a "reasonable basis" to proceed with an investigation and that crimes within the jurisdiction of the Court have been committed. Art. 15(4).

§ 1-11 THE REGISTRY

The Registry is the Court's administrative organ for non-judicial matters. Under Article 43 of the Statute, the Registrar, a full-time member of the Court, is elected by the judges for a five-year term and exercises his or her functions under the authority of the President of the Court. Although the Statute has little to say about either the Registrar or the Registry, this organ is by far the Court's largest, and it exercises a great deal of control over the Court's operations. The Registry is responsible for initiating staff regulations governing the Court's personnel, and for the establishment and operation of the

Victims and Witnesses Unit. In addition, it carries out the Court's outreach activities, is responsible for managing the Court's information technology infrastructure and, perhaps most importantly, supports the Court's defense counsel in its work, which includes creating and maintaining the list of defense attorneys from whom the accused may choose if counsel is to be provided.

VI. THE COURT'S CURRENT CASELOAD

§ 1-12 INVESTIGATIONS AND PRELIMINARY EXAMINATIONS

As of the summer of 2023, seventeen investigations involving sixteen situation countries have been opened at the ICC, and thirty-one cases have been brought. Six situations were referred to the Court by the States involved: the Central African Republic, Côte d'Ivoire, the Democratic Republic of the Congo, Mali, the State of Palestine, and Uganda. Two situations, Darfur (Sudan) and Libya, were referred to the ICC by the U.N. Security Council in 2005 and 2011, respectively. Pursuant to Article 15 of the Statute, the Office of the Prosecutor brought six situations *proprio motu*: Afghanistan, Bangladesh/Myanmar, Burundi, Georgia, Kenya, and the Philippines. Finally, a group of States Parties referred the situation involving Venezuela to the Court in 2018, and a second group of forty-three States referred the situation in Ukraine, following Russia's invasion of Ukraine on February 24, 2022.

Prior to opening a formal investigation, the Office of the Prosecutor, under Article 15(2) of the Rome Statute, may receive information from individuals or groups, States, intergovernmental organizations, or NGOs. He or she may also receive information from a State Party, the U.N. Security Council, or via a declaration from a non-State Party that it accepts the jurisdiction of the Court regarding the alleged commission of ICC crimes under Article 12(3). The Prosecutor will assess the information and decide whether to open a preliminary examination to determine whether or not there is a reasonable basis to open an investigation into the crimes. As of the summer of 2023, three preliminary examinations are ongoing (Democratic Republic of the Congo, Nigeria, and Venezuela II) and eight have been closed as the Prosecutor decided not to proceed. In 2013 the Office of the Prosecutor published a *Policy Paper on Preliminary Examinations* which set out the factors to be considered under Article 53(1) of the Rome Statute in determining whether there is a reasonable basis to proceed with an investigation. The *Policy Paper* states that preliminary examination activities "seek to contribute to the two overarching goals of the Rome Statute: the ending of impunity, by encouraging genuine national proceedings, and the prevention of crimes." INT'L CRIM. CT. OFF. OF THE PROSECUTOR, POLICY PAPER PRELIMINARY EXAMINATIONS, ¶ 16 (Nov. 2013). Preliminary examinations are addressed in more detail in Chapter 7.

§ 1-13 JUDICIAL PROCEEDINGS

In its first twenty-one years, the ICC has had thirty-one cases brought before it, some with multiple accused. It has convicted ten individuals and acquitted four. It has issued forty arrest warrants. Seventeen individuals have been detained and have appeared, and sixteen remain at large. Trials have taken longer than expected, and the addition of the pre-trial phase of the proceedings seems to have increased, rather than decreased, the time between arrest and the conclusion of trials. Several important reparations orders have been issued, and with the increase in activity at the Court due to the Ukraine situation, many States have seconded personnel to the Court, which is busier than ever.

VII. CURRENT AND FUTURE CHALLENGES

§ 1-14 LACK OF UNIVERSALITY AND STATE SUPPORT

With 124 States Parties, the ICC Statute has been widely ratified. Yet challenges remain. Three of the five permanent members of the U.N. Security Council have not ratified the Statute, and two, the United States and the Russian Federation, which signed the Statute, have given notice that they no longer intend to be bound by their signatures. India, Indonesia, and several other countries with large populations are also outside the Rome Statute system. This deprives the Court of financial and political support, and gives rise to allegations of double standards, particularly in the case of U.N.

Security Council referrals voted for by States that are not themselves parties to the Rome Statute.

Because all of the Court's early situations involved Africa, there was a significant backlash from the African Union and many African countries, which accused the ICC of double standards and, in its most extreme form, suggested that the Court represented yet another form of Western colonialism. At one point in 2016, three African States were poised to withdraw from the Court's jurisdiction; although two of those countries pulled back from that initiative, the pushback was a clear challenge to the ICC's legitimacy. The opening of investigations in non-African locations, including Afghanistan, the State of Palestine, the Philippines, Ukraine, and Venezuela, may have begun to change the perception of the Court in that regard.

§ 1-15 LENGTH OF PROCEEDINGS

The Court has also been accused of being too slow. It was initially thought that the addition of the Pre-Trial Chamber would assist with the streamlining of cases by doing more to prepare them for trial, thereby avoiding some of the procedural delays experienced at the *ad hoc* international criminal tribunals, which averaged three years between arrest and judgment. Thus far, however, the addition of the Pre-Trial Chamber seems not to have had this effect: in the *Lubanga* case, for example, which was the first case tried at the Court, the accused was transferred to The Hague on March 16, 2006, and the decision confirming the charges was issued in January 2007.

Trial did not begin until two years later, and the judgment was not issued until March 14, 2012, six years after arrest. Likewise, the *Katanga* case took nearly seven years between arrest and judgment. In contrast, the first case before the ICTY, *Prosecutor v. Duško Tadić*, took less than a year to try, and the trial judgment was rendered two years following the accused's transfer to the Tribunal. Prosecutor v. Duško Tadić, Case No. IT-94-1, *Judgment* (TC II, May 7, 1997).

An additional factor impacting the Court's efficiency may be the fact that the ICC is conceived of as a Court of last, not first resort. This gives both States and the accused the opportunity to challenge the admissibility of cases on the basis of complementarity, discussed below in Chapter 2, § 2-10. A recent study from the Nuremberg Academy concluded that ICC trial times were not disproportionately long, given their complexity, but that they could nonetheless be shortened and accelerated through the adoption of various measures.

§ 1-16 RESOURCE CHALLENGES

The ICC is funded through contributions by ICC States Parties. The ASP's Committee on Budget and Finance produces a draft budget, which is then approved by the ASP at its annual session each year. As the judicial and investigative operations of the Court have increased, States Parties have not provided resources proportionate to this uptick in activity. Most court-watchers believe this has hampered the ICC's ability to meet States' expectations. At the same time, States have complained that the Court must clearly demonstrate that it is meeting efficiency requirements and achieving success before they are willing to increase funding to it, noting their own precarious financial situations as a reason for restraint. The largest portion of the Court's budget is allocated to the Registry or administration of the Court (including payment of counsel for indigent accused)—this amounted to nearly € 76 million in 2020 (compared to € 12 million for the Judiciary and € 47 million for the Office of the Prosecutor).

Although international criminal justice is costly, the Court's approximately € 169 million (covering seventeen country-wide investigations) seems in line with expenditures by developed countries at the national level. For example, the trial of Timothy McVeigh who was accused of the Oklahoma City bombing in the United States was estimated at $ 13.8 million; the initial budget for the Bataclan terrorism trial in France was over € 60 million. These expenses do not include the costs of paying the judges, other ICC staff, translation services, investigations, witness protection programs and jail facilities covered by the ICC's annual budget.

§ 1-17 OBTAINING THE PRESENCE OF THE ACCUSED

As of this writing, the Court has also struggled with the arrest of its defendants, and sixteen remain at large, including, perhaps most famously, Russian

President Vladimir Putin and Minister Maria Lvova-Bulova. Because the Court cannot proceed against accused who are not physically present before it, obtaining the presence of the accused is critically important. The Court does not have its own police force and relies upon States for support. However, some States have refused to cooperate with the Court, and some accused continue to travel widely even following their indictments, such as former Sudanese President Omar Al-Bashir, who was indicted in 2009 and 2010 on charges of war crimes, crimes against humanity, and genocide. Following his indictment, President Al-Bashir visited not only non-States Parties, such as China, but even travelled to ICC States Parties, including South Africa.

§ 1-18 MANAGING EXPECTATIONS

The establishment of the Court in 1998 raised the expectations of victims and the international community that the age of impunity was over, and the commission of atrocities—especially against civilians—would stop. Since 1998, however, there has been continued conflict in many countries, and new situations have arisen that have resulted in hundreds of thousands of victims. While the ICC has given important hope to victim communities, it has been required, at the same time, to work within the limits of its judicial mandate. The Trust Fund for Victims, which is the first formal effort to attach reparations and material support to victims to an international criminal court, has helped to support victims, but there are more victims who need assistance than the TFV can support.

§ 1-19 THE 2020 INDEPENDENT EXPERT REPORT

In 2018, as the ICC celebrated the 20th anniversary of the Rome Statute's entry into force, criticism of the Court was increasing. A series of contentious judicial decisions and lengthy trials, together with the prosecution's seeming difficulties in achieving success in the courtroom, problems of state cooperation, and a lack of universal ratification of the Statute, caused the Court's President, on behalf of the principal officers of the Court, to request that the ASP conduct an "independent comprehensive expert review of the Court's performance." At its 18th Session, the ASP issued a mandate that a group of experts, chaired by Justice Richard Goldstone of South Africa, examine three clusters of issues: governance, the judiciary, and prosecution and investigation. The Independent Expert Review concluded its work and issued its final report on September 30, 2020. The report contains 384 recommendations and was taken up by the ASP at its 19th Session, in 2020. In response to the report, the ASP created an ICC Review Mechanism, which is continuing to work on reforms and improvements to the ICC's procedure, organs, and governance.

VIII. CONCLUSION

The International Criminal Court's establishment was an extraordinary achievement of the twentieth century. As the ICC approaches the 25th anniversary of the Statute's entry into force, it continues to face significant challenges. At the same time, the Court seems more essential than ever. As Portugal observed in the General Debate at the December 2022 session of the Assembly of States Parties, "the ICC . . . plays a central role in the fight against impunity, bringing justice to victims, and in the prevention of the commission of atrocity crimes, contributing, in a very significant way, to the advancement of the rule of law, and stable, peaceful societies." A key indicator of the Court's future will be how it handles the Ukraine situation. If it fails in Ukraine, it may lose State support. If it succeeds, meaning that it is able to bring cases within a reasonable period and prosecute them to a high degree of professionalism, without neglecting the other important situations on its docket, it will have done much to assure its future.

Selected Sources and Additional Reading

NEIL BOISTER & ROBERT CRYER, THE TOKYO INTERNATIONAL MILITARY TRIBUNAL: A REAPPRAISAL 17 (2008).

FANNY BENEDETTI, KARINE BONNEAU & JOHN L. WASHBURN, NEGOTIATING THE INTERNATIONAL CRIMINAL COURT 39 (2014).

WHITNEY R. HARRIS, TYRANNY ON TRIAL (2d ed., 1999).

FRANCINE HIRSCH, SOVIET JUDGMENT AT NUREMBERG (2020).

THE ELGAR COMPANION TO THE INTERNATIONAL CRIMINAL COURT (Margaret M. Deguzman & Valerie Oosterveld, eds., 2020).

THE INTERNATIONAL CRIMINAL COURT AND AFRICA (Charles Chernor Jalloh & Ilias Bantekas, 2017).

THE LEGISLATIVE HISTORY OF THE INTERNATIONAL CRIMINAL COURT (M. Cherif Bassiouni & William A. Schabas, eds., 2d ed. 2016).

LEILA NADYA SADAT, THE INTERNATIONAL CRIMINAL COURT AND THE TRANSFORMATION OF INTERNATIONAL LAW: JUSTICE FOR THE NEW MILLENNIUM (2002).

WILLIAM SCHABAS, THE INTERNATIONAL CRIMINAL COURT: A COMMENTARY ON THE ROME STATUTE (2d ed., 2016).

Laurent Barcelo, *Aux origines de la cour pénale internationale: le projet français de chambre criminelle internationale*, in GUERRES MONDIALES ET CONFLITS CONTEMPORAINS 103 (2006).

Geoff Dancy & Eric Wiebelhaus-Brahm, *The Impact of Criminal Prosecutions during Intrastate Conflict*, 55 J. PEACE RESEARCH 47 (2018).

Courtney Hillebrecht, *The Deterrent Effects of the International Criminal Court: Evidence from Libya*, 42 INT'L INTERACTIONS 616 (2016).

Philippe Kirsch, The Work of the Preparatory Commission, in THE INTERNATIONAL CRIMINAL COURT: ELEMENTS OF CRIMES AND RULES OF PROCEDURE AND EVIDENCE xiv (Roy S. Lee, ed., 2001).

Leila Nadya Sadat, *Summer in Rome, Spring in the Hague, Winter in Washington?: U.S. Policy Towards the International Criminal Court*, 21 WIS. INT'L L. J. 557 (2003).

Leila [Wexler] Sadat, The Proposed Permanent International Criminal Court: An Appraisal, 29 CORNELL INT'L L. J. 665 (1996).

Leila Nadya Sadat & S. Richard Carden, *The New International Criminal Court: An Uneasy Revolution*, 88 GEO. L. J. 381 (2000).

Commission on the Responsibility of the Authors of the War and on Enforcement of Penalties: Report presented to the Preliminary Peace Conference, 14 AM. J. INT'L L. 95 (1920).

Final Act of the United Nations Diplomatic Conference of Plenipotentiaries on the Establishment of the International Criminal Court on 17 July 1998, Annex I, Resolution F, U.N. Doc. A/CONF.183/10 (1998).

G.A. Res. 177(II), U.N. GAOR, 2d Sess., 123d plen. mtg. at 111–12, U.N. Doc. A/519 (1947).

International Criminal Tribunal for the former Yugoslavia, Weekly Press Briefing (Jan. 15, 2003), http://www.icty.org/sid/3446.

International Law Association Draft Statute for an International Criminal Court (1926).

International Military Tribunal (Nuremberg), Judgment and Sentence (October 1, 1946) reprinted in 41 AM. J. INT'L L. 172 (1947).

International Nuremberg Principles Academy, Length of the Proceedings at the International Criminal Court (Sept. 2022), https://www.nuremberg academy.org/projects/detail/adf9bc613be04825aa302

997f7aa35c6/length-of-the-proceedings-at-the-international-criminal-court-25/.

Int'l Crim. Ct., Assembly of States Parties Resolution ICC-ASP/21/Res.1, Proposed Programme Budget for 2023 of the International Criminal Court (Dec. 9, 2022).

INT'L CRIM. CT. OFF. OF THE PROSECUTOR, POLICY PAPER ON PRELIMINARY EXAMINATIONS (Nov. 2013), https://www.icc-cpi.int/sites/default/files/iccdocs/otp/OTP-Policy_Paper_Preliminary_Examinations_2013-ENG.pdf.

Principles of International Law Recognized in the Charter of Nuremberg and in the Judgment of the Tribunal, U.N. GAOR, 5th sess., Supp. No. 12, at 11, U.N. Doc. A/1316 (1950).

Report on the Completion Strategy of the International Criminal Tribunal for Rwanda, U.N. Doc. S/2009/247 (May 14, 2009).

Statement of Portugal, Twenty-first Session of the ICC Assembly of States Parties, December 2022, https://asp.icc-cpi.int/sites/asp/files/2022-12/ASP21.GD_.PRT_.05.12.pdf.

Study by the International Law Commission of the Question of an International Criminal Jurisdiction, G.A. Res. 260B(III), U.N. GAOR 6th Comm., 3d Sess., 179th plen. Mtg., at 177, U.N. Doc. A/810 (1948).

CHAPTER 2

JURISDICTION, ADMISSIBILITY, AND REFERRALS TO THE COURT

I. INTRODUCTION

A challenging aspect of the Rome Statute's negotiation was identifying the situations and cases that fall within the Court's jurisdiction and are admissible. The relevant provisions are found in Part 2 of the Statute. Articles 5–8 *bis* set forth the Court's subject matter or "prescriptive" jurisdiction (jurisdiction *ratione materiae*); Article 11 defines its temporal jurisdiction (jurisdiction *ratione temporis*); Articles 12–14 set out referral mechanisms and the preconditions to the exercise of jurisdiction by the Court, which also touch upon the Court's geographic jurisdiction (jurisdiction *ratione loci*); and Article 26 covers the Court's personal jurisdiction (jurisdiction *ratione personae*).

Article 17 elaborates the Court's admissibility requirements, which, in addition to other elements, embodies the principle of "complementarity," meaning that the ICC is a court of last, not first, resort. Under Article 17, a case at the ICC becomes inadmissible if it is being investigated or prosecuted by a State with jurisdiction over it, if the accused has already been tried for the same conduct, or if the case is not of sufficient gravity.

Finally, Articles 14–16, 18, and 19 detail the procedural mechanisms by which situations are referred to the Court by different parties and can be withdrawn from the Court by the Security Council. They also lay out the manner in which jurisdiction and admissibility may be challenged by the accused and States. Over time, the Office of the Prosecutor has developed policy papers detailing how cases proceed from communications of alleged ICC crimes under Article 15, through a preliminary process to evaluate jurisdictional and admissibility known as the "preliminary examination phase," and then to investigation and trial. This process is explored in more detail in Chapters 7 and 8.

II. NATURE OF THE COURT'S JURISDICTION

The jurisdiction of the International Criminal Court is of the same lineage and founded on the basic core principles expressed in the Charter of the International Military Tribunal at Nuremberg (IMT) and the Statutes of the Yugoslavia and Rwanda Tribunals created by the Security Council. Like the IMT, the ICC was established by a treaty and is an international judicial body, exercising jurisdiction "on behalf of the international community" which, as Egon Schwelb wrote in 1946, "was, and is now, represented for all practical purposes by the United Nations." This is expressed in Article 4 of the Rome Statute which provides that the Court shall have an independent legal personality and the legal capacity necessary for the exercise of its functions and the fulfilment of its purposes.

Thus, like other international criminal courts and tribunals that preceded it, the ICC was created to be an international court exercising jurisdiction over international crimes. Under the Nuremberg principles codified by the International Law Commission following World War II, this meant that it was enforcing law created by the international community (in the form of international crimes, created by treaty or customary international law) against individuals accused of violating this law, who could not plead their national law in defense or assert their immunity even if they were high ranking government officials. Thus, the International Criminal Court's jurisdiction, like the jurisdiction of other international courts, rests on a universalist foundation, a concept sometimes referred to as constituting the *ius puniendi* (right to punish) of the international community. For this reason, is it is correct to say that the ICC exercises universal (international) jurisdiction, but this universality is only relative as it is limited by the Rome Statute itself and, as a practical matter, by the fact that only 123 States as of this writing (2023) have joined the Court. As the ICC Appeals Chamber recently confirmed in its judgment regarding the arrest warrants issued by the Court against Sudan's former President, Omar Al-Bashir, international courts, "when adjudicating international crimes, do not act on behalf of a particular State or States. . . [but] on behalf of the international community as a whole." Prosecutor v. Omar Hassan Ahmad Al-Bashir, Case No. ICC-02/05-01/09, *Judgment in the Jordan Referral re Al-Bashir Appeal*, ¶ 115 (AC, May 6, 2019). Questions regarding the appropriateness of the Court's jurisdiction in a particular case or over a particular situation are governed by international law and the Rome Statute itself, and, under the principle of *Kompetenz Kompetenz* (in German) or *la compétence de la compétence* (in French), it is the Court itself that rules upon challenges to its own jurisdiction. Request Under Regulation 46(3) of the Regulations of the Court, Case No. ICC-RoC46(3)-01/18-37, *Decision on the Prosecution's Request for a Ruling on Jurisdiction under Article 19(3) of the Statute*, ¶ 30 (PTC I, Sept. 6, 2018).

In considering the jurisdictional regime of the Rome Statute, it is useful to recognize that the term "jurisdiction" or *compétence* (in French) has three separate components: prescriptive, adjudicative, and enforcement jurisdiction. As outlined in Section 401 of the *Restatement (Third) of the Foreign Relations Law of the United States,* prescriptive jurisdiction refers to principles permitting the international community to "make its law applicable to the activities, relations, or status of persons, or the interests of persons in things. . . ." In the context of the Rome Statute, this refers to the subject matter jurisdiction of the Court (jurisdiction *ratione materiae*). Jurisdiction to adjudicate means to subject persons—particularly criminal defendants—to the process of the Court, which address the referral system and preconditions to jurisdiction. Enforcement jurisdiction means to induce or compel compliance or to punish noncompliance with the orders and decisions of the ICC.

III. SCOPE OF THE COURT'S JURISDICTION

§ 2-1 JURISDICTION *RATIONE MATERIAE*

§ 2.1.1 Jurisdiction over Core Crimes

Article 5 of the 1998 Rome Statute extends the Court's subject matter jurisdiction to four crimes: genocide (Article 6), crimes against humanity (Article 7), war crimes (Article 8), and aggression (Article 8 *bis*). Each of these crimes was defined in the Rome Statute in the article referenced above, except for the crime of aggression, which was not defined until the Court held its first Review Conference in Kampala in 2010.

These four crimes are often referred to as "core" crimes by international criminal lawyers, because they are created and defined by international law (and directly justiciable before international as well as national courts). They are understood to embody non-derogable *jus cogens* norms, meaning that they are universally applicable and binding upon States. These norms are found in customary international law as well as well as certain international treaties, such as the genocide convention. A handful of States, including the United States, dispute the *jus cogens* status of the prohibition on aggression, arguing that there are some circumstances in which acts of aggression are permissible, notably in the case of so-called "humanitarian intervention," generally defined as the use of military force to protect civilian populations from the commission of atrocity crimes. Although most States and scholars disagree and believe all four core crimes have *jus cogens* status (as they did at Nuremberg), the controversy regarding the crime of aggression resulted in an unusual jurisdictional regime regarding this crime at the ICC, as set forth in subsection 2.1.3, below.

§ 2.1.2 Inherent Jurisdiction over Three of the Four Core Crimes

Under Article 12(1) of the 1998 Rome Statute, jurisdiction over genocide, crimes against humanity, and war crimes is automatic and without reservation (subject to the State consent regime and complementarity principle, as detailed below), with one exception. When the Statute was adopted in 1998, Article 124 permitted a State to opt out of the war crimes jurisdiction of the Court regarding its own nationals or crimes committed on its territory for seven years after the Statute entered into force for that State. Only two States, France and Colombia, ever availed themselves of Article 124's opt-out provision. France withdrew its declaration and Colombia's expired at the end of seven years. Article 124 was reviewed at the Court's 2010 Kampala Review Conference and was retained until the Assembly of States Parties meeting in 2015, when it was finally deleted. *See* Int'l Crim. Ct., Assembly of States Parties Resol. ICC-ASP/14/Res.2, *Resolution on Article 124* (Dec. 14, 2017).

§ 2.1.3 A Special Regime for the Crime of Aggression

The Statute has a special jurisdictional regime for the Kampala amendments on the crime of aggression, which departs from the inherent jurisdiction applicable to the other three crimes. After the adoption of a definition of the crime of aggression in Article *8 bis* of the Rome Statute in 2010, Articles 15 *bis* and 15 *ter*, introduced at the same time, detail the nature of the Court's jurisdiction over aggression, providing that the aggression amendments would not enter into force until two additional steps had been taken. First, the aggression amendments would not enter into force until one year following their acceptance or ratification by at least thirty States. Second, the Court's States Parties had to "activate" the amendments by a separate vote that could not be taken before January 1, 2017.

On December 14, 2017, the Court's Assembly of States Parties activated the jurisdiction of the Court over the crime of aggression, effective July 17, 2018. Additionally, although the regime governing the Court's jurisdiction over the crime of aggression is almost identical to the regime governing jurisdiction over the other three crimes in case of a Security Council referral to the Court under Article 13(b) of the Statute (see *infra* § 4.2), that is not true for referrals by States Parties or by the Prosecutor, *proprio motu*. In the latter two circumstances, if the Security Council has not decided that aggression has taken place, the Prosecutor must seek authorization from a Pre-Trial Chamber to proceed under Article 15 *bis*(8). In addition, paragraph 5 of Article 15 *bis* provides that the Court may not exercise jurisdiction over the nationals of non-States Parties or with respect to the territory of a non-State Party—even in cases involving acts of aggression against a State Party to the Statute. This limitation has already proven challenging in practice, as it has prevented the ICC from exercising jurisdiction over Russian nationals implicated in alleged acts of aggression against Ukraine, as Russia is not a State Party to the Statute.

Finally, Article 15 *bis*(4) allows States to opt out of the Court's jurisdiction over the crime of aggression by lodging a declaration to such effect with the Registrar. Unlike Article 124, there is no "sunset" clause built into the opt-out proviso other than the requirement that the State "consider" its declaration within a three-year period. While the language of Article 15 *bis*(4) is clearly framed as an "opt-out," the Assembly Resolution adopted by consensus on December 15, 2017, activating the Court's jurisdiction over the crime, supports the view of some States that only an affirmative "opt-in" to the Court's aggression jurisdiction suffices to bring their territory and their nationals under the Court's aggression jurisdiction in cases of Article 13(a) (State Party) or Article 13(c) (Prosecutorial) referrals. The resolution provides that the Court "shall not exercise its jurisdiction regarding a crime of aggression when committed by a national or on the territory of a State Party that has not ratified or accepted" the amendments. *See* Int'l Crim. Ct., Assembly of States

Parties Resol. ICC-ASP/16/Res.5, *Activation of the Jurisdiction of the Court over the Crime of Aggression* (Dec. 14, 2017). Another group of States has argued that the proper construction of the amendments provides that all States Parties not affirmatively opting out of the aggression amendments are bound thereby.

In the end, the controversy surrounding the crime of aggression, and its differential treatment in the Rome Statute, has largely been due to opposition from States reluctant to give up the option to use force in circumstances they believe advance their national interests.

§ 2.1.4 Jurisdiction over Treaty Crimes

In addition to jurisdiction over the four core crimes currently set forth in the Rome Statute, during the Statute's negotiation, many argued that the Court should be able to hear cases involving treaty crimes, such as terrorism and drug trafficking. In fact, the 1989 impetus for the international criminal court project's resurrection was a resolution from a group of Caribbean nations seeking the establishment of a court to address those crimes. During the negotiations, however, it was decided that it was premature to take on these additional crimes, in part because their inclusion could have encumbered the Court's jurisdiction (by complicating the notion of inherent jurisdiction and possibly requiring the addition of special chambers), and because at least some of the additional crimes were not clearly defined. Recognizing, however, that treaty crimes present serious problems for the international community and that some countries felt particularly strongly about their inclusion, Resolution E, which was adopted by the Diplomatic Conference in its Final Act, provides that the issues of terrorism and drug crimes should be taken up at a Review Conference, with a view to their ultimate inclusion in the jurisdiction of the Court. Although the Assembly of States Parties has periodically considered the addition of these crimes, no concrete action has been taken, although prominent international lawyers have recently advanced a proposal for a new international criminal court on grand corruption.

§ 2-2 TEMPORAL JURISDICTION (*RATIONE TEMPORIS*)

Under Article 11(1) of the Statute, the Court's jurisdiction is limited to crimes committed after the Statute entered into force. Pursuant to Article 126(1) the Statute entered into force on July 1, 2002, the first day of the month after the 60th day following the date of the deposit of the 60th instrument of ratification received by the U.N. Secretary General. For States becoming parties after that date, under Article 11(2), the Court may exercise jurisdiction only with respect to crimes committed after the entry into force of the Statute with respect to that State, unless the State declares otherwise under Article 12(3), *i.e.*, by making a declaration that it accepts the Court's jurisdiction retroactively.

Retroactive acceptance of the Court's jurisdiction happened, for example, in the case of Palestine, which acceded to the Rome Statute on January 2, 2015, meaning that the Statute entered into force for that State on April 1, 2015 (the 1st day of the month after the 60th day following the deposit of its instrument of accession). However, prior to the deposit of its instrument of accession, Palestine lodged a declaration under Article 12(3) of the Statute accepting the jurisdiction of the Court over crimes committed "in the occupied Palestinian territory, including East Jerusalem, since June 13, 2014." DECLARATION OF PALESTINE UNDER ARTICLE 12(3) OF THE ICC STATUTE (Dec. 31, 2014).

The principle of non-retroactivity in the Statute is thus an absolute bar to jurisdiction in the case of crimes committed prior to July 1, 2002; but conduct prior to a State's accession or ratification can be reached if the State so desires. This firm temporal bar precluded the transfer of cases from the two *ad hoc* tribunals for the former Yugoslavia and Rwanda to the Court, an option that had been considered earlier in the Statute's negotiation.

§ 2-3 GEOGRAPHIC JURISDICTION (*RATIONE LOCI*)

The geographic scope of the Court's jurisdiction, *ratione loci*, varies depending on the mechanism by which the case comes to the Court. As indicated in § 4.1 below, if the Security Council refers the matter to the Court under Article 13(b), the ICC's jurisdiction extends to the territory of every State in the world, whether or not the State is a party to the Rome Statute. Under Article 13(b) of the Statute, the

Security Council may refer cases only if it is "acting under Chapter VII of the Charter of the United Nations." This presumably means that the Council must be taking a measure "not involving the use of force" to maintain international peace and security, following the precedent of the International Criminal Tribunal for the former Yugoslavia (ICTY) in the *Tadić* case, which held that establishing an international criminal tribunal was a lawful use of the Security Council's powers under Article 41 of the U.N. Charter. Prosecutor v. Duško Tadić, Case No. IT-94-1, *Decision on the Defence Motion on Jurisdiction*, ¶¶ 26–29 (T.C., Aug. 10, 1995).

If the matter is referred by a State Party or initiated *proprio motu* by the Prosecutor, the Court's jurisdiction is more restricted. In such instances, under Article 12 of the Statute (Preconditions to the exercise of jurisdiction), jurisdiction extends to the territory of a non-State Party only if that State consents to the jurisdiction of the Court, and either the conduct occurred on the territory of the consenting State, or the accused is a national of the consenting State.

Recent jurisprudence has expanded the territorial scope of the Court's jurisdiction. In 2018, the ICC Prosecutor sought a ruling from the Court that it could assert jurisdiction under Article 12(2)(a) of the Statute in the situation involving the attack on the Rohingya in Myanmar (a non-State Party) that had resulted in their alleged deportation to Bangladesh (a State Party), as well as other ICC crimes. The Pre-Trial Chamber answered in the affirmative, finding that it had the power to determine its own jurisdiction under the principle of *la compétence de la compétence* and other core principles of public international law. Request Under Regulation 46(3) of the Regulations of the Court, Case No. ICC-RoC46(3)-01/18-37, *Decision on the Prosecution's Request for a Ruling on Jurisdiction under Article 19(3) of the Statute*, ¶ 30 (PTC I, Sept. 6, 2018). The Court also concluded that the ICC had independent and "objective legal personality" that "engaged and cooperated not only with States Parties," but with non-States Parties as well. *Id.* ¶ 48. Thus, the Pre-Trial Chamber found that, because the crime of "deportation" in Article 7(1)(d) required "displacement across a border," and given that this element had taken place within the jurisdiction of Bangladesh, a State Party, the Court's jurisdiction over that crime was established, particularly given the 'inherently transboundary nature of the crime of deportation." *Id.* ¶¶ 64–71. As for other crimes, the Pre-Trial Chamber indicated that the crime of persecution against the Rohingya under Article 7(1)(h) of the Statute might also be chargeable, as well as other inhumane acts under Article 7(1)(k), based upon the "appalling conditions" in which the members of the Rohingya people live in Bangladesh following their deportation. *Id.* ¶¶ 75–77.

In 2019, following the decision of Pre-Trial I, Pre-Trial Chamber III authorized the ICC Prosecutor to proceed with an investigation for alleged crimes committed by individuals in Myanmar (a non-State Party) against the Rohingya if "at least one element of a crime within the jurisdiction of the Court or part of such a crime is committed on the territory of a State Party to the Statute." Situation in the People's Republic of Bangladesh/Republic of the Union of Myanmar, Case No. ICC-01/19-27, *Decision Pursuant to Article 15 of the Rome Statute,* ¶ 43 (PTC III, Nov. 14, 2019). Basing its ruling both on principles of customary international law and the proper interpretation of the Rome Statute, the Chamber found that the territoriality principle expressed in Article 12(2)(a) of the Statute properly included—as a matter of public international law and textual interpretation—situations in which the conduct embodying the criminal act was committed in part on the territory of a State Party to the Rome Statute. *Id.* ¶ 59. The Chamber concluded that when States conferred jurisdiction upon the ICC, there was no evidence they wished to constrain the Court in a manner that they were not themselves constrained, and that the only "clear limitation" in the Statute required that at least "part of the conduct (i.e., the *actus reus* of the crime) take place in the territory of a State Party." *Id.* ¶ 61.

§ 2-4 PERSONAL JURISDICTION (*RATIONE PERSONAE*)

Under Articles 1 and 25(1), the Statute provides for jurisdiction *ratione personae* over natural persons only (thereby excluding business entities, organizations, or States). Furthermore, under Article 63, trials *in absentia* are not permitted, requiring that the Court have the accused in custody to exercise personal jurisdiction over them. Although early discussions concerning the question of an international criminal court at the International Law Commission proposed adding a provision on State culpability, the idea was rejected as "science fiction."

Under Article 26 of the Statute, the Court's jurisdiction is limited to persons eighteen years or older, following Article 1 of the Convention on the Rights of the Child, defining a "child" as a human being under the age of 18. The Rome Statute expressly avoids referring to this age limit as an age of criminal responsibility. Rather, to accommodate sharp differences of view as to the appropriate age of criminal responsibility, as well as the argument that atrocities are often committed by minors, the Statute takes the view that the age threshold is jurisdictional in nature, rather than normative. Thus, the provision arguably neither takes a position on whatever age of responsibility exists in national systems, nor condones offenses by minors.

IV. REFERRALS TO THE COURT AND PRE-CONDITIONS TO JURISDICTION

§ 2-5 REFERRALS TO THE COURT

The Rome Statute provides three ways for situations to be referred to the Court: referral by a State Party to the Statute under Article 13(a); referral by the Prosecutor acting on their own initiative (*proprio motu*) under Article 13(c); and referral of a situation by the Security Council acting under Chapter VII of the U.N. Charter pursuant to Article 13(b).

As an initial matter, the Statute distinguishes between "situations," which the Prosecutor's *Policy Paper on Case Selection and Prioritisation* has noted "are generally defined in terms of temporal, territorial and in some cases personal parameters," and "cases," which "comprise specific incidents within a given 'situation' during which one or more crimes within the jurisdiction of the Court may have been committed." INT'L CRIM CT. OFF. OF THE PROSECUTOR, POLICY PAPER ON CASE SELECTION AND PRIORITISATION (Sept. 15, 2016). In the case of referrals under Articles 13(a) and (c), the Statute directs the reader to Article 12 on "Preconditions to the exercise of jurisdiction," which imposes limits on the situations sent to the Court by either the Prosecutor or a State Party, but not on situations sent to the Court by the Security Council.

In practice, this means that the ICC is a true "universal jurisdiction" court only with respect to situations referred to it by the Security Council. If the Security Council refers a situation to the Court, the Court may be asked to pass judgment on the commission of crimes anywhere in the world. The consent of no State is required, even if the potential accused are nationals of non-States Parties to the Court's Statute and the crimes did not take place on the territory of a State Party.

§ 2-6 PRECONDITIONS TO JURISDICTION

However, if the Prosecutor or a State refers a situation, although the universality principle does not disappear, preconditions to the Court's exercise of jurisdiction, as set forth in Article 12(2) of the Statute, are layered upon it. These preconditions are based on two additional disjunctive principles of jurisdiction: the territoriality principle and the nationality principle.

Under Article 12(2)(a), the Court may exercise its jurisdiction if the State on the territory of which the conduct in question occurred either is a Party to the Rome Statute or has accepted the jurisdiction of the Court under Article 12(3). Alternatively, under Article 12(2)(b), the Court may also exercise its jurisdiction if the accused is a national of a State Party. The Statute does not permit custodial States to consent to jurisdiction. That is, if a defendant of a State that is a non-State Party to the Statute travels to a State that is a State Party, the State to which the suspect has traveled may not serve as a jurisdictional nexus to the ICC, even though it could, under international law, likely try the accused itself under the principle of universal jurisdiction.

Although the notion of "territory" seems clear, issues have arisen in practice relating to the application of Article 12(2)(a). First, "territory" includes a vessel or aircraft registered to a State Party. Indeed, in an application by the Union of the Comoros challenging the Prosecutor's decision not to proceed with an investigation into the *Situation on Registered Vessels of the Union of the Comoros, the Hellenic Republic of Greece and the Kingdom of Cambodia,* it was common ground that the Court would have jurisdiction over crimes allegedly committed on those vessels by members of the Israeli

Defense Forces "irrespective of the nationalities of the alleged perpetrators or victims," because the vessels were registered to ICC States Parties. Situation on Registered Vessels of the Union of the Comoros, the Hellenic Republic of Greece and the Kingdom of Cambodia, Case No. ICC-01/13, *Application for Review pursuant to Article 53(3)(a) of the Prosecutor's Decision of 6 November 2014 not to initiate an investigation in the Situation,* ¶ 3 (PTC I, Jan. 29, 2015).

Second, in the Palestine situation, the ICC Prosecutor contended that the Court's "territorial jurisdiction extends to the Palestinian territory occupied by Israel during the Six-Day War in June 1967, namely the West Bank, including East Jerusalem, and Gaza." Situation in the State of Palestine, Case No. ICC-01/18, *Decision on the 'Prosecution request pursuant to article 19(3) for a ruling on the Court's territorial jurisdiction in Palestine,* ¶ 22 (PTC I, Feb. 5, 2021). The Prosecutor had asked the Court for a preliminary ruling on this question, which it issued in February 2021. *Id.* Israel contended that there was no Palestinian State that could confer jurisdiction on the Court as Palestine's boundaries were not yet settled, and it did not exercise full sovereignty over some of the territory in question. The Pre-Trial Chamber disagreed. It found dispositive the opinion of the U.N. Office of Legal Affairs, which concluded that the General Assembly's decision of December 4, 2012, according Palestine "non-member observer State status in the United Nations," meant that Palestine could become a party to any treaties open to "any State." *Id.* ¶ 98. Palestine thereupon acceded to the Rome Statute and, the Chamber found, could therefore accept the jurisdiction of the Court with respect to its territory without the ICC having in any way to adjudicate "a border dispute under international law nor prejudging the question of any future borders." *Id.* ¶ 113. Finally, the Chamber found that the territory could be delimitated based upon the General Assembly's earlier resolution affirming Palestinian sovereignty over the territory occupied since 1967 including East Jerusalem, Gaza, and the West Bank. *Id.* ¶¶ 117–118.

§ 2-7 ARTICLE 12(3) DECLARATIONS

As mentioned above, Article 12(3) allows a non-State Party to the Statute to accept the Court's jurisdiction. Lodging a declaration does not automatically trigger an investigation; however, it will be the basis for initiating a preliminary examination by the Prosecutor. INT'L CRIM. CT. OFF. OF THE PROSECUTOR, POLICY PAPER ON PRELIMINARY EXAMINATIONS ¶ 76 (Nov. 2013). Although the Statute is not clear, the Prosecutor has treated an Article 12(3) declaration as a *proprio motu* referral under Article 13(c) and Article 15 of the Statute, rather than a State Party referral under Article 13(a) and Article 14, and subsequent cases appear to align with this approach. For example, Côte d'Ivoire used Article 12(3) to accept the jurisdiction of the Court prior to its ratification of the Rome Statute, and in 2011, the Prosecutor requested that an investigation be authorized *proprio motu* pursuant to Article 15 of the Statute. Situation in the Republic of Côte d'Ivoire, Case No. ICC-02/11, *Request for authorization of an investigation pursuant to article 15* (PTC III, June 23, 2011). The request was granted by Pre-Trial Chamber III. Situation in the Republic of Côte d'Ivoire, Case No. ICC-02/11, *Corrigendum to "Decision Pursuant to Article 15 of the Rome Statute on the Authorisation of an Investigation into the Situation in the Republic of the Côte d'Ivoire* (PTC III, Nov. 15, 2011). Palestine also filed an Article 12(3) declaration, later followed by accession to the Rome Statute.

Ukraine filed two Article 12(3) declarations, one in 2014 and a second in 2015 with prospective effective, following Russia's annexation of Crimea in 2014. The Prosecutor took the position, following Russia's invasion of Ukraine, that unless he received a referral of the situation from States Parties under Article 13(a), he would require authorization from a Pre-Trial Chamber to proceed with an investigation. The Prosecutor invited States Parties to refer the situation to him, which they did almost immediately. Forty-one States formally referred the situation in Ukraine to the office, based upon Ukraine's Article 12(3) declaration.

Although the language of Article 12(3) seems to permit States to consent to jurisdiction over specific "crimes" relating to a particular situation without subjecting themselves to jurisdiction with respect to any other relevant ICC crimes in the same case, this was clearly not the drafters' intent, as the Chair of the drafting committee, the late M. Cherif Bassiouni, observed in remarks he gave at the annual meeting of the American Society of International Law in Spring 1999. The Rules of Procedure and Evidence (RPE) 44(2) were ultimately amended to correct the problem by requiring the Registrar to inform States lodging a declaration with the Court pursuant to Article 12(3) that the consequence of making such a declaration is acceptance of the Court's jurisdiction with respect to any Article 5 crimes of relevance to the situation in question. Concerns have been raised, nonetheless, about the possible politicization of the Court by a State's use of Article 12(3) declarations as opposed to relying on State accession or ratification of the Statute, as it may be a tactical move by a particular government in power against its internal opponents. Although the declaring State is required to cooperate with the Court "without any delay or exception" in accordance with Part 9 of the Statute, it remains, nonetheless, a non-State Party in many respects.

§ 2-8 JURISDICTION AND THE U.N. SECURITY COUNCIL: ARTICLE 16 OF THE STATUTE

Article 16 permits the U.N. Security Council to adopt a resolution under Chapter VII of the U.N. Charter requesting that the Court not commence an investigation or prosecution, or that it defer any proceeding already in progress, for a period up to twelve months. The Council may renew the request "under the same conditions." Although there were efforts to convince the Security Council to use its Article 16 power in the case involving Kenyan President Uhuru Kenyatta, that resolution failed.

See Press Release, U.N. Dep't of Pub. Info.: News and Media Div., *Security Council Resolution Seeking Deferral of Kenyan Leaders' Trial Fails to Win Adoption, with 7 Voting in Favor, 8 Abstaining*, SC/11176 (Nov. 15, 2013).

V. ADMISSIBILITY

§ 2-9 GENERAL ADMISSIBILITY REQUIREMENTS OF THE ROME STATUTE

Admissibility is defined in Article 17 of the Statute. Cases are inadmissible in four situations: (1) the case is being investigated by a State with jurisdiction; (2) the case has been investigated by a State with jurisdiction which has decided not to prosecute; (3) the person has already been tried for the conduct which is the subject of the complaint; or (4) the case is of insufficient gravity to warrant pursuit. Each of these categories is subject to further explication in the Statute. Although an extensive debate took place during the Preparatory Commission meetings as to whether the RPE should articulate admissibility criteria or factors to be considered by the Court in making determinations under Article 17, no additional criteria were added to the Rules.

§ 2-10 THE PRINCIPLE OF COMPLEMENTARITY

Unlike the *ad hoc* tribunals for Rwanda and the former Yugoslavia, which operated on the basis of primacy jurisdiction—meaning that States had to defer to their proceedings if so requested—the International Criminal Court is a court of last, not first, resort. Both the Preamble to the Statute and Article 1 express this fundamental principle, providing that the Court is to be complementary to national criminal jurisdictions. That said, States and the ICC may sometimes exercise jurisdiction concurrently in a situation as has occurred with the investigations following the invasion of Ukraine by the Russian Federation in 2022.

Complementarity is not defined in the Statute, but it has been implemented in practice during the Court's first twenty-five years. As a formal matter, under Article 17, the Court may exercise jurisdiction if: (1) national jurisdictions are "unwilling or unable" to; (2) the crime is of sufficient gravity; and (3) the person has not already been tried for the conduct on which the complaint is based. Although States and the accused in a particular case can challenge admissibility on the grounds of complementarity, as detailed in Section VI below, it is the Prosecutor that assesses a situation first under Article 17 when deciding to proceed with an investigation or a case.

For example, in 2014, the Prosecutor received complaints regarding war crimes allegedly committed by U.K. armed forces in Iraq and determined to re-open the preliminary examination of the situation. Six years later, despite finding that there was a reasonable basis to believe that war crimes had been committed, the Prosecutor concluded that the situation was not admissible and the preliminary examination would be closed because the U.K. authorities were "not unwilling genuinely to carry out relevant investigative inquiries and/or prosecutions (Article 17(1)(a)) or that decisions not to prosecute in specific cases resulted from unwillingness genuinely to prosecute (Article 17(1)(b))." INT'L CRIM CT. OFF. OF THE PROSECUTOR, SITUATION IN IRAQ/UK: FINAL REP., ¶ 1 (Dec. 9, 2020). Thus, complementarity may operate to deprive the Court of cases within its jurisdiction, both as a consequence of State sovereignty and to preserve the important relationship between the ICC and national systems.

Under the principle of *positive complementarity*, developed by the Court over the past twenty years, the ICC can undertake activities and actions, in cooperation with States, which are aimed at promoting national proceedings, and often does so. The principle of positive complementarity is sometimes referred to as the "looking over the shoulder" function of the Court, whereby the ICC Prosecutor's office will engage with governments and civil society in situations where ICC crimes are being committed and the government is at least attempting to redress them. This was the case with Colombia, which was under preliminary examination from June of 2004 to October 28, 2021, when the Office "concluded that there was not a reasonable basis to believe that potential cases arising from an investigation of the situation would be admissible." Press Release, International Criminal Court, *ICC Prosecutor, Mr Karim A.A. Khan QC, concludes the preliminary examination of the situation in Colombia with a Cooperation Agreement with the Government charting the next stage in support of domestic efforts to advance transitional justice*, ICC-CPI-20211028-PR1623 (Oct. 28, 2021).

VI. CHALLENGES TO JURISDICTION AND ADMISSIBILITY

§ 2-11 INTRODUCTION

The Rome Statute contains a complex procedure for challenging jurisdiction and admissibility. Articles 18 and 19 permit challenges to jurisdiction and admissibility by States and are complemented by RPE 31 to 62. At every stage of the proceeding up to trial, including the vetting of the case by the Pre-Trial Chamber if the Prosecutor is investigating *proprio motu* under Article 15(4), challenges to admissibility and jurisdiction are permitted and, for the most part, are subject to interlocutory appeal. That said, decisions of the Pre-Trial Chamber under Article 15 regarding authorization of an investigation do not appear to be subject to interlocutory appeal, *see* Arts. 15, 82; *cf.* RPE 50(5), although the Prosecutor was given leave to appeal upon the denial by the Pre-Trial Chamber of her request to open an investigation into the Afghanistan situation. Situation in the Islamic Republic of Afghanistan, Case No. ICC-02/17, *Decision on the Prosecutor and Victims' Requests for Leave to Appeal the 'Decision Pursuant to Article 15 of the Rome Statute on the Authorisation of an Investigation into the Situation in the Islamic Republic of Afghanistan'* (Sept. 17, 2019). Given that, at most stages of the proceedings, there are several parties (including the Court) with a right of challenge, the Court spends a great deal of time on motions relating to admissibility and jurisdiction, which has undoubtedly contributed to the slow pace of proceedings.

Under Article 18 on "preliminary admissibility issues," in situations referred by a State or by the Prosecutor *proprio motu,* the Prosecutor must notify all States Parties and those States which would normally exercise jurisdiction over the crime concerned that he or she has a reasonable basis to commence an investigation. States then have a one-month period to request that the Prosecutor defer opening the investigation—a decision that the Prosecutor may challenge before the Pre-Trial Chamber. Article 18 was added to the Statute quite late in the negotiations as a response to concerns about the Prosecutor's *proprio motu* powers. In the event of a referral of a situation by a State under Article 13(a), the operation of Article 18 has been uncontroversial. In the case of the Prosecutor commencing a case *proprio motu,* however, an issue has arisen regarding whether the Prosecutor must comply with Article 18 even prior to approval of the investigation by the Pre-Trial Chamber. In 2017, Pre-Trial Chamber III found that, under Article 18 "a State acquires rights of participation only once the Prosecutor initiates an investigation following authorization by a Pre-Trial Chamber," settling, at least for the time being, the debate. Situation in the Republic of Burundi, Case No. ICC-01/17, *Public Redacted Version of "Decision Pursuant to Article 15 of the Rome Statute on the Authorization of an Investigation into the Situation in the Republic of*

Burundi", ICC-01/17-X-9-US-Exp, 25 October 2017, ¶ 17 (PTC III, Publ. Red. Nov. 9, 2017).

Under Article 19 on "Challenges to the jurisdiction of the Court or the admissibility of a case," the Court must satisfy itself that it has jurisdiction in any case before it. Article 19(1). It *may*, on its own motion, determine the admissibility of a case under Article 17. *Id.* The Pre-Trial Chambers of the Court have generally considered the question of admissibility under Article 19(1) when the Prosecutor has requested arrest warrants, for example, but without prejudice to any subsequent challenge to admissibility under Article 19. Prosecutor v. Joseph Kony, Vincent Otti, Okot Odhiambo, Dominic Ongwen, Case No. ICC-02/04-01/05, *Decision on the admissibility of the case under article 19(1) of the Statute,* ¶ 19 (PTC II, Mar. 10, 2009).

The Pre-Trial Chambers have also, to date, examined the question of admissibility, *sua sponte*, in rendering Article 15 decisions permitting the Prosecutor to open an investigation in cases brought under his or her *proprio motu* powers under Article 13(c). It seems that they are no longer required to do so, however, after the decision of the Appeals Chamber authorizing an investigation into the situation in Afghanistan, which found that the factors in Article 53(1) of the Statute (Initiation of an Investigation), which include the question of admissibility (Article 53(1)(b)), apply only in situations referred to the Prosecutor by a State Party or the Security Council. Situation in the Islamic Republic of Afghanistan, Case No. ICC-02/17,

Judgment on the appeal against the decision on the authorization of an investigation into the situation in the Islamic Republic of Afghanistan, ¶ 34 (AC, Mar. 5, 2020). The Appeals Chamber noted that, in its view, "it is sufficient for the purposes of the Article 15 procedure that the Prosecutor considers the admissibility of potential cases in determining whether she should request authorization for an investigation . . . there is no basis for the Pre-Trial Chamber to consider that question as well." *Id.* ¶ 40.

Article 19 permits several parties, in addition to the Court and the Prosecutor, to bring challenges, including (1) "an accused or a person for whom a warrant or summons has been issued,"; (2) a State with jurisdiction that has or is prosecuting or investigating the crime; or (3) "a State from which acceptance of jurisdiction is required under article 12." Under Article 19(4), each party may challenge jurisdiction only once, except by leave of the Court in exceptional circumstances. Parties must bring challenges prior to the commencement of the trial or risk losing them (subject to special permission, and only on grounds of *ne bis in idem* (double jeopardy) if the challenge is to admissibility rather than jurisdiction). Pre-Trial Chamber II, in the *Kony* case, noted that "multiple determinations of admissibility may be made in a given case," ¶ 25, and that the accused "will always be entitled to raise a challenge under article 19(2) of the Statute, whether or not the Chamber has exercised its powers under article 19(1)." Prosecutor v. Joseph Kony, Vincent Otti, Okot Odhiambo, Dominic Ongwen, Case No. ICC-02/04-01/05, *Decision on the admissibility of the case under article 19(1) of the Statute*, ¶ 26 (PTC II, Mar. 10, 2009).

In the *Katanga* case, Trial Chamber II suggested that the Statute envisaged a "three-phase approach" to admissibility challenges. Phase I extends until the decision on the confirmation of the charges (DCCC) has been filed with the Registry, and permits all types of challenges, subject to the requirement that States must make them "at the earliest opportunity." Phase II, which is relatively brief, extends from the DCCC until the constitution of the Trial Chamber, during which time challenges are permissible only on *ne bis in idem* grounds. Phase III, which begins with the constitution of the Trial Chamber, only permits challenges on the grounds of *ne bis in* idem, and only with special permission. Prosecutor v. Germain Katanga and Mathieu Ngudjolo Chui, Case No. ICC-01/04-01/07, *Reasons for the Oral Decision on the Motion Challenging the Admissibility of the Case (Article 19 of the Statute)*, ¶ 49 (TC II, June 16, 2009).

Challenges by States suspend the Prosecutor's investigation of the case, subject to the Prosecutor's right to seek permission from the Court to pursue certain investigative measures to preserve evidence and prevent the absconding of persons. Article 19(8). This right applies only if the Prosecutor has already requested a warrant of arrest with respect to the person in question.

The Prosecutor may ask for a ruling from the Court regarding a question of jurisdiction or admissibility. Article 19(3). Prosecutor Bensouda did so on two occasions: with respect to the Bangladesh/Myanmar and Palestine situations. Given that the Prosecutor is under an independent obligation to determine admissibility in all cases, it seems clear that jurisdiction and admissibility (as defined in Article 17) are mandatory requirements from the Prosecutor's perspective for all prosecutions before the Court, although admissibility (but not jurisdiction) may be waivable by other parties, as explained below. Although a rule was proposed that would require the Pre-Trial Chamber authorizing an investigation pursuant to Article 15 to consider the case's ultimate admissibility, it was criticized on the grounds that it could lead to unnecessary delay and was rejected.

Article 53 of the Statute (on reasonable basis) clearly requires the Prosecutor to consider admissibility before launching an investigation. The Prosecutor's *Policy Paper on Preliminary Examinations* (November 2013) takes this view, noting that Article 53(1)(a)–(c) of the Statute establishes the legal framework for a preliminary examination and requires the Prosecutor to consider jurisdiction, admissibility, and the interests of justice.

§ 2-12 INADMISSIBILITY

§ 2.12.1 Test for Inadmissibility

With respect to investigation or prosecution, State action will render a case inadmissible unless the State is unwilling or unable *genuinely* to conduct the investigation or prosecution. Article 17(1)(a)–(b).

Unwillingness is defined as situations in which the proceedings were undertaken for the purpose of shielding the person concerned from criminal responsibility where "there has been an unjustified delay in the proceedings [that is] inconsistent with an intent to bring the person concerned to justice," or where "the proceedings were not, or are not being, conducted independently or impartially" *and* in a manner that is consistent "with an intent to bring the person concerned to justice." Article 17(2)(a)–(c). Inability to prosecute does not raise quite the same problem, for the Statute is clear that inability concerns the total or substantial collapse of a State's judicial system. Article 17(3). In determining if "unwillingness" is present, the Court is admonished by the Statute to "hav[e] regard to the principles of due process recognized by international law." Article 17(2).

The ICC Appeals Chamber has articulated a "same person, same conduct" test to determine admissibility in a particular case. Prosecutor v. Saif Al-Islam Gaddafi, Case No. ICC-01/11-01/11, *Judgement on Appeal on Admissibility Challenge*, ¶¶ 55–63 (AC, Mar. 9, 2020). Interestingly, although the *Gaddafi* case was found admissible, Libya successfully challenged the admissibility of the ICC's case against another defendant, Abdullah Al-Senussi, arguing that its national judicial system was actively investigating Al-Senussi for the same crimes that were the basis of the case in the ICC. The Court found that both prongs of the admissibility test under Article 17(1)(a) were fulfilled: (i) there was an ongoing investigation or prosecution of Al-Senussi at the national level; and (ii) the State was not unwilling or unable genuinely to carry out the investigation or prosecution. Prosecutor v. Abdullah Al-Senussi, Case No. ICC-01/11-01/11, *Decision on the Admissibility of the Case Against Al-Senussi*, ¶ 26 (PTC I, Oct. 11, 2013). According to the Court's clarification of this rule, the national system need not charge the accused with the same "crime," but must be addressing "substantially the same conduct." *Id.* ¶ 79. Thus, the case was inadmissible before the ICC, even though there were significant concerns about the fairness of the proceedings before the Libyan courts.

§ 2.12.2 Meaning of "Genuinely"

The term "genuinely" was drawn from the Zutphen intersessional draft (one of the precursors of the Rome Statute). It is problematic for two reasons. First, it permits a State to prevent a case from proceeding before the Court merely by launching an investigation. Indeed, although the word "genuinely" appears to require some good faith element on behalf of the State, it is perfectly proper under the Statute for a State to open an investigation for the sole purpose of depriving the ICC of jurisdiction, so long as the State does not exhibit "unwillingness" in doing so (or its "inability" is not apparent). The decision of the Prosecutor to close the preliminary examination involving the alleged crimes of U.K. armed forces in Iraq underscores this: Assuming States are actively investigating, the ICC will not function as "a human rights body" or assess whether "the Prosecutor or a Chamber of this Court would have come to a different conclusion [than U.K. authorities] on the evidence and proceeded differently." Instead, the Office will determine "whether the facts, on their face, demonstrate an intent to shield persons from criminal responsibility." INT'L CRIM CT. OFF. OF THE PROSECUTOR, SITUATION IN IRAQ/UK: FINAL REP., ¶¶ 9–10 (Dec. 9, 2020).

§ 2.12.3 *Ne Bis In Idem*

Article 20(1) of the ICC Statute provides that no one shall be tried before the Court if they were either previously convicted or acquitted by the Court with respect to "conduct which formed the basis" of the crimes charged in the second proceeding. This "double jeopardy" provision at the ICC was added to the Statute as an additional protection for the accused before the Court and is consistent with Article 14(7) of the International Covenant on Civil and Political Rights, as well as with comparable provisions in the Statutes of the *ad hoc* tribunals for the former Yugoslavia and Rwanda and the Special Court for Sierra Leone.

Article 20(3) extends the bar to retrial before the Court if the person was tried "by another court for conduct also proscribed under article 6, 7, 8, or 8 *bis*" unless the trial in the other court were either "for the purpose of shielding the person concerned from criminal responsibility," or were otherwise not conducted "independently or impartially in accordance with the norms of due process recognized by international law and were conducted in a manner which, in the circumstances, was inconsistent with an intent to bring the person concerned to justice." (Article 20(3)(a) & (b)). Article 20(2) provides that no person who has been convicted or acquitted of a crime by the ICC shall be tried "by another court" for the same Article 5 crime. Note that the bar in Article 20(2) requires that the two prosecutions be for the same "crime," as opposed to the bar in Articles 20(1) and (3) which apply to the "same conduct." The ICC provision is broader than the double jeopardy standard in the United States, which does not apply between two different sovereigns, for example the states and the federal government. Article 20 does not, however, bar direct appeals by the prosecution, which are explicitly permitted by Article 81(1)(a) of the Statute.

Article 20 was the subject of extensive negotiations regarding both the triggering and the extent of the bar on subsequent proceedings, yet there is very little jurisprudence on the provision to date. It was raised in passing by defense lawyers in Prosecutor v. Mathieu Ngudjolo Chui, Case No. ICC-01/04-02/12, *Transcript of Initial Appearance*, at 20 (Feb. 11, 2008), who initially argued that the charges against the accused were inadmissible because he had already been charged with the same conduct in the Democratic Republic of the Congo. The Pre-Trial Chamber rejected his claim and confirmed the charges against Ngudjolo. Prosecutor v. Mathieu Ngudjolo Chui, Case No. ICC-01/04-02/12, *Decision on Warrant of Arrest*, ¶ 22 (PTC I, July 6, 2007). He was subsequently acquitted by the Trial Chamber, and his acquittal was upheld on appeal. Prosecutor v.

Germain Katanga and Mathieu Ngudjolo Chui, Case No. ICC-01/04-02/07 *Judgment* (AC, July 14, 2009).

The issue also arose in two separate decisions in the *Kenyatta* case: first, upon the Prosecutor's decision to seek an adjournment of the trial based upon the Kenyan government's failure to cooperate with the Court, and subsequently, when the Prosecutor withdrew the charges against Kenyatta without prejudice. In the first decision, the Trial Chamber stated that if the Prosecutor withdrew the charges, "the principle of *ne bis in idem* would not attach." Prosecutor v. Uhuru Muigai Kenyatta, Case No. ICC-01/09-02/11, *Decision on Prosecution's Application for Further Adjournment*, ¶ 56 (TC V(B), Dec. 3, 2014). In its *Decision on the withdrawal of charges against Mr. Kenyatta,* issued a few months later, the Trial Chamber confirmed that if the Prosecutor withdrew the charges prior to trial, *ne bis in idem* would not bar a future prosecution. Prosecutor v. Uhuru Muigai Kenyatta, Case No. ICC-01/09-02/11, *Decision on the Withdrawal of Charges Against Mr. Kenyatta,* ¶ 9 (TC V(B), Mar. 13, 2015). This case suggests that the Court takes the position that a case is only inadmissible on *ne bis in idem* grounds if the person has been "tried or acquitted" elsewhere, and that jeopardy will not attach to earlier proceedings.

§ 2-13 GRAVITY

The Statute has always had threaded through it the idea of gravity—that the Court should hear only the most serious cases of truly international concern.

This is expressed in the Preamble, as well as in Articles 1, 5, and 17. This was the International Law Commission's position, and it remains true for the Rome Statute. Nevertheless, gravity is not a defined term, and it has been for the Court to elaborate its meaning over time. The test adopted is that "(i) a gravity determination involves a generic assessment. . . of whether the groups of persons that are likely to form the object of the investigation capture those who may bear the greatest responsibility for the alleged crimes committed; and (ii) that gravity must be assessed from both a 'quantitative' and 'qualitative' viewpoint. Factors such as nature, scale and manner of commission of the alleged crimes, as well as their impact on victims are indicators of the gravity of a given case." Situation on Registered Vessels of the Union of the Comoros, the Hellenic Republic of Greece and the Kingdom of Cambodia, Case No. ICC-01/13, *Decision on the Request of the Union of Comoros to Review the Prosecutor's Decision not to Initiate an Investigation*, ¶ 21 (PTC I, July 16, 2015) citing Situation in the Republic of Kenya, Case No. ICC-01/09, *Decision Pursuant to Article 15 of the Rome Statute on the Authorization of an Investigation into the Situation in the Republic of Kenya*, ¶¶ 60–62 (PTC II, Mar. 31, 2010); *see also* INT'L CRIM. CT. OFF. OF THE PROSECUTOR, POLICY PAPER ON PRELIMINARY EXAMINATIONS, ¶¶ 60–66 (Nov. 2013); INT'L CRIM CT. OFF. OF THE PROSECUTOR, POLICY PAPER ON CASE SELECTION AND PRIORITISATION, ¶¶ 35–41 (Sept. 15, 2016).

In the *Situation on Registered Vessels of the Union of the Comoros,* the Comoros challenged the ICC Prosecutor's decision concluding that an attack by members of the Israeli Defense Forces on the *Mavi Marmara*, a ship in a humanitarian aid flotilla bound for the Gaza Strip, was not admissible because the case was not of sufficient gravity. During the raid, ten persons were killed, around 50–55 were injured, and a number suffered outrages upon personal dignity both on the vessel and during their subsequent detention in Israel. Pre-Trial Chamber I ordered the Prosecutor to revisit her estimation of the gravity of the case. Situation on Registered Vessels of the Union of the Comoros, the Hellenic Republic of Greece and the Kingdom of Cambodia, Case No. ICC-01/13, *Decision on the Request of the Union of Comoros to Review the Prosecutor's Decision not to Initiate an Investigation* (PTC I, July 16, 2015). The Prosecutor appealed, and the Appeals Chamber decided by majority to dismiss her appeal. Situation on Registered Vessels of the Union of the Comoros, the Hellenic Republic of Greece and the Kingdom of Cambodia, Case No. ICC-01/13, *Decision on the Admissibility of the Prosecutor's Appeal Against the "Decision on the Request of the Union of Comoros to Review the Prosecutor's Decision Not to Initiate an Investigation* (AC, Nov. 6, 2015). On November 6, 2017, the Prosecutor notified Pre-Trial Chamber I of her "final decision," under RPE 108(3), coming to the same conclusion based upon a review of all the evidence, including evidence newly made available in 2015–2017. The decision to close the preliminary examination disappointed the Union of Comoros and was criticized by some commentators, but it fits within the recommendations issued by the Independent Expert Review of the ICC that the Court should, to the extent possible, "focus[ ] on situations of the highest gravity on those most responsible for the crimes." INT'L CRIM. CT., INDEPENDENT EXPERT REVIEW OF THE INTERNATIONAL CRIMINAL COURT AND THE ROME STATUTE SYSTEM: FINAL REPORT, ¶¶ 646–650 (Sept. 30, 2020). This is now the stated policy of the Office, as set forth in its *Policy Paper on Case Selection and Prioritisation,* ¶ 6 (Sept. 15, 2016).

§ 2-14 THE INTERESTS OF JUSTICE

Article 53(1)(c) of the Statute, applicable to the initiation of an investigation, provides that the Prosecutor may decline to pursue an investigation if there are "substantial reasons to believe" that the investigation would not be in the "interests of justice," taking into account all the circumstances, including the gravity of the crime, and the interests of victims. Article 53(2) has a similar provision. It applies to the initiation of a prosecution, and adds as a factor to be considered, the age or infirmity of the alleged perpetrator.

In 2007, the Prosecutor adopted a *Policy Paper on the Interests of Justice* that set out several factors: (a) the Prosecutor should decline to proceed with an investigation only in exceptional circumstances, (b) a presumption exists in favor of investigation or prosecution; and (c) the necessity of interpreting the 'interests of justice" language in the Statute, considering the Statute's object and purpose of the

Rome Statute. The policy paper also sets out additional factors that the Office will used in making such an assessment, including gravity, the interests of victims, and, in a case involving the initiation of a prosecution, the age and infirmity of the alleged perpetrator.

The *Policy Paper* recognizes that the interests of justice consideration is not a positive requirement of initiating an investigation or a case; thus, it is distinguishable from jurisdiction and admissibility, both of which the Office are required to establish. The *Policy Paper* also points to a "consistent trend" imposing a duty upon States to prosecute international crimes. *Id.* at p. 7. Finally, the *Policy Paper* welcomes other justice mechanisms, and the "complementary role that can be played by domestic prosecutions, truth seeking, reparations programs, institutional reform and traditional justice mechanisms in the pursuit of a broader justice." *Id.* at p. 8.

The ICC Prosecutor has never relied upon "the interests of justice," to decline to pursue an investigation or prosecution. However, in 2019, Pre-Trial Chamber II issued a decision rejecting the Prosecutor's Article 15 request to open an investigation into the situation in Afghanistan on the grounds that it found the investigation would not serve the interests of justice. Situation in the Islamic Republic of Afghanistan, Case No. ICC-02/17, *Decision Pursuant to Article 15 of the Rome Statute on the Authorisation of an Investigation into the Situation in the Islamic Republic of Afghanistan*

(PTC II, Apr. 12, 2019). The Pre-Trial Chamber took the view that the Chamber was obliged to make a "positive determination to the effect that investigations would be in the interests of justice," *id.* ¶ 35, because the "current circumstances of the situation in Afghanistan are such as to make the prospects for a successful investigation and prosecution extremely limited." *Id.* ¶ 96.

The Appeals Chamber, however, reversed the decision of the Pre-Trial Chamber and authorized the opening of the investigation. Situation in the Islamic Republic of Afghanistan, Case No. ICC-02/17, *Judgment on the appeal against the decision on the authorization of an Investigation into the Situation in the Islamic Republic of Afghanistan* (AC, Mar. 5, 2020). It noted that earlier decisions of the Pre-Trial Chamber authorizing an investigation had also considered the Article 53(1) factors, including the interests of justice, in assessing whether an investigation could be opened under the Statute. *Id.* ¶ 24. It concluded however, agreeing with the victims' representatives, that the "reasonable basis" determination under Article 53(1), including an assessment of the interests of justice, should not feature in the Pre-Trial Chamber's analysis under Article 15(4). According to the Appeals Chamber, Article 53(1) applies to situations referred to the Prosecutor by a State Party or the Security Council, whereas Article 15(4) is the relevant provision for the authorization of an investigation by the Pre-Trial Chamber, which makes no reference to the interests of justice criteria. *Id.* ¶¶ 26–37.

VII. AMNESTIES

The Rome Statute is silent regarding the effect of national amnesties on prosecutions before the Court. The United Nations has taken the position that amnesties for war crimes, crimes against humanity, and genocide are not permitted under international law; however, jurists and policymakers continue to debate whether so-called "conditional amnesties" adopted as part of a transition to democratic governance, as opposed to blanket or self-amnesties, might be permissible under certain circumstances. In an admissibility challenge brought by Saif Al-Islam Gaddafi in the Libyan situation, he raised the question whether Libya's general amnesty law (applicable to even the most serious perpetrators) prevented his prosecution before the ICC. Pre-Trial Chamber I found that it did not, holding that there "is a strong, growing, universal tendency that grave and systematic human rights violations—which may amount to crimes against humanity by their very nature—are not subject to amnesties or pardons under international law." Prosecutor v. Saif Al-Islam Gaddafi, Case No. ICC-01/11-01/11, *Decision on the Admissibility Challenge by Dr. Saif Al-Islam Gaddafi pursuant to Articles 17(1)(c), 19 and 20(30 of the Rome Statute,* ¶ 61 (PTC I, Apr. 5, 2019). The Pre-Trial Chamber surveyed international law sources on the question, as well as the jurisprudence of the Special Court for Sierra Leone (SCSL), which had rejected the Lomé Amnesty Agreement as a bar to prosecution before the SCSL in Prosecutor v. Morris Kallon and Brima Bazzy Kamara, Case No. SCSL-2004-15 and Case No. SCSL-2004-16, *Decision on*

Challenge to Jurisdiction: Lomé Accord Amnesty (AC, Mar. 13, 2004). The Pre-Trial Chamber concluded that "[a]mnesties and pardons intervene with States' positive obligations to investigate, prosecute and punish perpetrators of core crimes . . . and deny victims the right to truth, access to justice, and to request reparations where appropriate." *Prosecutor v. Gaddafi, supra,* ¶ 77.

The Appeals Chamber unanimously affirmed the finding of admissibility in the case; however, in paragraph 96 of its judgment, it summarily noted that the Pre-Trial Chamber's holdings on the Libyan amnesty law's compatibility with international law were *obiter dicta*, observing that "international law is still in the developmental stage on the question of acceptability of amnesties." Prosecutor v. Saif Al-Islam Gaddafi, Case No. ICC-01/11-01/11, *Judgment on the appeal of Mr. Saif Al-Islam Gaddafi against the decision of Pre-Trial Chamber I entitled 'Decision on the Admissibility Challenge by Dr. Saif Al-Islam Gaddafi pursuant to Articles 17(1)(c), 19 and 20(3) of the Rome Statute' of April 4, 2019,* ¶ 96 (AC, Mar. 9, 2020). Judge Carranza issued a lengthy separate opinion challenging paragraph 96, concluding that "there is well-established law, principles and standards confirming that general amnesties and equivalent measures for grave human rights violations, such as those caused by the commission of crimes under the jurisdiction of the Court, are incompatible with international law." Prosecutor v. Saif Al-Islam Gaddafi, Case No. ICC-01/11-01/11, *Separate and Concurring Opinion of Judge Luz del Carmen Ibanez Carranza dated April 21, 2020, on the*

Judgment on the appeal of Mr. Saif Al-Islam Gaddafi against the decision of Pre-Trial Chamber I entitled 'Decision on the Admissibility Challenge by Dr. Saif Al-Islam Gaddafi pursuant to Articles 17(1)(c), 19 and 20(3) of the Rome Statute' of April 4, 2019, ¶ 5 (AC, Mar. 9, 2020). Thus, this question remains unsettled.

As to whether the Prosecutor is permitted to take national amnesties into consideration in deciding whether or not an investigation serves "the interests of justice," the negotiating history of the Statute suggests that Article 53(1)(c) was inserted at least in part to address concerns that a regime transitioning from a genocidal or conflict-ridden past may contemplate granting amnesties and adopting a truth and reconciliation process, either instead of or in addition to bringing criminal prosecutions. The Statute is "creatively ambiguous" on this point according to Philippe Kirsch, who presided over the Rome Conference as the Chair of the Committee of the Whole and, like many other delegates, evidently had the South African experience with a Truth and Reconciliation Commission in mind.

VIII. IMMUNITIES: ARTICLE 27 OF THE STATUTE

A fundamental principle of the Rome Statute is that all defendants are equal under it, and before the Court. Following the example of Article IV of the 1948 Convention on the Prevention and Punishment of the Crime of Genocide, Article 27(1) (Irrelevance of Official Capacity) of the Rome Statute provides:

> This Statute shall apply equally to all persons without any distinction based on official capacity. In particular, official capacity as a Head of State or Government, a member of a Government or parliament, an elected representative or a government official shall in no case exempt a person from criminal responsibility under this Statute, nor shall it, in and of itself, constitute a ground for reduction of sentence.

This provision codifies the customary international law rule that whatever immunities an official might otherwise have under international law cannot be pleaded as a bar or a defense to criminal responsibility, *ratione materiae*.

Article 27(1) complements Article 27(2), which reads as follows: "Immunities or special procedural rules which may attach to the official capacity of a person, whether under national or international law, shall not bar the Court from exercising its jurisdiction over such a person." A former President of the Court's Assembly of States Parties, H.E. Zeid Ra'ad Zeid al-Hussein of Jordan, has referred to Article 27 as the "most profound article ever to be written into a multilateral treaty." Yet the article was, during the ICC negotiations, "uncontested throughout the discussions, and [ ] relatively easy to agree on." Per Saland, *International Criminal Law Principles, in* THE MAKING OF THE ROME STATUTE 189, 202 (Roy S. Lee, ed., 1999). The International Criminal Tribunals for the former Yugoslavia and Rwanda, which had similar provisos in their

Statutes, found the provision represented "a rule of customary international law," Prosecutor v. Slobodan Milošević, Case No. IT-99-37-PT, *Decision on Preliminary Motions*, ¶ 28 (TC, Nov. 8, 2001) as did the Special Court for Sierra Leone in the *Charles Taylor* case. Prosecutor v. Charles Taylor, Case No. SCSL-2003-01, *Decision on Immunity from Jurisdiction*, ¶ 52 (AC, May 31, 2004).

Although Article 27 was easily agreed to during the Rome Statute's negotiations, throughout the Statute's twenty years of operation, individuals on the receiving end of the Court's investigations, subpoenas, and warrants have protested its application to them, leading several States Parties to assert that they are unable (and unwilling) to surrender individuals who may have immunity under international law to the ICC without the consent of their State of nationality. In 2019, the ICC Appeals Chamber settled, at least for the time being, the application of Article 27 in a case involving the Hashemite Kingdom of Jordan's refusal to execute an arrest warrant of the Court against Sudan's former President Omar Al-Bashir. The Appeals Chamber held that Jordan should have arrested Al-Bashir. Prosecutor v. Omar Hassan Ahmad Al-Bashir, Case No. ICC-02/05-01/09, *Judgment in the Jordan Referral re Al-Bashir Appeal* (AC, May 6, 2019). The Chamber relied upon customary international law, holding:

> There is neither state practice nor *opinio juris* that would support the existence of head of state immunity under customary international law

> vis-à-vis an international court. To the contrary, such immunity has never been recognized in international law as a bar to the jurisdiction of an international court. *Id.* ¶ 113.

The Appeals Chamber noted that the burden of proving such a rule would be on the party arguing for its existence, consistent with classic doctrines of public international law. *Id.* ¶ 116; *see also* Lotus Case (Fr. v. Turk.), *Judgment*, 1927 P.C.I.J. (ser. A) No. 10 (Sept. 7, 1927). The Appeals Chamber noted that the absence of a rule of customary international law recognizing head of state immunity before international courts is "explained by the different character of international courts when compared with domestic jurisdictions." Prosecutor v. Omar Hassan Ahmad Al-Bashir, Case No. ICC-02/05-01/09, *Judgment in the Jordan Referral re Al-Bashir Appeal*, ¶ 115 (AC, May 6, 2019).

The Appeals Chamber also found that although domestic jurisdictions "constitute an expression of a State's sovereign power, which is necessarily limited by the sovereign power of other States," international courts, conversely, "act on behalf of the international community as a whole." *Id.* Thus, the Appeals Chamber rejected the arguments of the African Union and amici who took the position that "the immunity *ratio personae* [sic] of Heads of State is absolute, even in the case of genocide, on the basis that any arrest or prosecution will inevitably interfere with their functions on behalf of the State, for so long as they remain in office." *Id.* ¶ 84. Because the Appeals Chamber's judgment was unanimous, it seems unlikely that this issue will continue to be litigated at the International Criminal Court, although there will undoubtedly be continued discussion of it given the controversy it generated at the time.

Selected Sources and Additional Reading

MARGARET M. DEGUZMAN, SHOCKING THE CONSCIENCE OF HUMANITY: GRAVITY AND THE LEGITIMACY OF INTERNATIONAL CRIMINAL LAW (2020).

MARC HENZELIN, LE PRINCIPE DE L'UNIVERSALITE EN DROIT PENAL INTERNATIONAL 63 (2000).

ROSALYN HIGGINS, PROBLEMS AND PROCESS: INTERNATIONAL LAW AND HOW WE USE IT (1994).

LAWYERS' COMMITTEE FOR HUMAN RIGHTS, ISSUES OF JURISDICTION AND ADMISSIBILITY IN THE RULES OF PROCEDURE AND EVIDENCE 2–4 (2000).

ROME STATUTE OF THE INTERNATIONAL CRIMINAL COURT, ARTICLE-BY-ARTICLE COMMENTARY (Kai Ambos, ed., 4th ed., 2021).

VICTOR TSILONIS, THE JURISDICTION OF THE INTERNATIONAL CRIMINAL COURT (2019).

Dapo Akande, *The Legal Nature of Security Council Referrals to the ICC and its Impact on Al Bashir's Immunities*, 7 J. INT'L. CRIM. J. 333 (2009).

Michael Akehurst, *Jurisdiction in International Law,* 46 BRIT. Y.B. INT'L L. 145 (1972–73).

M. Cherif Bassiouni, *The Normative Framework of International Humanitarian Law: Overlaps, Gaps and Ambiguities*, 8 TRANSNAT'L L. & CONTEMP. PROBS. 199, 201–02 (1998).

Neil Boister, *Treaty Crimes, International Criminal Court,* 12 NEW CRIM. L. REV. 341 (2009).

D. W. Bowett, *Jurisdiction: Changing Patterns of Authority over Activities and Resources*, 1982 BRIT. Y. B. INT'L L. 1, 12–13.

Linda E. Carter, *The Principle of Complementarity and the International Criminal Court: The Role of* Ne Bis in Idem, 8 SANTA CLARA J. INT'L. L. 165 (2010).

Roger S. Clark, *Amendments to the Rome Statute of the International Criminal Court Considered at the first Review Conference on the Court, Kampala, 31 May–11 June 2010*, 2 GOETTINGEN J. INT'L L. 690 (2010).

Kamari Maxine Clarke & Sarah-Jane Koulen, *The Legal Politics of the Article 16 Decision: The International Criminal Court, the UN Security Council and Ontologies of a Contemporary Compromise*, 7 AFR.J. LEGAL STUD. 297 (2014).

Gerard Conway, Ne Bis in Idem *and the International Criminal Tribunals,* 14 CRIM. L. F. 351 (2003).

Lorraine Finlay, *Does the International Criminal court Protect against Double Jeopardy: An Analysis of Article 20 of the Rome Statute*, 15 U.C. DAVIS J. INT'L L. & POL'Y 221 (2009).

A.J.J. de Hoogh, *The Relationship between Jus Cogens, Obligations Erga Omnes and International Crimes: Peremptory Norms in Perspective*, 42 AUSTRIAN J. PUBL. INT'L. L. 183 (1991).

Shabtai Rosenne, *The Jurisdiction of the International Criminal Court*, 2 YBK. INT'L HUM. L. 119 (1999).

Leila Nadya Sadat, *Exile, Amnesty & International Law,* 81 NOTRE DAME L. REV. 955 (2006).

Leila Nadya Sadat, *Commentary on Parts 1 and 2 of the Zutphen Intersessional Draft: Establishment of the Court, Complementarity, Jurisdiction and Admissibility, in* OBSERVATIONS ON THE CONSOLIDATED ICC TEXT BEFORE THE FINAL SESSION OF THE PREPARATORY COMMITTEE, 13bis NOUVELLES ÉTUDES PÉNALES 17, 22 (Leila Sadat Wexler, special ed., 1998).

Leila Sadat, *First Committee Report on Jurisdiction, Definition of Crimes and Complementarity*, *in* THE INTERNATIONAL CRIMINAL COURT: OBSERVATIONS AND ISSUES BEFORE THE 1997–98 PREPARATORY COMMITTEE; AND ADMINISTRATIVE AND FINANCIAL IMPLICATIONS, 13ter NOUVELLES ÉTUDES PÉNALES 163, 164–65 (M. Cherif Bassiouni, ed., 1997) (formerly Wexler).

Leila [Wexler] Sadat, *The Proposed Permanent International Criminal Court: An Appraisal*, 29 CORNELL INT'L L. J. 665 (1996).

Leila Nadya Sadat & S. Richard Carden, *The New International Criminal Court: An Uneasy Revolution,* 88 GEO. L. J. 381, 394–95 (2000).

Per Saland, *International Criminal Law Principles, in* THE INTERNATIONAL CRIMINAL COURT: THE MAKING OF THE ROME STATUTE 189 (Roy S. Lee, ed., 1999).

Michael P. Scharf, *Justice vs. Peace, in* THE UNITED STATES AND THE INTERNATIONAL CRIMINAL COURT 186 (Sarah B. Sewall & Carl Kaysen, eds., 2000).

Michael P. Scharf, *Swapping Amnesty for Peace: Was there a Duty to Prosecute International Crimes in Haiti?*, 31 TEX. INT'L L. J. 1 (1996).

Jean-Eric Schoettl, *Décisions du Conseil Constitutionnel: Cour pénale internationale,* L'ACTUALITE JURIDIQUE: DROIT ADMINISTRATIF 230 (Mar. 20, 1999).

Egon Schwelb, *Crimes against Humanity*, 23 BRIT. Y.B. INT'L L. 178 (1946).

Carsten Stahn, *Response: The ICC, Pre-Existing Jurisdictional Treaty Regimes, and the Limits of the* Nemo Dat Quod Non Habet *Doctrine—A Reply to Michael Newton*, 49 VAND. J. TRANSNAT'L. L. 443 (2016).

Carsten Stahn, Mohamed M. El Zeidy & Hector Olasolo, *The International Criminal Court's* Ad Hoc *Jurisdiction Revisited*, 99 AM. J. INT'L. L. 421 (2005).

Christian Tomuschat, *Crimes Against the Peace and Security of Mankind and the Recalcitrant Third State*, 24 ISR. Y.B. HUM. RTS. 41, 52 (1994).

Herman von Hebel & Darryl Robinson, *Crimes within the Jurisdiction of the Court*, *in* THE INTERNATIONAL CRIMINAL COURT: THE MAKING OF THE ROME STATUTE 79 (Roy S. Lee, ed., 1999).

DAPO AKANDE, MAX DU PLESSIS & CHARLES CHERNOH JALLOH, INSTITUTE FOR SECURITY STUDIES, AN AFRICAN EXPERT STUDY ON THE AFRICAN UNION CONCERNS ABOUT ARTICLE 16 OF THE ROME STATUTE OF THE ICC (2010).

Convention on the Rights of the Child, Nov. 20, 1989, G.A. Res. 44/25, U.N. GAOR, 44th Sess., Supp. No. 49, art. 1, U.N. Doc. A/44/49 (1989), *reprinted in* 28 I.L.M. 1456 (1989).

DECLARATION OF PALESTINE UNDER ARTICLE 12(3) OF THE ICC STATUTE (Dec. 31, 2014), https://www.icc-cpi.int/iccdocs/PIDS/press/Palestine_A_12-3.pdf.

Int'l Crim. Ct., Assembly of States Parties Resol. ICC-ASP/14/Res.2, *Resolution on Article 124* (Dec. 14, 2017).

Int'l Crim. Ct., Assembly of States Parties Resol. ICC-ASP/16/Res.5, *Activation of the Jurisdiction of the Court over the Crime of Aggression* (Dec. 14, 2017).

INT'L CRIM. CT., INDEPENDENT EXPERT REVIEW OF THE INTERNATIONAL CRIMINAL COURT AND THE ROME STATUTE SYSTEM: FINAL REPORT (Sept. 30, 2020), https://asp.icc-cpi.int/sites/asp/files/asp_docs/ASP19/IER-Final-Report-ENG.pdf.

INT'L CRIM CT. OFF. OF THE PROSECUTOR, POLICY PAPER ON CASE SELECTION AND PRIORITISATION (Sept. 15, 2016), https://www.icc-cpi.int/items Documents/20160915_OTP-Policy_Case-Selection_Eng.pdf.

INT'L CRIM CT. OFF. OF THE PROSECUTOR, SITUATION IN IRAQ/UK: FINAL REP. (Dec. 9, 2020), https://www.icc-cpi.int/sites/default/files/items Documents/201209-otp-final-report-iraq-uk-eng.pdf.

Press Release, International Criminal Court, *Ukraine Accepts ICC Jurisdiction over Alleged Crimes Committed Since 20 February 2014*, ICC-CPI-20150908-PR1146 (Sept. 8, 2015).

Press Release, International Criminal Court, *Ukraine Accepts ICC Jurisdiction over Alleged Crimes Committed Between 21 November 2013 and 22 February 2014*, ICC-CPI-20140417-PR997 (Apr. 17, 2014).

Press Release, U.N. Dep't of Pub. Info.: News and Media Div., *Security Council Resolution Seeking Deferral of Kenyan Leaders' Trial Fails to Win Adoption, with 7 Voting in Favor, 8 Abstaining*, SC/11176 (Nov. 15, 2013).

Report of The Intersessional Meeting Form 19–30 January 1998 in Zutphen, the Netherlands, art. 11, at 140 n.53., U.N. Doc. A/AC.249/1998/L.13 (1998).

RESTATEMENT (THIRD) OF THE FOREIGN RELATIONS LAW OF THE UNITED STATES §§ 401(a), 404, 421(1) (1987).

Rome Statute of the International Criminal Court, United Nations Diplomatic Conference of Plenipotentiaries on the Establishment of an International Criminal Court, preamble, cls. 1 & 3; arts. 1, 5, 17, 20, July 17, 1998, Annex II U.N. Doc. A/CONF.183.9 (1998).

U. N. Diplomatic Conference of Plenipotentiaries on the Establishment of an Int'l Crim. Ct., *Final Act of the United Nations Diplomatic Conference of Plenipotentiaries on the Establishment of an International Criminal Court*, UN Doc. A/CONF.183/10, Resol. E (July 17, 1998).

CHAPTER 3

THE COURT'S OPERATIONS—ORGANS, STRUCTURE AND ADMINISTRATION

I. INTRODUCTION

The International Criminal Court is a unique institution, unlike domestic courts or other international tribunals. Now located in a permanent building, constructed in a sustainable manner and reflective of the Court's ethos and priorities, the four formal organs of the Court set forth in Article 34 of the Statute are the Presidency, the Judiciary, the Office of the Prosecutor, and the Registry. Additional organs include the Defense and the Assembly of States Parties. In addition, the Rome Statute of the ICC contemplated the creation of a Trust Fund for Victims, which was created in 2002 by the Assembly of States Parties and whose mandate is to ensure that victims of atrocity crimes receive appropriate reparations and assistance. The Trust Fund for Victims (TFV) is a body functionally separate from the ICC itself; thus, its functioning will not be addressed in this Chapter but is taken up in Chapter 9.

Each of the Court's organs plays a different and key role in the Court's operations. This Chapter builds upon Chapter 1 by expanding upon their role and operation.

II. THE PRESIDENCY

The Presidency is one of the four organs of the Court. Art. 34(a). It has a complex and key role, providing oversight of judicial processes, functioning as a court administrator, and serving as one of the most important external faces of the ICC. Composed of the President and First and Second Vice-Presidents, who are, pursuant to Article 38 of the Statute, elected by an absolute majority of the judges for three-year terms, which are renewable only once pursuant to Article 38(1). As a result of criticism published by the Court's Assembly of States Parties in the 2020 Independent Expert Review, which focused specifically on the Presidency election process, the Court's judges adopted *Guidelines on the Procedure for the Election of the Presidency*, which entered into force as of January 19, 2021, and provide specific election procedures regarding the Presidency in order to promote better collegiality, transparency and openness. INT'L CRIM CT., GUIDELINES ON THE PROCEDURE FOR THE ELECTION OF THE PRESIDENCY (Jan. 19, 2021).

§ 3-1 PRESIDENCY'S AREAS OF RESPONSIBILITY

Pursuant to the Rome Statute, the Presidency is required to perform various judicial tasks, assigned to it by the Rome Statute itself. It is also responsible for the proper administration of the Court, with the exception of the Office of the Prosecutor. Art. 38(3)(a). The President is known as the President of the Court and performs an important external relations task, often traveling to represent the Court abroad and presiding over ceremonial events. The Presidency also maintains relations with States and other entities and promotes public awareness and understanding of the Court. An important example of such functions of the Presidency is its mandate to conclude enforcement agreements with States Parties, described further below. Art. 103; *see also* INT'L CRIM. CT., RULES OF PROCEDURE AND EVIDENCE, Doc No. ICC-PIOS-LT-03-004/19, Rule 199 (2019) (RPE).

In its administrative functions, the Presidency has responsibility for the proper administration of the court, and it also oversees the work of the Registry. Art. 38(3)(a); *see also* INT'L CRIM. CT., REGULATIONS OF THE COURT, Doc. No. ICC-BD/01-05-16, Regs. 15-18 (2018) (Court Regulations). On matters of mutual concern, the Presidency must consult with and seek agreement from the Office of the Prosecutor. Art. 38(4).

In exercising its judicial functions, the Presidency constitutes Chambers and assigns cases to them, reviews certain Registry decisions, and concludes cooperation agreements with States. Court Regulations, Regs. 46(1), 46(2) & 107. The Presidency routinely reviews certain Registry decisions, pursuant to the *Rules of Procedure and Evidence (RPE)* (RPE 21(3)), as well as the *Regulations of the Court* (Court Regulations, Reg. 72), and the *Regulations of the Registry*. Court Regulations, Regs. 3(2)(h), 11, 56(2), 125(4), 126(3), 137(5), 219(4), and 220; *see also* INT'L CRIM. CT., REGULATIONS OF THE

REGISTRY, Doc. No. ICC-BD/03-03-13 (2018). The Presidency's judicial review of Registry decisions encompasses a range of subject areas, including matters related to detention, the legal assistance to be paid by the Court, and matters related to the maintenance of the lists of counsel, assistants to counsel, and experts. The Presidency also decides upon judges' requests to be excused from the exercise of their functions, under Article 41(1). In addition, the Presidency has authority over the temporary extradition of a convicted person to a third state for the purposes of prosecution. Rome Statute, Art. 109 & 111; RPEs 214, 215(1), & 225. If a convicted person has escaped, the Presidency has the authority to work with the relevant State in order to locate the escaped person. Art. 111; RPE 225(1). Finally, the Presidency plays a key role in the enforcement of sentences, fines, forfeitures, and reparation orders.

In particular, every State wishing to be considered as a penal jurisdiction where a convicted person will serve their sentence must first be placed on a list of States of enforcement maintained by the Registrar ("the List"), subject to the Presidency's acceptance of the conditions that the State attaches to its agreement. Art. 103(a); RPE 200(2). At the 2010 ICC Review Conference at Kampala, a resolution was adopted urging States Parties to join the List. Resolution on Strengthening the enforcement of sentences, ICC Resolution RC/Res. 3, June 8, 2010. To date, only fourteen States have entered into agreements with the ICC to accept prisoners. Mali was the first African State to enter into an agreement on the enforcement of sentences. ASSEMBLY OF

STATES PARTIES, REPORT OF THE BUREAU ON COOPERATION, ICC-ASP/11/28, ¶ 12 (Oct. 23, 2012).

The Presidency has the discretion to include or not include a particular State on the List; the Presidency may also request additional information from any interested State before taking a decision. RPE 200(2). In practice, the ICC enters into bilateral agreements with States which establish a framework for the acceptance of sentenced persons; such agreements are concluded by the President and the relevant State. Some are general agreements to enforce sentences; others are *ad hoc* arrangements relating to the enforcement of a particular convicted individual; and a handful of States have agreed to accept their own nationals or residents if sentenced by the Court when they ratified the Statute. The general agreements are concluded based upon a Model Enforcement Agreement ("MEA") used by the Presidency to facilitate the conclusion of such bilateral agreements, which are typically preceded by negotiations between the Presidency's Enforcement Unit and the relevant State Party. Thus far, most States Parties have agreed to the general terms of the MEA, without suggesting fundamental modifications thereto.

§ 3-2 COMPOSITION

As of this writing, the ICC has had four Presidents. The current President is Judge Piotr Hofmański (Poland), preceded by Judge Chile Eboe-Osuji (Nigeria), Judge Sang-Hyun Song (South Korea) and Judge Philippe Kirsch (Canada). Given the vital role of the ICC's President, and the Presidency, it is surprising that, although much attention has been paid to the selection of the ICC Prosecutor, relatively little scholarly discussion has taken place about the selection of the ICC President.

Another concern regarding the composition of the Presidency has focused upon the lack of equitable gender representation on the ICC bench, including within the Presidency. All four Presidents of the Court have been male, and in 2018, an all-male Presidency was elected, consisting of Judges Chile Eboe-Osuji as President, and Judges Robert Fremr and Marc Perrin de Brichambaut as First and Second Vice-Presidents, respectively. This lack of gender representation drew criticism and has been partially rectified with the election of the current members thereof, one of whom is female.

III. THE JUDICIARY

§ 3-3 JUDICIAL QUALIFICATIONS AND ELECTIONS

The ICC's eighteen judges are elected by the Assembly of States Parties and serve nine-year non-renewable terms. Art. 36(9)(a). ICC judges are elected based on their qualifications, impartiality, and integrity. Article 36(3)(a) requires that judges be "persons of high moral character, impartiality and integrity who possess the qualifications required in their respective States for appointment to the highest judicial offices." They must "have an excellent knowledge of and be fluent in at least one of the working languages of the Court" (English and French). Art. 36(3)(c). No two judges may be nationals of the same State Party. Art. 36(7).

Judges are elected from two lists of candidates: List A comprises candidates who have competence in criminal law and the necessary relevant experience as judges, prosecutors, or advocates in criminal proceedings, and List B comprises candidates who have competence in relevant areas of international law, such as international humanitarian law, human rights law, and experience in a professional legal capacity relevant to the judicial work of the Court. Art. 36(5). Elections are organized so that there are always at least nine serving judges from List A and at least five from List B. *Id.*

Finally, the Assembly of States Parties is required to consider geographic representation and gender parity; thus, established voting requirements provide that each regional group of the United Nations has at least two judges, and that at least six judges shall be female and at least six shall be male. Art. 36(8). During the past few years, concern about the quality of some judges nominated to serve at the Court has led to calls for increasing both the standards applied to judicial elections, and to vetting of all candidates to ensure their integrity and high quality.

§ 3-4 JUDICIAL FUNCTIONS

Judges are responsible for ensuring fair proceedings for all involved in cases, including the prosecution, the defense and the accused, and the victims. They must conduct fair trials, render decisions that the parties and other stakeholders can understand, issue arrest warrants and summonses to appear, authorize victims to participate, and order witness protection measures, in addition to other tasks. The judges elect the President and the two Vice-Presidents, whose functions are described above. The ICC's judges serve on Pre-Trial Chambers, Trial Chambers, and Appeals Chambers. Under Article 39 of the Rome Statute, the Presidency assigns judges to different Divisions (Appeals, Trial and Pre-Trial divisions) based on the nature of the functions to be performed by each Division and the qualification and experience of the judges, so that each Division contains an appropriate level of expertise in both international and criminal law. Although Article 39(3) notes that judges assigned to the Trial and Pre-Trial Divisions can serve on both Trial and Pre-Trial Chambers and serve for a period of three years, and judges assigned to the Appeals Division serve only on Appeals Chambers and remain in this Division for their entire term of office, in fact, the judges have developed a practice of permitting judges to rotate from the Pre-Trial and Trial Divisions to Appeals. Judge Christine Van Den Wyngaert, for example, served in all three Divisions during her tenure in office.

ICC judges have thus far issued seven editions of the so-called *Chambers Practice Manual*, which is a practice manual that reflects judicial agreement on various matters related to pre-trial, trial, and appellate issues. The most recent update, published in July 2023, adds a new section (Part VI) on *Principles and procedures governing the issuance of dissenting and separate opinions.* INT'L CRIM. CT., CHAMBERS PRACTICE MANUAL (7th ed. 2023). Paragraph 104 notes that "dissenting and separate opinions should be a measure of last resort," and should have as their primary aim "to contribute to the progressive development of the law." *Id.*, at ¶ 105. They should, in principle, not exceed the length of the majority judgment or decision, *id.*, at ¶ 108, and should be issued "simultaneously with the majority judgment." *Id.*, at ¶ 108. These reforms respond to the criticisms of scholars and the 2020 Independent Expert Report that seriatim judgments and overly long and tendentious dissents were not serving the Court well in its mission of delivering justice.

§ 3-5 PRE-TRIAL CHAMBERS

The functions of the Pre-Trial Chamber are carried out either by three judges of the Pre-Trial Division or by a single judge of that division where the Statute or the Rules so permits. Art. 39(2)(b)(iii). The Trial and Pre-Trial Divisions are to be composed predominantly of judges with criminal trial experience. Art. 39(1). They decide if there is enough evidence for a case to go to trial, and if so, confirm the charges and commit the case to trial under Article 61 of the Statute. The Court's Pre-Trial Chambers also issue arrest warrants or summonses to appear, preserve evidence, protect suspects, and safeguard information affecting national security. In addition, Pre-Trial Chamber judges are charged with guaranteeing the rights of all persons during the investigation phase, including suspects, victims, and witnesses. They grant protection measures for victims and witnesses, appoint counsel for the defense, ensure that suspects are not detained for an unreasonable period of time prior to trial, and decide on requests for interim release pending trial.

The Pre-Trial Chambers play a pivotal role in determining whether a case proceeds to trial. They authorize the Prosecutor to open an investigation *proprio motu*, or to continue an investigation when a State requests that the ICC defer to national investigations, or to take steps in an investigation without a State's cooperation. Pre-Trial Chambers judges also review the Prosecutor's decision not to investigate where there is a referral, and they decide on challenges to jurisdiction or the admissibility of a case. Most Pre-Trial Chamber decisions can be reviewed by the Appeals Chamber.

In 2019, a Pre-Trial Chamber played a key role in deciding a State's admissibility challenge. In a decision later affirmed by the Appeals Chamber, the Pre-Trial Chamber held that the case against Saif Al-Islam Gaddafi in the Libya situation was admissible before the Court. Prosecutor v. Saif Al-Islam Gaddafi, Case No. ICC-01/11-01/11, *Decision on the 'Admissibility Challenge by Dr. Saif Al-Islam Gadaffi pursuant to Articles 17(1)(c), 19 and 20(3) of the Rome Statute'* (PTC I, Apr. 5, 2019). Gaddafi had been accused of committing crimes against humanity for his alleged role in the suppression of civilian demonstrations during the 2011 uprising in Libya; he had claimed that the ICC could not exercise jurisdiction over him because he had already been tried and convicted by a national court for the same conduct. The Pre-Trial Chamber rejected this argument and Libya's admissibility challenge, showing the power the Pre-Trial Chamber has to determine if cases are able to proceed.

In one of the Court's most controversial decisions to date, in 2019, Pre-Trial Chamber II rejected the Prosecutor's request to open an investigation in the situation of Afghanistan. Situation in the Islamic Republic of Afghanistan, Case No. ICC-02/17, *Decision Pursuant to Article 15 of the Rome Statute on the Authorisation of an Investigation into the Situation in the Islamic Republic of Afghanistan* (PTC II, Apr. 12, 2019). This was the first time that any Pre-Trial Chamber had refused to grant an authorization to investigate in the context of a situation initiated *proprio motu*. The decision came at the end of a 13-year-long proceeding in the Afghanistan situation, which had begun when the preliminary examination was opened in 2006, but the Prosecutor's request for authorization to open an investigation regarding alleged Taliban crimes, crimes of Afghan national forces, and allegations of torture committed by U.S. forces in 2003–2004 had not been submitted until late in 2017.

Pre-Trial Chamber II held that the supervisory mechanism of the Rome Statute's Article 15, coupled with Article 53(1), must include a determination that the investigation would be in the interests of justice, which encompassed the criterion of likelihood that the investigation would be feasible and meaningful under the relevant circumstances. According to Pre-Trial Chamber II, the investigation would not be in the interests of justice because significant time had elapsed between the alleged crimes and the request, because of limited cooperation that the Prosecutor had received throughout this time, and because of the likelihood that relevant evidence and suspects would no longer be available, particularly as regards potential U.S. persons given the status of the United States as a non-State Party and its general opposition to the Court and the investigation. In imposing a substantive standard before authorizing the requested investigation, Pre-Trial Chamber II demonstrated its willingness to control the Prosecutor's ability to bring cases forward by performing an autonomous review of the merits of the Prosecutor's assessment of the likelihood of bringing a successful case. This Pre-Trial Chamber decision was widely criticized and was overturned on appeal.

On April 15, 2020, the Prosecution notified Pre-Trial Chamber II that the Government of Afghanistan had requested a deferral, pursuant to Article 18(2) of the Rome Statute, which allows States to seek a deferral if they are investigating the crimes within the ICC's jurisdiction on their own, and the situation was placed on hold. Two years later, after the fall of the government to the Taliban, the Prosecutor requested authorization to resume the investigation. In October 2022, Pre-Trial Chamber II authorized the ICC Prosecutor to resume its investigation, finding that the material submitted by Afghanistan did not demonstrate that the latter was investigating appropriately. Situation in the Islamic Republic of Afghanistan, Case No. ICC-02/17,

Decision pursuant to article 18(a) of the Statute authorising the Prosecution to resume investigation (PTC II, Oct. 31, 2022). In December 2021, the ICC Prosecutor announced that its investigation would prioritize alleged crimes committed by the Islamic State and the Taliban, and that it would not focus on alleged crimes committed by United States' forces in Afghanistan.

§ 3-6 TRIAL CHAMBERS

Trial Chambers are composed of three judges per Article 39(2)(b)(iii). Their main role is to conduct fair trials: to decide if there is enough evidence to prove beyond a reasonable doubt that the accused is guilty as charged; to sentence those found guilty, which includes pronouncing such sentences in public; and to order reparations to victims, which may include restitution, compensation, and rehabilitation. Art. 64.

One of the most significant roles that the Trial Chambers play regards evidentiary issues. The Rome Statute provides a legal framework, whereby Trial Chambers collect, manage, and evaluate all of the presented evidence. Article 74 (2) states that "[t]he Trial Chamber's decision shall be based on its evaluation of the evidence and the entire proceedings." Trial Chambers have thus played key roles within specific proceedings, such as in the *Lubanga* case, where the Trial Chamber had to manage multiple delays driven by evidentiary disclosure issues, as well as in the *Katanga* and *Ngudjolo* cases. Managing evidentiary issues is closely tied to another fundamental role that Trial Chambers play under Article 64 of the Rome Statute, "[t]he Trial Chamber shall ensure that a trial is fair and expeditious and is conducted with full respect for the rights of the accused."

Trial Chambers have discretion and flexibility to rule on evidentiary issues during trials. They are not bound by rulings of other Trial or Pre-Trial Chambers with respect to evidence. Article 69(3) permits the submission of all evidence "relevant to the case," subject to the evaluation of its probative value and potential prejudice to the accused or the testimony of a witness. Art. 69(4). As the *Lubanga* Trial Chamber held, "the Chamber has concluded that it enjoys a significant degree of discretion in considering all types of evidence." Prosecutor v. Thomas Lubanga Dyilo, Case No. ICC-01/04-01/06, *Decision on the admissibility of four documents*, ¶ 24 (June 13, 2008). This is subject to the specific provisions of the Court's *Rules of Procedure and Evidence*.

§ 3-7 APPEALS CHAMBER

The Appeals Chamber, which handles appeals lodged by all parties, consists of five judges, including the President of the Court. Appeals Chamber judges confirm, reverse, or amend decision on guilt or innocence of the accused. The Appeals Chamber may also confirm, reverse, or modify a sentence pronounced by the Trial Chamber, and, if necessary, may order a new trial before a different Trial Chamber. Art. 81. The Appeals Chamber is charged with ensuring that the conviction was not materially affected by errors or by unfairness of proceedings, and they also ensure that the sentence is proportionate to the crimes. Art. 81(2). In addition, Appeals Chamber judges can confirm, reverse, or amend an order for reparations, art. 82(4), and also revise the final judgement or sentence if, for example, new evidence is subsequently found. Art. 84. Finally, subject to the *Rules of Procedure and Evidence*, the Appeals Chamber may hear appeals on jurisdiction and admissibility decisions, interim release decisions, and interlocutory matters. Art. 82(1).

IV. THE OFFICE OF THE PROSECUTOR

The Office of the Prosecutor (OTP) examines situations under the Court's jurisdiction and conducts investigations and prosecutions of individuals accused of ICC crimes. It is the first such office in history to have been given the mandate by the Court's States Parties to select situations independently and impartially for investigation, without direct oversight by the States Parties.

The OTP has approximately 380 staff members from over 80 different nations, including legal professionals, investigators, analysts, psycho-social support experts, diplomacy and international relations experts, and public information and communication professionals. The Prosecutor and the Deputy Prosecutors head the office, each of which are elected by the Assembly of States Parties for a non-renewable nine-year mandate. The Current Prosecutor is Karim A.A. Khan (United Kingdom), who was elected in a contested vote, receiving 72 of 123 votes, on February 12, 2021. His predecessors were Fatou Bensouda (The Gambia) and Luis Moreno Ocampo (Argentina), who were selected by consensus. Traditionally the OTP was served by one Deputy Prosecutor, also elected by the ASP. In the last round of elections, however, two Deputy Prosecutors were chosen: Mame Mandiaye Niang (Senegal) and Nazhat Shameem Khan (Fiji), bringing expertise, gender, and regional diversity to the Office.

§ 3-8 ORGANIZATION OF THE OFFICE OF THE PROSECUTOR

Prior to 2021, the OTP was composed of three main divisions: the Jurisdiction, Complementarity, and Cooperation Division (JCCD); the Investigation Division; and the Prosecution Division. JCCD conducted preliminary examinations, provided advice on issues related to jurisdiction, admissibility, and cooperation, and coordinated the OTP's judicial cooperation and external relations. The Investigation Division was charged with providing investigative expertise and support, including the coordination of staff field deployment, creating security plans and protection policies, and analyzing crimes and relevant evidence. The Prosecution Division was tasked with developing OTPs advocacy and litigation strategies and conducted prosecutions, including through written and oral submissions to the Court's judges.

In July 2021, Prosecutor Khan announced a reorganization of the OTP with the aim of creating a more effective, united, and cohesive Office. The OTP has implemented a new governance model built on two Prosecution Pillars, each headed by a Deputy Prosecutor. The Prosecution Pillars merge the competencies and skills of staff previously allocated to separate Divisions of the Office into Unified Teams. According to OTP's 2022 Annual Report, "bringing together investigators, analysts, cooperation advisers, and lawyers, [will] encourage[ ] greater integration and strengthening of situation or case specific knowledge that will maintain a continuity of resources and expertise and increase results." INT'L CRIM CT. OFF. OF THE PROSECUTOR, ANNUAL REPORT OF THE OFFICE OF THE PROSECUTOR, 2022: TOWARDS A MORE JUST WORLD EVERY DAY (Dec. 1, 2022).

According to this recent reorganization, the Appeals and Prosecution Legal Coordination Section and the Gender and Children Unit report to one of the Deputy Prosecutors, while also providing comprehensive support to all Unified Teams. The OTP's Prosecution Pillars, as well as the units, sections and teams that report directly to the Prosecutor, are reinforced by a newly created Integrated Services Pillar that centralizes the support functions of the OTP and the provision of specialized expertise. The former Jurisdiction, Complementarity and Cooperation Division has also been reorganized, reallocating the International Cooperation Advisors to the Unified Teams while bringing together political cooperation, external relations and judicial cooperation in the newly created Office of External Affairs. The new structure became operational as of Spring 2022. *Id.* Unlike the other situations, the Ukraine investigation has its own "pillar" within the OTP.

§ 3-9 SELECTION OF CASES AND SITUATIONS

The Prosecutor selects situations and cases pursuant to specific policies and priorities. In 2016, in an effort to render its decisions more transparent and standardized, the Office of the Prosecutor published a *Policy Paper on Case Selection and Prioritisation*, in which it emphasized that it would conduct case selection and prioritization on the basis of the overarching principles of independence, impartiality, and objectivity. INT'L CRIM CT. OFF. OF THE PROSECUTOR, POLICY PAPER ON CASE SELECTION AND PRIORITISATION, ¶ 16 (Sept. 15, 2016). The predominant criterion for case selection is gravity. *Id.*, at ¶ 6.

As a matter of law, the *Policy Paper on Case Selection* sets out the legal criteria that the OTP must follow under the Rome Statute in order to select a case for investigation and prosecution. Under Article 58(1)(a), the OTP will ensure that the person concerned has committed a crime within the jurisdiction of the Court, and that the case falls within the scope of, or be sufficient linked to a situation that has been properly referred to the Court. INT'L CRIM CT. OFF. OF THE PROSECUTOR, POLICY PAPER ON CASE SELECTION AND

PRIORITISATION, ¶ 26 (Sept. 15, 2016). In addition, all cases selected for investigation and prosecution must be admissible in terms of complementarity, *id.*, at ¶¶ 30–31, and gravity as required by Article 17(1)(d), *id.*, at ¶ 32, and that they would not be contrary to the interests of justice, as set out in the OTP's *Policy Paper on the Interests of Justice. Id.*, at ¶ 33. Finally, under Regulation 34(1) and the 2015 Strategic Plan of the Office, the Office will conduct its investigations towards "those persons who appear the most responsible for the identified crimes." *Id.*, at ¶ 42. This requires an assessment of the degree of responsibility of the alleged perpetrator(s), and the potential charges and modes of liability.

In the same policy paper, the OTP announced, for the first time, that it would seek to prosecute environmental crimes, although it has yet to do so. INT'L CRIM CT. OFF. OF THE PROSECUTOR, POLICY PAPER ON CASE SELECTION AND PRIORITISATION, ¶ 7 (Sept. 15, 2016). More recently, in December 2022, the OTP launched its first-ever Policy on the Crime of Gender Persecution; in it, the Office of the Prosecutor announced that "the Office will ensure that charges for gender persecution are brought wherever there is sufficient evidence" and "[T]he Office will . . . investigate and prosecute those most responsible for gender persecution that fall under the Court's jurisdiction." INT'L CRIM CT. OFF. OF THE PROSECUTOR, POLICY ON THE CRIME OF GENDER PROSECUTION, ¶ 82 (Dec. 2022). This policy paper is built upon the OTP's prior adoption of a policy on sexual and gender-based crimes, INT'L CRIM CT. OFF. OF THE PROSECUTOR, POLICY PAPER ON SEXUAL AND

GENDER-BASED CRIMES (June 2014), and the subsequent policy on children. INT'L CRIM CT. OFF. OF THE PROSECUTOR, POLICY ON CHILDREN (Nov. 2016).

Most recently, in its 2023–25 strategic plan, the OTP declared, as its primary goal, the delivery of results in the courtroom. As part of its announced strategy to achieve this goal, the OTP specified that it would prioritize cases and situations through an overall strategic planning cycle and completion targets. It pledged to meet this goal by stating that it "will prioritize situations and cases systematically and objectively with the overall goal of reducing the total number of situations, thereby ensuring increased focus and resources on earmarked situations and cases. . . .the Office will prioritize cases according to factors such as their relative gravity and prospect of success. It will progress each situation to complete its investigations appropriately, with the aim of reducing, overall, the number of open investigations." INT'L CRIM CT. OFF. OF THE PROSECUTOR, STRATEGIC PLAN 2023–2025.

In the same strategic plan, the OTP announced, as an additional strategic goal, the enhancement of efforts by national authorities to fight impunity. The OTP stated that it will "work closely with situation and other countries, accountability mechanisms and other partners to ensure a coordinated and effective effort towards closing the impunity gap." *Id.*, at ¶ 33. This particular strategy may influence the OTP's selection and prioritization of cases and situations as well. Finally, the most recent Strategic Plan announced as one of its primary objectives is to ensure effective investigations and prosecutions of sexual and gender-based crimes and crimes against children; the OTP will thus "prioritize the effective investigation and prosecution of SGBV and CAC crimes by ensuring that these crimes are considered. . . from the initial investigative and prosecutorial stages when developing case theories, investigation plans and charging strategies." *Id.*, at ¶ 59.

V. THE DEFENSE

§ 3-10 RIGHTS OF THE ACCUSED

The Rome Statute confers extensive protections on those accused before the Court. Article 67 sets out a complete set of rights, most of which are familiar to U.S. students and practitioners: The right to a public and fair hearing, conducted impartially, art. 67(1); to be informed promptly of the charges against him or her in a "language which the accused fully understands and speaks," art. 67(1)(a), including a right to have an interpreter and translations, art. 67(1)(f); to be tried without undue delay, art. 67(1)(c); to be present at trial and have a right to legal counsel of their choosing, art. 67(1)(d); and, perhaps more surprisingly to common-law lawyers, the right to make "an unsworn oral or written statement in his or her defense," art. 67(1)(f).

Article 66 guarantees that everyone before the Court is "presumed innocent until provided guilty," beyond a reasonable doubt. Art. 66(1) & 66(3). The burden is on the Prosecutor to prove the guilt of the accused. Art. 66(2). Respect for these rights are fundamental to the legitimacy of the ICC itself, and during the Statute's negotiation, the minimum guarantees set out in Article 14 of the International Covenant on Civil and Political Rights were expanded upon and enlarged so that the ICC would be seen as a model jurisdiction to which national systems might look. In addition to the specific provisions of Article 67 and 68, Article 21(3) provides that the "application and interpretation of law [before the ICC] must be consistent with internationally human rights." Thus, in interpreting the provisions of the Rome Statute, particularly as regards the rights of the accused, reference must be made to international human rights law.

§ 3-11 DEFENSE COUNSEL

When the Rome Statute was negotiated, proposals were made to have the defense become a full organ of the Court. As was the case, however, with respect to the *ad hoc* international criminal tribunals, a decision was made not to do so. This means that the counsel for the defense are not Court employees. In order to practice before the Court, however, they must be on the List of Counsel, which is maintained by the Registry pursuant to RPE 21(2). Under RPE 22(1), they must have "established competence in international or criminal law and procedure, as well as the necessary relevant experience" and, under Regulation 67, they must have served at least ten years to be lead counsel and at least eight years to be associate counsel.

The right of suspected perpetrators to freely choose their lawyers is a fundamental principle in the ICC. When a suspect or accused person needs legal representation and wishes to appoint their own counsel, they may either choose from the List maintained by the Registry or choose another lawyer who meets the criteria established by the *Regulations of the Court* and is willing to be included on the List. Court Regulations, Reg. 75. As of this writing, the List of Counsel includes more than 400 lawyers from a variety of jurisdictions, including counsel from non-State Parties such as the United States and Russia.

Pre-Trial Chambers can also appoint counsel in certain circumstances. For example, the Court can appoint *ad hoc* counsel to represent the general interest of the defense where there is a unique investigative opportunity under Article 56(1) of the Statute to "take testimony or a statement from a witness or to examine, collect or test evidence, which may not be available subsequently" at trial. Moreover, a Chamber can appoint counsel when the interests of justice so require, and the Registry can appoint duty counsel in urgent situations.

Although defense teams are not members of the ICC staff, the Registry provides services to them, as well as limited office space. The ICC's legal aid system ensures that the Court pays the cost of legal representation for defendants who do not have the means to pay for it themselves. The Registry's services can include helping counsel maintain confidential communications with their clients and providing support during investigative activities. It also assists with interpretation and translation services and provides training on the e-court technology system. Finally, the Office of Public Counsel for the Defense (OPCD) established by Court Regulation 77, may assist teams with legal research and advice, and advance submissions on behalf of unrepresented suspects or on specific issues. Court Regulation, Reg. 77(4)(f).

Most defense counsel are members of the International Criminal Court Bar Association (ICCBA), which is an independent professional organization representing the interests of counsel and other support staff who represent defendants, victims, or other actors before the ICC. The ICCBA provides a range of support and services for its members, and also acts as a discussion forum on all matters related to the ICC.

VI. THE REGISTRY

As noted in Chapter 1, pursuant to Article 43(1) of the Statute, the Registry is responsible for the "non-judicial aspects of the administration and servicing of the Court." The head of this organ is the Registrar, who is the principal administrative officer of the Court, and who is elected by the judges by an absolute majority, taking account of any recommendation from the ICC ASP. Art. 43(4). He or she serves a five-year term, renewable once. Art. 43(5). The current Registrar is Osvaldo Zavala Giler (Ecuador), who was preceded by Peter Lewis (United Kingdom), Herman von Hebel (the Netherlands), and Silvana Arbia (Italy). The Registry is responsible for three main categories of services: judicial support, external affairs, including dissemination of news and live-streaming Court proceedings, and Court management. The Registry is the largest of the Court's organs.

VII. THE ASSEMBLY OF STATES PARTIES

The Court's Assembly of States Parties (ASP) is composed of States Parties and serves as the Court's management oversight and legislative body. The ASP meets annually either at the seat of the court in The Hague, Netherlands, or at the United Nations Headquarters in New York; the ASP may also hold special sessions if circumstances so require. Each State Party holds one vote, although every effort is made to reach decisions by consensus. Non-States Parties to the Rome Statute may participate in the work of the ASP as observers, without the right to vote, if they signed the Final Act of the Rome Diplomatic Conference. The ICC President, the Prosecutor, and the Registrar, or their representatives, may also participate in the meetings of the ASP, as appropriate.

Article 112 of the Rome Statute tasks the ASP to provide management oversight to the Presidency, the Prosecutor, and the Registrar with regards to the Court's administration. The ASP also adopts the *Rules of Procedure and Evidence* and the *Elements of Crimes*. These two documents are of prime importance for the Court and for the effective and fair functioning of its judicial processes. The *Rules of Procedure and Evidence* delineate how various procedural and evidentiary issues are to be resolved; this is a particularly significant development at the ICC, as such procedural matters had mostly been left to judges under the structures of other *ad hoc* tribunals. The *Elements of Crimes* document assists the Court in the interpretation and application of Articles 6, 7, 8, and 8 *bis* of the Rome Statute, thereby providing further clarity as to the meaning of each substantive crime.

The ASP meets annually, and at these meetings considers budgetary issues and audit reports, as well as other reports on the activities of various organs of the Court. The ASP is also tasked with the election of judges, the Prosecutor, and the Deputy Prosecutor(s), and has the power to decide, by secret ballot, on their removal from office under Article 46 of the Statute.

VIII. PREMISES AND *IN SITU* PROCEEDINGS

The seat of the Court is located in The Hague, the Netherlands. In December 2015, the Court moved to its current location, near the International Court of Justice, Europol, the International Criminal Tribunal for the former Yugoslavia, and other international organizations, occupying a site generously donated to it by The Netherlands. In addition to its main building in The Hague, the ICC also maintains a liaison office to the United Nations, located in New York City, and has operated field offices in Bangui (Central African Republic), Abidjan (Côte d'Ivoire), Kinshasa, Bunia, and Ituri (Democratic Republic of the Congo), Nairobi (Kenya), and Kampala (Uganda). It is permissible under the Statute to hold trials outside of The Hague, if the judges so determine under Article 62, but to date that has not occurred, although judges have visited crime scenes in situation countries.

In 2023 the ICC concluded agreements with Ukraine and with Venezuela to establish additional field offices. Press Release, International Criminal Court, *Ukraine and International Criminal Court sign an agreement on the establishment of a country office*, ICC-CPI-20230323-PR17 (Mar. 23, 2023); Karim A.A. Khan KC, *ICC Prosecutor Karim A.A. Khan KC concludes visit to Colombia, signing Action Plan for renewed cooperation with national authorities in pursuit of accountability* (June 9, 2023). The Prosecutor recently identified an increase in the OTP's field presence as one of its key strategic goals. INT'L CRIM CT. OFF. OF THE PROSECUTOR, STRATEGIC PLAN 2023–2025.

Selected Sources and Additional Reading

LOUISE CHAPPELL, GENDER AND JUDGING AT THE INTERNATIONAL CRIMINAL COURT (2010).

IDENTITY AND DIVERSITY ON THE INTERNATIONAL BENCH: WHO IS THE JUDGE? (Freya Baetens ed., 2020).

THE INTERNATIONAL CRIMINAL COURT AND COMPLEMENTARITY: FROM THEORY TO PRACTICE (Carsten Stahn & Mohamed El Zeidy eds., 2010).

MARK KLAMBERG, EVIDENCE IN INTERNATIONAL CRIMINAL TRIALS: CONFRONTING LEGAL GAPS AND THE RECONSTRUCTION OF DISPUTED EVENTS (2013).

KARIM A. A. KHAN, CAROLINE BUISMAN & CHRISTOPHER GOSNELL, PRINCIPLES OF EVIDENCE IN INTERNATIONAL CRIMINAL JUSTICE (2010).

Hirad Abtahi & Steven Arrigg Koh, *The Emerging Enforcement Practice of the International Criminal Court*, 45 CORNELL J. INT'L L. 1 (2012).

Nancy Combs, *Dissent and Legitimacy in International Criminal Law,* 57 WAKE FOREST L. REV. 1061 (2023).

Volker Roben, *The Procedure of the ICC: Status and Function of the Prosecutor*, 7 MAX PLANCK Y.B. U.N. L. 513 (2003).

Leila Sadat, *Meeting Challenges: Politics, Trial Processes, and Early Judicial Work, in* THE INTERNATIONAL CRIMINAL COURT: CONTEMPORARY CHALLENGES AND REFORM PROPOSALS 319 (Richard H. Steinberg, ed., 2020).

Gerard A.M. Strijards & Robert O. Harmsen, *Article 103: Role of States in enforcement of sentences of Imprisonment, in* THE ROME STATUTE OF THE INTERNATIONAL CRIMINAL COURT: A COMMENTARY 2173 (Otto Trifterrer & Kai Ambos, 3d ed., 2016).

Yvonne Dutton & Milena Sterio, *The United States Can and Should Broadly Contribute to the Trust Fund for Victims (Part IV)*, JUST SEC. (Feb. 16, 2023), https://www.justsecurity.org/85156/the-united-states-can-and-should-broadly-contribute-to-the-trust-fund-for-victims-part-iv/.

Gregory Gordon, *Selecting the ICC's Next ASP President: High Scrutiny for High Stakes*, OPINIO JURIS (Nov. 16, 2020), http://opiniojuris.org/2020/11/16/selecting-the-iccs-next-asp-president-high-scrutiny-for-high-stakes/.

Angela Mudukuti, *IER Blog Series: The Next ICC President: Watch This Election Closely*, INT'L JUST. MONITOR (Mar. 1, 2021), https://www.ijmonitor.org/2021/03/ier-blog-series-the-next-icc-president-watch-this-election-closely/.

Assembly of States Parties to the Rome Statute of the International Criminal Court, Strengthening the Enforcement of Sentences, ICC 2010 Review Conference Resolution RC/Res.3 (9th Plenary Meeting, June 8, 2010), http://www.icc-cpi.int/iccdocs/asp_docs/Resolutions/RC-Res.3-ENG.pdf.

Assembly of States Parties to the Rome Statute of the International Criminal Court, Report of the Bureau on Cooperation, ICC-ASP/11/28, ¶ 12 (Oct. 23, 2012).

INDEPENDENT EXPERT REVIEW OF THE INTERNATIONAL CRIMINAL COURT AND THE ROME STATUTE SYSTEM: FINAL REPORT (Sept. 30, 2020), https://asp.icc-cpi.int/sites/asp/files/asp_docs/ASP19/IER-Final-Report-ENG.pdf.

INTERNATIONAL BAR ASSOCIATION, EVIDENCE MATTERS IN ICC TRIALS (Aug. 2016), https://www.ibanet.org/document?id=Evidence-matters-in-icc-trials.

INTERNATIONAL BAR ASSOCIATION, IBA/ICC MONITORING AND OUTREACH PROGRAMME (June 2011), https://www.ibanet.org/document?id=June-2011-ICC-External-Communications.

International Criminal Court, *The Presidency*, https://www.icc-cpi.int/about/presidency.

Resolution on Strengthening the enforcement of sentences, ICC Resolution RC/Res. 3, June 8, 2010, https://asp.icc-cpi.int/sites/asp/files/asp_docs/Resolutions/RC-Res.3-ENG.pdf.

Press Release, International Criminal Court, *ICC and Spain conclude Agreement on the Enforcement of Sentences*, ICC-CPI-20221208-PR1692, https://www.icc-cpi.int/news/icc-and-spain-conclude-agreement-enforcement-sentences#:~:text=Similar%20agreements%20on%20the%20enforcement,Great%20Britain%20and%20Northern%20Ireland.

Press Release, International Criminal Court, *ICC Judges Authorize Prosecution to Resume Investigation in Afghanistan*, ICC-CPI-20221031-PR1680 (Oct. 31, 2022), https://www.icc-cpi.int/news/icc-judges-authorise-prosecution-r.esume-investigation-afghanistan.

The Trust Fund for Victims, *About us*, https://www.trustfundforvictims.org/en/about/vision.

THE WOMEN'S INITIATIVE FOR GENDER JUSTICE, GENDER REPORT CARD ON THE INTERNATIONAL CRIMINAL COURT 2018 (Dec. 2018), https://4genderjustice.org/ftp-files/publications/Gender-Report_design-full-WEB.pdf.

Al Jazeera, *ICC Prosecutor Defends Dropping US from Afghan War Crime Probe* (Dec. 6, 2021), https://www.aljazeera.com/news/2021/12/6/icc-prosecutor-defends-dropping-us-from-afghan-investigation.

CHAPTER 4

THE COURT AND THE UNITED NATIONS

I. INTRODUCTION

As the world's first permanent international criminal court, the negotiators of the Rome Statute recognized that the ICC needed to be independent from the political workings of the United Nations. They also realized that to be effective, and to ensure its legitimacy, the Court would need the U.N.'s active support. The ICC was created at a U.N. Diplomatic Conference, but as a separate institution that is formally outside of the U.N. framework. It was established by a multilateral treaty rather than by endeavoring to amend the United Nations Charter, a difficult and probably unachievable possibility, and the negotiators also rejected attempting to establish the court through a Security Council or General Assembly resolution as an insufficiently firm legal basis for the establishment of a permanent institution. Article 2 of the Rome Statute mandated that the ICC enter into a cooperation agreement with the United Nations, which was adopted as the Negotiated Relationship Agreement Between the International Criminal Court and the United Nations (Relationship Agreement) on October 4, 2004. The Rome Statute also allows the Security Council to refer cases to the Court, and to defer them under limited circumstances. Yet the Court's relationship with the Security Council remains challenging, largely because the Security Council has done little to support it, even with respect to the two situations referred to the Court by the Security Council—Libya and Sudan. The process by which the ICC was created is addressed in Chapter 1. This Chapter focuses on the ongoing relationship between the ICC and the United Nations.

II. THE RELATIONSHIP AGREEMENT

The ICC's formal relationship with the U.N. is governed by a Relationship Agreement which entered into force on October 4, 2004. Under this Agreement, the United Nations recognized the Court as an independent permanent judicial institution with international legal personality and legal capacity. Two themes permeate the Relationship Agreement. First, the ICC is an independent judicial organ and functions separately from the United Nations; second, the United Nations has a duty to cooperate with and support the ICC.

§ 4-1 MUTUAL OBLIGATIONS IN THE RELATIONSHIP AGREEMENT

The Relationship Agreement imposes specific obligations on each party. In addition, Article 3 imposes a general obligation of cooperation, according to which both parties pledge to consult with each other on important issues. Article 4 provides for reciprocal representation. It grants the Court the right to attend and participate in the work of the General Assembly as an observer and allows the President or Prosecutor of the Court to address the Security Council when it is considering matters related to the Court's activities. For example, the ICC Prosecutor has addressed the Security Council several times on the issue of the outstanding arrest warrants against the former president of Sudan, Omar Al-Bashir, as well as more generally regarding the Situation in Darfur, referred to the Court by the Council under Security Council Resolution 1593. Press Release, International Criminal Court, *Statement of ICC Prosecutor, Karim A.A. Khan KC, to the United Nations Security Council on the situation in Darfur, pursuant to Resolution 1593* (July 13, 2023). Article 4 also grants the U.N. Secretary General (or his or her representative) a standing invitation to attend public proceedings of the Court.

The United Nations and the ICC share information, and Article 5 provides for the exchange of information between the parties. The Secretary-General must transmit to the Court information on developments related to the Rome Statute which are relevant to the Court's work. The Court's Registrar must provide the United Nations with information and documentation related to pleadings, proceedings, judgments, and orders of the Court for cases which may be of interest to the United Nations. Article 5 also requires the ICC Registrar to provide information about the ICC's work if the International Court of Justice requests it. Article 6 permits the Court to submit reports on its activities to the United Nations, which the Court has done annually since 2005. These reports describe the Court's activities, including updates on situations, cases and preliminary examinations. The reports also describe the state of the Court's cooperation with the United Nations, including any challenges. Article 7 allows the Court to propose items for the United Nations to consider. Finally, the Office of the Prosecutor provides annual reports to the U.N. Security Council regarding cases which the Security Council has referred to the Court. In cases involving the prosecution of the crime of aggression, if the investigation is initiated by the Prosecutor *proprio motu* or referred by a State Party, the Prosecutor must inform the Security Council about the investigation and give the Security Council six months to determine if an act of aggression has occurred. If the Security Council fails to make such a determination, the Prosecutor may only proceed if authorized by a Pre-Trial Chamber. Art. 15 *bis*.

The ICC and the United Nations have also agreed to cooperate on more practical matters. Article 8 requires the parties to consult and cooperate regarding personnel arrangements. This includes consulting on the employment of their officers and staff, cooperating in the temporary interchange of personnel, and making most efficient use of specialized personnel, systems, and services. Article 9 requires the parties to consult on administrative matters to avoid the creation of overlapping or competing facilities or services. Article 10 obligates the United Nations to provide the Court with facilities and services as may be required, including for Assembly of States Parties meetings, with translation and interpretation services, as well as documentation and conference services. In fact, the Assembly of States Parties has been meeting at the

U.N. headquarters in New York City at least as often as every third year. Article 12 allows the Court's judges, the Prosecutor, Deputy Prosecutor, and Registrar, in addition to Registry and Office of the Prosecutor staff and officials, to use the *laissez-passer* of the United Nations as a valid travel document where such use is recognized by States.

The ICC and the United Nations must also cooperate on sensitive case-related matters. Article 15 addresses general cooperation obligations between the parties and specifies that the United Nations is to cooperate with the Court and provide it with information or documents it requests. Article 16 provides that the United Nations shall cooperate with the Court should the latter request the testimony of a U.N. official. Article 17 provides for cooperation between the Security Council and the ICC in referrals of situations to the Court by the Security Council under its powers in Chapter VII of the U.N. Charter. Article 17 also addresses issues of State non-cooperation with the Court; in such cases, the Court shall inform the Security Council of the matter, and the Security Council may take appropriate action. Article 18 obligates the United Nations to cooperate with the Prosecutor, and to enter into additional cooperation agreements with the Prosecutor as may be necessary. Article 10 requires the United Nations to waive privileges and immunities attached to a person who may enjoy them if the person is alleged to be criminally responsible for a crime within the Court's jurisdiction, thereby allowing the Court to actually exercise its jurisdiction over this person. Finally, Article 20 provides for confidentiality, and allows the United Nations to seek the consent of a person or entity that possesses information before disclosing such information to the Court.

§ 4-2 INFORMATION SHARING AND ARTICLE 18 OF THE RELATIONSHIP AGREEMENT

Article 18 of the Relationship Agreement permits the United Nations to provide information to the ICC Prosecutor on a confidential basis, and Article 54(3)(e) permits the Prosecutor to enter into such confidentiality agreements for the purpose of generating "lead evidence." In *Prosecutor v. Lubanga*, these agreements came into conflict with the Prosecutor's duty under Article 67(2) of the Rome Statute to disclose exculpatory information to the defense. Throughout the investigation of the situation in the Democratic Republic of Congo (DRC), the Prosecutor entered into numerous agreements under Article 54(3)(e), with both the United Nations and other so-called "information providers," such that approximately fifty percent of the evidence gathered in the DRC was obtained under an obligation of confidentiality. In light of uncertainty regarding the Prosecutor's disclosure obligations, the Trial Chamber stayed the proceedings against Lubanga, holding that the trial process had been affected to such a degree that it was impossible to guarantee the defendant a fair trial. Prosecutor v. Thomas Lubanga Dyilo, Case No. ICC-01/04-01/06, *Decision on the consequences of non-disclosure of exculpatory materials covered by Article 54(3)(e)* *agreements and the application to stay the prosecution of the accused, together with certain other issues raised at the Status Conference on **10** June **2008*** (TC I, June 15, 2008).

The Trial Chamber's decision was subsequently upheld by the Appeals Chamber, which stressed that, under the language of the Rome Statute, Article 54(3)(e) confidentiality agreements should only be made for the purpose of gathering lead evidence. Prosecutor v. Thomas Lubanga Dyilo, Case No. ICC-01/04-01/06, *Judgment on the appeal of the Prosecutor against the decision of Trial Chamber I entitled "Decision on the consequences of non-disclosure of exculpatory materials covered by Article 54(3)(e) agreements and the application to stay the prosecution of the accused"* (AC, Oct. 21, 2008). That said, the Appeals Chamber ultimately allowed the trial to continue, although it found that the Prosecutor must use Article 54(3)(e) in such a manner that allows *the Court*, rather than the Prosecutor, to resolve the potential tension between confidentiality and the demands of a fair trial.

III. THE COURT AND THE SECURITY COUNCIL

The ICC's relationship with the Security Council continues to be one of the most important and challenging aspects of its operation. Article 13(b) of the Rome Statute permits the U.N. Security Council to refer situations to the ICC. While these referrals expand the Court's ability to investigate and prosecute cases, they also create additional complex legal issues. The U.N. Security Council's ability to refer cases to the ICC was the subject of controversy at the time of the 1998 Rome Statute negotiations. Powerful States, including the United States, were in favor of subjecting the Court's exercise of jurisdiction to the approval of the Security Council. Other States, however, supported a politically independent Court, and did not want to rely heavily on the Security Council in jurisdictional matters. The compromise reached in Rome resulted in the ability of the Security Council to refer cases to the Court under Article 13(b) and permitted the Prosecutor to initiate certain cases *proprio motu*.

§ 4-3 SECURITY COUNCIL REFERRALS

Article 13(b) provides that the Security Council may, acting under its power granted by Chapter VII of the U.N. Charter, refer a situation to the ICC. The Security Council has done this twice. In March 2005, the Security Council adopted Resolution 1593 referring the situation in Darfur, Sudan, which is not an ICC State Party, to the Court. The vote on Resolution 1593 was divided, but sufficient to adopt the resolution. In February 2011, the Security Council unanimously adopted Resolution 1970 referring the situation in Libya, which is also not an ICC State Party, to the ICC. These two referrals, however, represent the exception and not the rule. Security Council referrals to the ICC remain rare because of the ability of any one of the permanent members—China, France, Russia, the United Kingdom, and the United States—to veto a resolution based upon its own national priorities. In May 2014, for example, Russia and China vetoed a proposed resolution which would have referred the Syria situation to the ICC.

§ 4-4 THE LEGALITY PRINCIPLE AND SECURITY COUNCIL REFERRALS

Article 22 provides that are not liable under the Statute unless their conduct was "at the time it takes place, a crime within the jurisdiction of the Court." Because the negotiators of the Rome Statute were careful to rely upon customary international law in their codification of ICC crimes, Security Council referrals regarding crimes committed on the territory of non-States Parties, or the exercise of jurisdiction by the Court over the nationals of non-States Parties should not, in principle, pose a problem under Article 22 which encompasses the principle of *nullum crimen sine lege* (no punishment without law or the "legality principle," as it is known in international human rights law).

That said, defense counsel have raised challenges to Security Council referrals on this basis. In *Prosecutor v. Ali Kushayb*, the Appeals Chamber held that the general legal framework of the Rome Statute, as well as human rights law, applies in situations referred to the Court by the Security Council. Prosecutor v. Ali Muhammad Ali Abd-Al-Rahman ("Ali Kushayb"), Case No. ICC-02/05-01/20, *Judgment on the Appeal of Mr Abd-Al-Rahman against the Pre-Trial Chamber II's "Decision on the Defence 'Exception d'incompetence'* (ICC-02/05-01/20-302)," (AC, Nov. 1, 2021). Thus, the doctrine of *nullum crimen sine lege* applies to all ICC cases, including those referred to by the Security Council. In a somewhat confusing opinion, the Appeals Chamber held that the ICC can only exercise jurisdiction over an individual who could have reasonably expected to face prosecution under national or international law. Controversially, the Appeals Chamber seemed to suggest that in cases involving the commission of alleged crimes on the territory of a non-State Party, to determine "foreseeability," the Court must look beyond the Rome Statute to factors such as the domestic law of the territorial State, international law, and even the position of the accused himself to determine if it were foreseeable (to them) that their conduct could lead to criminal charges.

In the case of *Ali Kushayb,* the Court found that not only was Sudan a party to various treaties that applied, and that Ali Kushayb himself was a commander who appreciated the framework of laws applicable to the conflict in Darfur, but that the "crimes under the Statute were intended to be generally representative of the state of customary international law when the Statute was drafted." *Id.,* at ¶ 89. Thus, the Chamber was satisfied that it was foreseeable to Ali Kushayb that he risked criminal liability for his conduct, especially because of his high rank. *Id.,* at ¶ 90.

The Appeals Chamber's reasoning is curious. The Appeals Chamber's approach suggests that the application of the Rome Statute may be contingent (as to non-State Party nationals), and that it might not apply to lower-ranking individuals. It also suggests that for at least some members of the Appeals Chamber, these are not *jus cogens* offenses that are universal and peremptory. This is contrary to the jurisdictional reach of the Statute established at Rome, as well as the decision of the Appeals Chamber in the *Al Bashir* immunity decision discussed in Chapter 2, and could, for example, allow Russian troops to commit war crimes or crimes against humanity in Ukraine with impunity on the grounds that Russia had not ratified the Rome Statute, had repudiated its signature thereto, and that therefore it would not be "foreseeable" to Russian forces that their conduct violated the criminal law of the Rome Statute.

§ 4-5 SECURITY COUNCIL REFERRALS AND THE CRIME OF AGGRESSION

A Security Council referral allows the ICC to investigate all crimes within the Court's jurisdiction, including the crime of aggression. Under Article 15 *ter*, the Security Council's powers under the U.N. Charter constitute the legal basis upon which the ICC can investigate the crime of aggression, without any consent requirement by the States involved. A Security Council determination that the crime of aggression has taken place is not binding on the ICC, which retains the ability to make its own assessment as to whether aggression has occurred. For more information about the crime of aggression, see Chapter 5.

§ 4-6 SECURITY COUNCIL REFERRALS AND ARTICLE 16

Article 16 grants the Security Council the ability to request that the ICC suspend, for a renewable period of twelve months, any investigation or prosecution either about to be commenced or already commenced, if the Security Council believes that this is necessary in order to maintain or restore international peace and security. As mentioned in Chapter 2, ¶ 2–8, an unsuccessful effort was made to invoke Article 16 in the Kenya situation.

In the Darfur situation, after the Prosecutor asked an ICC pre-Trial Chamber to issue an arrest warrant for then-Sudanese President Al-Bashir, the government of Sudan, supported by Russia, China, Libya, the African Union, and the League of Arab States, argued that the Security Council should exercise its authority under Article 16 to request the suspension of the ICC proceedings related to Darfur. These States and organizations claimed that the issuance of an arrest warrant against Al-Bashir would undermine ongoing efforts to find a peaceful resolution to the conflict in Darfur. In contrast, a number of States, including the United Kingdom, the United States, and Croatia, as well as some non-governmental organizations, opposed any action by the Security Council on the ground that, *inter alia*, intervention by the Security Council would be contrary to the rule of law. In the case of Al-Bashir, this issue has been settled as the Security Council has not intervened and has not requested the suspension of ICC proceedings in the Darfur situation.

More generally, the debate over whether the Security Council should invoke Article 16 to request deferral of a prosecution implicates two relevant issues: (i) whether the Rome Statute permits the Security Council to request that the ICC defer ongoing investigations or prosecutions when the Security Council has itself referred them to the ICC; and (ii) assuming an affirmative answer to the first question, whether the Security Council, as a matter of policy, should request such a deferral. In the context of the Darfur situation, some scholars have concluded that while the Security Council has the authority to request a deferral, it should only do so in exceptional circumstances.

§ 4-7 CHALLENGES RELATED TO SECURITY COUNCIL REFERRALS

Several challenges remain regarding the Security Council's ability to refer situations to the ICC. First, the Security Council is a political body limited by its veto structure; thus, referrals are always selective and shield some States from the Court's jurisdiction. The situations in North Korea and Sri Lanka are examples of situations in which atrocity crimes may have been committed according to official reports, but there is a strong likelihood that an attempt to refer those situations to the ICC would be vetoed by China and/or Russia. France's draft resolution to authorize an ICC investigation into the Syrian situation was vetoed by Russia and China, Press Release, United

Nations, *Referral of Syria to International Criminal Court Fails as Negative Votes Prevent Security Council from Adopting Draft Resolution,* SC/11407 (May 22, 2014). Likewise, any attempt to refer the Ukraine situation to the ICC would undoubtedly be subject to vetoes by Russia and, most likely, China as well.

Second, the Security Council may sometimes have to limit its own referral to obtain political support for a proposed resolution. In the case of Libya, paragraph 5 of Security Council Resolution 1970 allowed the Court to investigate Libyan nationals while excluding from the Court's jurisdiction the nationals of other non-State Parties. This language was the result of negotiations within the Security Council and seen as necessary to secure the political buy-in of the United States and other veto-wielding Council members. In addition, paragraph 8 of Resolution 1970, like paragraph 7 of Resolution 1953, provides that the expenses from the Libyan investigation would have to borne by the Court and not by the United Nations, depriving the Court of much needed resources.

Finally, one of the most important challenges facing the ICC is the lack of sufficient cooperation from States, which has also been seen with respect to Security Council referrals. Although Security Council referrals are based on Chapter VII of the U.N. Charter, and thereby binding on all U.N. Member States, neither Resolution 1593 nor 1970 specifically required States Parties to the Rome Statute to cooperate with the Court (although other provisions of the Statute do require them to cooperate as detailed in Chapter 7, *infra*), but only urged them to do so. The resolutions also noted that "States not party to the Rome Statute have no obligation under the Statute." S.C. Resolution 1970, ¶ 5; S.C. Resolution 1593, ¶ 2.

In the Darfur and Libya situations, ICC progress has been slow, in part due to non-cooperation by ICC non-States Parties, and in particular regarding the non-enforcement of ICC arrest warrants. In the Darfur situation, the ICC arrest warrants respecting former President Al-Bashir have not been enforced by several States—including ICC States Parties and non-States Parties, allowing him to travel extensively with relative impunity. The particular challenge of head-of-state immunity is addressed in Chapter 2.

IV. CALLS FOR REFORM

§ 4-8 OPPORTUNITIES FOR ENHANCED COOPERATION BY THE SECURITY COUNCIL

The United Nations could develop a coherent strategy to support the ICC's work related to situations it refers to the Court. For example, the Security Council could assist the Court in carrying out arrest warrants by putting pressure on States through sanctions, asset freezes, and other diplomatic tools. Such pressure through the Security Council can isolate the leaders of the affected States and increase the impact of the Court's decisions. Frozen assets can also eventually be used to cover defendants' legal fees or to pay reparations to the victims. The Security Council can also support the Court politically by issuing statements of support toward the Court and by refusing to endorse amnesties; moreover, permanent members of the Security Council could abstain from using the veto in situations where atrocity crimes appear to have been committed. Finally, future referral resolutions could delete the paragraph forbidding the United Nations from contributing to ICC expenses regarding Security Council referrals, thereby permitting the General Assembly to allocate funds for future ICC situations.

§ 4-9 GENERAL ASSEMBLY "UNITING FOR PEACE" RESOLUTIONS AS A REFERRAL MECHANISM

In the context of Russia's invasion of Ukraine, and in light of the Security Council's veto structure, some experts have suggested that the U.N. General Assembly should be authorized to refer situations to the ICC. The General Assembly has already adopted a resolution condemning Russian actions in Ukraine and in doing so, it has invoked the 1950 "Uniting for Peace" Resolution, according to which the Assembly can act in situations of Security Council paralysis. G.A. Res. 377(V) (Nov. 3, 1950). Allowing the General Assembly to refer situations to the ICC would require an amendment to the Rome Statute; it was an option considered and rejected during the Statute's negotiation. It is conceivable that bestowing such powers on the General Assembly would be consistent with the "Uniting for Peace" principles and with the

Assembly's general role in maintaining peace and security; at the same time, considerable practical obstacles and legal questions are raised by this proposal.

§ 4-10 LIMITATIONS ON THE USE OF THE VETO IN THE WAKE OF ATROCITY CRIMES

Another option to enhance the ICC and the United Nation's effectiveness is to somehow require the permanent members of the security to limit their use of the veto. In April 2023, France and Mexico, reiterating earlier initiatives, proposed that all five permanent members of the Security Council voluntarily and collectively suspend the use of the veto in cases of mass atrocities. Scholars have also argued that vetoes involving mass atrocities are actually illegal under international law. Because the veto power of the permanent members derives from the United Nations Charter, which is subsidiary to *jus cogens* norms and violates that Charter's purposes and principles, it has been argued that use of the veto in mass atrocity situations violates international law.

Selected Sources and Additional Reading

DAPO AKANDE, INTERNATIONAL LAW IMMUNITIES AND THE INTERNATIONAL CRIMINAL COURT (2017).

WILLIAM A. SCHABAS, INTERNATIONAL CRIMINAL COURT: A COMMENTARY ON THE ROME STATUTE (2ND ED. 2016).

ALEXANDER SKANDER GALAND, UN SECURITY COUNCIL REFERRALS TO THE INTERNATIONAL

CRIMINAL COURT: LEGAL NATURE, EFFECTS AND LIMITS (2019.

INTERNATIONAL PEACE INSTITUTE, THE RELATIONSHIP BETWEEN THE ICC AND THE SECURITY COUNCIL: CHALLENGES AND OPPORTUNITIES (MAR. 2013), https://www.ipinst.org/wp-content/uploads/publications/ipi_e_pub_relationship_bet__icc_and_sc__2_.pdf.

JENNIFER TRAHAN, EXISTING LEGAL LIMITS TO SECURITY COUNCIL VETO POWER IN THE FACE OF ATROCITY CRIMES (2020).

Louise Arbour, *The Relationship between the ICC and the UN Security Council*, 20 GLOBAL GOVERNANCE 195 (2014).

Miguel Lemos, *The Appeal's Chamber's Jurisdiction Judgment in Abd-Al-Rahman and the Issue of Applicable Law at the International Criminal Court*, 22 CHINESE J. INT'L. L. 223 (2023).

Marko Milanovic, *Is the Rome Statute Binding on Individuals? (And Why We Should Care)*, 9 J. INT'L CRIM JUST. 25 (2011).

Shane Darcy, *Aggression by P5 Security Council Members: Time for ICC Referrals by the General Assembly*, JUST SEC. (Mar. 16, 2002), https://www.justsecurity.org/80686/aggression-by-p5-security-council-members-time-for-icc-referrals-by-the-general-assembly/.

Lukas Emanuel Muller, *Recapitulating the History of the SC-ICC Relationship*, VÖLKERRECHTSBLOG (July

12, 2022), https://voelkerrechtsblog.org/referrals-deferrals-and-many-double-standards/.

The Global Campaign for Ratification and Implementation of the Kampala Amendments on the Crime of Aggression, *The ICC and the Security Council*, https://crimeofaggression.info/role-of-the-icc/the-icc-and-the-un-security-council/.

Leila Nadya Sadat, *Heads of State and Other Government Officials Before the International Criminal Court: The Uneasy Revolution Continues, in* THE ELGAR COMPANION TO THE INTERNATIONAL CRIMINAL COURT 96 (Margaret M. deGuzman & Valerie Oosterveld eds., 2020).

William A. Schabas, *United States Hostility to the International Criminal Court: It's All About the Security Council*, 15 EUROPEAN JOURNAL OF INTERNATIONAL LAW 701 (2004).

Press Release, International Criminal Court, *Statement of ICC Prosecutor, Karim A.A. Khan KC, to the United Nations Security Council on the situation in Darfur, pursuant to Resolution 1593* (July 13, 2023).

United Nations, *Russia, China block Security Council referral of Syria to International Criminal Court* (May 22, 2014), https://news.un.org/en/story/2014/05/468962-russia-china-block-security-council-referral-syria-international-criminal-court.

United Nations, *General Assembly Holds First-Ever Debate on Historic Veto Resolution, Adopts Texts on Infrastructure, National Reviews, Council of Europe*

Cooperation, GA/12500 (Apr. 26, 2023), https://press.un.org/en/2023/ga12500.doc.htm#:~:text=In%20that%20spirt%2C%20the%20representative,in%20cases%20of%20mass%20atrocities.

S.C. Res. 1593 (Mar. 31, 2005).

S.C. Res. 1970 (Feb. 26, 2011).

Jennifer Trahan, *UNSC Veto Power Symposium: New Perspective for Tackling a Core Challenge to the UN System on the 75th Anniversary of the United Nations*, OPINIO JURIS (Nov. 30, 2020), http://opiniojuris.org/2020/11/30/unsc-veto-power-symposium-new-perspective-for-tackling-a-core-challenge-to-the-un-system-on-the-75th-anniversary-of-the-united-nations/.

Talita de Souza Dias, *The Principle of Legality in the ICC's Appeals Judgment on Abd-Al-Rahman's Jurisdictional Challenge: A Follow-up on Merits and Shortcomings*, EJIL:TALK! (Dec. 1, 2021), https://www.ejiltalk.org/the-principle-of-legality-in-the-iccs-appeals-judgment-on-abd-al-rahmans-jurisdictional-challenge-a-follow-up-on-merits-and-shortcomings/.

WAR CRIMES RESEARCH OFFICE, INTERNATIONAL CRIMINAL COURT LEGAL ANALYSIS AND EDUCATION PROJECT, THE RELATIONSHIP BETWEEN THE INTERNATIONAL CRIMINAL COURT AND THE UNITED NATIONS (AUG. 2009), https://www.wcl.american.edu/wcl-american-edu/assets/WCRO_Report_on_ICC_and_UN_August2009.pdf.

CHAPTER 5

SUBSTANTIVE LAW OF THE COURT: THE CORE CRIMES

I. INTRODUCTION

As noted in Chapter 1, §§ 1-3 to 1-6, the Rome Statute was negotiated on the basis of a text submitted to States by the U.N. International Law Commission (ILC). The ILC's 1994 draft statute originally proposed including two categories of crimes: the first category would have been "core crimes" under international law; namely, genocide, aggression, serious violations of the laws of war, and crimes against humanity. The second category was "treaty" crimes, which included transnational crimes such as terrorism and drug trafficking, but also, confusingly, apartheid and grave breaches of the 1949 Geneva Conventions on the laws of war. As negotiation of the Rome Statute progressed, States decided to limit the ICC's jurisdiction to the core crimes, based upon their understanding of the contours of these crimes under customary international law. The crimes of genocide, crimes against humanity, and war crimes was easily agreed upon by those present. Aggression, however, proved challenging, and was therefore included, but not defined (or justiciable) in the text of the Statute adopted in 1998.

II. GENOCIDE

§ 5-1 ELABORATING THE DEFINITION

Genocide was the least controversial and simplest of the core crimes to include in the Rome Statute, as it had been codified in the Convention on the Prevention and Punishment of the Crime of Genocide, adopted by the U.N. General Assembly in 1948, and incorporated into the Statutes of the International Criminal Tribunals for the former Yugoslavia and Rwanda unchanged. The International Court of Justice found the convention definition to be part of customary international law, "binding on States, even without any conventional obligation," *Reservations to the Genocide Convention,* Advisory Opinion, 1951 I.C.J. 15, 23 (May 23).

Article I of the Genocide Convention states that genocide is a crime, whether committed in "time of peace or in time of war," and requires States to prevent and punish it. Article II defines genocide as a series of acts, "committed with intent to destroy, in whole or in part, a national, ethnical, racial or religious group." The prohibited acts include killing, causing serious bodily or mental harm, deliberately inflicting "conditions of life calculated to bring about" the physical destruction of the group in whole or in part, imposing measures intended to prevent births within the group, and forcibly transferring children of the group to another group. This provision was incorporated into Article 6 of the Rome Statute verbatim, as it had been in Articles 4 and 2, respectively, of the Statutes of the ICTY and the

ICTR. The crime of genocide, therefore, requires the commission of a criminal act (*actus reus*) with criminal intent (*mens rea*), and, in addition, under the jurisprudence of the ICTY and the ICTR, requires the act to have been committed with the specific intent (*dolus specialis*) to destroy, in whole or in part, a specific group.

Until the ICTR handed down the *Akayesu* case on September 2, 1998, there had been no prosecutions in national or international courts for the crime of genocide, although the term was used in the *Einsatzgruppen case* in 1946 to describe the crimes committed by Nazi death squads, and in the *Eichmann* case in Israel in 1968. Prosecutor v. Jean-Paul Akayesu, Case No. ICTR-96-4, *Judgment* (TC I, Sept. 2, 1998). Thus, there was no jurisprudence to inform the negotiations in Rome, although scholars and victim communities employed the term "genocide" extensively, and the preparatory works (*travaux préparatoires*) of the Genocide Convention and the work of the International Law Commission offered some insight.

Article III of the Genocide Convention makes genocide a crime, as well as other offenses including conspiracy to commit genocide, direct and public incitement, attempt, and complicity. However, this provision did not find its way into the Rome Statute as such. Rather, the modes of liability for genocide, like those of the other crimes, are found in Article 25 of the ICC Statute, which deleted conspiracy to commit genocide, but included direct and public incitement to genocide as Article 25(e) of the Rome Statute.

By its terms, Article II of the Genocide convention only protects four groups from genocide, and omits social and political groups. This narrow ambit leaves out many of the most severe atrocities of the twentieth century, including the so-called "Cambodian Genocide" during which the Khmer Rouge regime killed an estimated 21 percent of the population (1.7 million people), largely on social and political grounds. During the preparatory meetings for the Rome Statute some delegations suggested adding social and political groups to the treaty; this suggestion did not receive widespread support, however, and they were added to Article 7(1)(h) as part of the crime against humanity of persecution instead.

§ 5-2 INTERPRETATION BY THE COURT

Following the adoption of the Rome Statute in 1998, the ICC Assembly of States Parties adopted so-called "Elements of Crimes," a document setting out the elements to be established to prove each crime, in accordance with Article 9 of the Rome Statute. These Elements are meant to elaborate on and make more specific exactly what the prosecution must prove to obtain a conviction. The Elements for the crime of genocide follow the text of Article 6 of the ICC Statute, with one exception—the *actus reus* must be committed "in the context of a manifest pattern of similar conduct directed against that group or was conduct that could itself effect such destruction." This provision is not found either in the text of the Rome Statute or the jurisprudence of the *ad hoc* tribunals.

Furthermore, for the each of the genocidal acts in Article 6 of the Statute (which track Article II of the Genocide Convention), specific provisions regarding those crimes have been added to the Elements of Crimes. These sometimes provide more definitions and context for terms that might not be clear from the text of the Statute. For example, footnote 4 of the Elements states that, with respect to the crime of genocide committed by deliberately inflicting conditions of life calculated to bring about physical destruction, the term "conditions of life" may include "deliberate deprivation of resources indispensable for survival, such as food or medical services, or systematic expulsion from homes." This could potentially cover situations involving siege warfare, cutting off access to humanitarian assistance, or ethnic cleansing.

With respect to the transfer of children, footnote 5 of the Elements provides that forcible transfer is not limited to physical force, "but may include threat of force or coercion, such as that caused by fear of violence, duress, detention, psychological oppression or abuse of power, against such person or persons or another person, or by taking advantage of a coercive environment." Element 6(e) requires individuals to be under the age of 18 at the time of the transfer, and that the perpetrator knew or should have known that.

As noted above, the "manifest pattern" provision in the Elements of Crimes means that the crime of genocide, as defined by the ICC is without precedent. In 2009, Pre-Trial Chamber I had the opportunity to consider it as it examined the Prosecutor's application for an arrest warrant against Omar Al-Bashir, the former President of Sudan. Al-Bashir was accused of intending to destroy, in part, the Fur, Masalit and Zaghawa ethnic groups, not only through killing and causing serious bodily or mental harm, but also by deliberately inflicting conditions of life calculated to bring about the groups' physical destruction. A Majority of Pre-Trial Chamber I's judges found that, although neither the Genocide Convention itself, nor the jurisprudence of the ICTY and the ICTR required any evidence of a genocidal policy or plan, the heightened standard imposed by the Elements of Crimes was not *per se* contrary to Article 6 of the Statute. Moreover, the Chamber found that it was consistent with Article 22(2)'s requirement that the Statute be "strictly construed," and in "case of ambiguity" interpreted in favor of the accused, and with the idea that genocide is the "crime of crimes." Prosecutor v. Omar Hassan Ahmad Al-Bashir, Case No. ICC-02/05-01/09, *Decision on the Prosecution's Application for a Warrant of Arrest against Omar Hassan Ahmad Al Bashir,* ¶ 133 (PTC I, Mar. 4, 2009).

The Pre-Trial Chamber also noted that the group must be defined "in the positive" and that "negative definitions of the targeted group" do not suffice for the purposes of Article 6. *Id.* ¶ 135. The Pre-Trial Chamber also applied an extraordinarily demanding evidentiary test, concluding that the warrant should not issue against Al Bashir for the crime of genocide because it could not be shown that genocide was the only reasonable conclusion drawn from the evidence (but permitting the warrant's issuance on other charges). *Id.* ¶¶ 158, 159, 203–206. This latter finding (on genocide) was set aside, Prosecutor v. Omar Hassan Ahmad Al-Bashir, Case No. ICC-02/05-01/09, *Judgment on the appeal of the Prosecutor against the "Decision on the Prosecution's Application for a Warrant of Arrest against Omar Hassan Ahmad Al Bashir"* (AC, Feb. 3, 2010), and the Appeals Chamber corrected the heightened evidentiary standard applied by the Pre-Trial Chamber. As of this writing, Al-Bashir has not been surrendered to the ICC and the case has yet to be confirmed.

The ease at which a definition of genocide was agreed is in contrast with the likely utility of genocide charges at the ICC. Indeed, it is safe to say that genocide will be one of the most difficult crimes to allege and prove at the Court. Acquittals on genocide counts at the ICTY in important cases, such as Prosecutor v. Goran Jelisić, Case No. IT-95-10, *Judgment* (TC, Dec. 14, 1999) (upheld on appeal) and Prosecutor v. Ratko Mladić, Case No. MICT-13-56, *Judgment* (AC, June 8, 2021) suggest that charges of genocide at the ICC are likely to be brought only in cases involving mass slaughter where the specific intent to destroy the group *qua* group is manifest and beyond question. The jurisprudence at the ICTY and the ICTR has required compelling evidence of specific intent to destroy the group, proof of the group's existence as a "stable" group, and that a "substantial" part of the group was destroyed. Thus, although allegations of genocide involving certain of the ICC's current situations abound, such as in the Bangladesh/Myanmar situation, the Prosecutor has only requested permission to investigate charges of crimes against humanity at this time.

III. CRIMES AGAINST HUMANITY

§ 5-3 ELABORATING THE DEFINITION

Crimes against humanity materialized as positive law during the Nuremberg and Tokyo tribunals established after World War II, but the concept has a long history. American and European jurists used it during the first half of the nineteenth century to describe slavery and the slave trade; to describe King Leopold's atrocities in the Congo; and in official declarations regarding the massacre of the Armenians in the early twentieth century. The concept was also given voice in the "Martens Clauses" inserted in the preambles of the 1899 and 1907 Hague Treaties, which declared the applicability of the "dictates of the public conscience" and the "laws of humanity" regarding prohibitions on the means and methods of warfare in armed conflict.

Article 6(c) of the Charter of the International Military Tribunal defined them as:

> CRIMES AGAINST HUMANITY: namely, murder, extermination, enslavement, deportation, and other inhumane acts committed against any civilian population, before or during the war; or persecutions on political, racial or religious grounds in execution

> of or in connection with any crime within the jurisdiction of the Tribunal, whether or not in violation of the domestic law of the country where perpetrated.

Unlike the crime of genocide, prior to the adoption of the International Criminal Court Statute in Rome, crimes against humanity had never been formally codified in a specialized convention. Crimes against humanity were included in the statutes of the *ad hoc* international criminal tribunals, including the ICTY and the ICTR, but varied from codification to codification. Thus, the negotiators in Rome had to define crimes against humanity during the Statute's negotiation. Article 7 of the Rome Statute represents their consensus as to which elements of the crime represented customary international law.

They eliminated the armed conflict nexus, found in the ICTY but not the ICTR Statute, but nonetheless retained, in Article 7(1), the requirement of an "attack" directed against a civilian population. They also eliminated the discriminatory intent requirement found in the ICTR Statute. Moreover, they added the requirement that the crime be committed "pursuant to or in furtherance of a state or organizational policy" in Article 7(2)(a). Finally, the list of offenses in Article 7(1)(a) through (k) requires the *actus reus* of the offense be limited to violent attacks upon corporal integrity (and similar offenses), tracking the Statutes of the *ad hoc* tribunals, but with important additions. It was not expanded to cover environmental and/or economic crimes, as some States had urged during the negotiations.

Like other core international crimes, crimes against humanity are composite offenses, comprising a material element (an *actus* reus), a mental element (*mens rea*) and context elements that internationalize the offense. The list of prohibited acts is found in Article 7(1) of the Statute, and includes murder, extermination, deportation and forcible transfer, imprisonment, torture, rape, and other forms of sexual, gender-based and reproductive violence, persecution, and a catch-all provision, other inhumane acts. The mental element is found in Article 30 of the Statute, except for command responsibility, which is addressed in Article 28.

Article 7 contains four separate preconditions that must be satisfied before jurisdiction attaches in a particular case in which crimes against humanity are charged. The ICC Elements of Crimes refer to these as "context" elements. Some of these are arguably jurisdictional in character, meaning that once they have been proven as regards a particular situation, they should not need to be reestablished *ab initio* with respect to each charge, or potentially, with respect to each accused. The four preconditions are (1) the commission of the crime as part of a "widespread or systematic attack;" (2) against a civilian population; (3) with knowledge of the attack [directed against any civilian population]; (4) and involving "a course of conduct involving the multiple commission of acts . . . against any civilian population pursuant to or in furtherance of a State or organization policy to commit such attack."

The text of Article 7, together with the preambular paragraphs of the Elements of Crimes for Article 7, evince an intent to clarify its application; unfortunately, however, they omit definitions for critical terms including "civilian population," "widespread," or "systematic" attacks, and offer little guidance as to the meaning of "state or organizational policy." Thus, the job of definition, interpretation, and application of Article 7 fell by default to the Prosecutor in the first instance, and to the Court's judiciary upon review.

§ 5-4 INTERPRETATION BY THE COURT

§ 5.4.1 Context Elements

The early case law of the ICC defined the terms "widespread" and "systematic" with relative ease, relying upon jurisprudence from the *ad hoc* international criminal tribunals to do so. It also concluded that the "attack" against the civilian population need not be a military operation. In the 2021 case of *Prosecutor v. Dominic Ongwen*, confirming earlier jurisprudence, the Trial Chamber held that an attack under Article 7 must be "a course of conduct," by which is meant a "series or overall flow of events, as opposed to a mere aggregate of random or isolated acts[,]" committed by a State or "organization;" the latter requiring only that "the organization has a set of structures or mechanisms, whatever those may be, that are sufficiently efficient to ensure the coordination necessary to carry out an attack directed against a civilian population." Prosecutor v. Dominic Ongwen, Case No. ICC-02/04-01/15, *Judgment*, ¶ 2674 (TC IX, Feb. 4, 2021).

The meaning of "state or organizational policy" has presented more difficulty of interpretation as it was not included as a context element in the *ad hoc* tribunals for the former Yugoslavia or Rwanda. It is, however, a requirement of Article 7, and it is still debated whether it is part of customary international law. The Court addressed it first in connection with a request to open an investigation into the 2007 post-election violence that took place in Kenya, which the Office of the Prosecutor argued was characterized by the commission of crimes against humanity. In considering the Prosecutor's request, the Majority of Pre-Trial Chamber II noted that the policy element had been eventually abandoned by the *ad hoc* tribunals but drew upon earlier cases in examining the Rome Statute. Situation in the Republic of Kenya, Case No. ICC-01/09, *Decision Pursuant to Article 15 of the Rome Statute of the Authorization of an Investigation into the Situation in the Republic of Kenya*, ¶ 86 (PTC II, Mar. 31, 2010). Finding that the plan to commit the attack may be inferred from the commission of "a series of events," including a variety of factors, *id.* ¶ 87, the Majority read "state or organizational," in Article 7(2)(a) disjunctively, rejecting the notion that only "State-like organizations may qualify." Rather, it focused upon "whether a group has the capability to perform acts which infringe on basic human values," adding that the organization need not be "State-like," and that the policy need not have been conceived at the highest level of the State, for "regional or even local organs of the State could satisfy the requirement of a State policy." *Id.* ¶¶ 89–90. Although Judge Hans-Peter Kaul penned an influential dissent, contending that the organization must be "State-like" for its policies to fall within the ambit of article 7, the Majority view has prevailed at the Court.

At the Rome Conference, some delegations wanted to delete the words "civilian population," arguing that they were imprecise and unnecessary, but this traditional limit on the ambit of crimes against humanity has remained. Thus far the ICC has followed the ICTY, holding that the definition of "civilian" in Article 50 of Additional Protocol I to the Geneva Conventions on the laws of war sets forth the relevant standard. That said, as the ICTY has also held, "despite the requirement that the attack be directed against a civilian population, there is no requirement that the *individual* victims of crimes against humanity be civilians for the purpose of IHL but may include persons otherwise protected under this body of law." Prosecutor v. Bosco Ntaganda, Case No. ICC-01/04-02/06, *Judgment*, ¶ 669 (TC VI, July 8, 2019). The Extraordinary Chambers in the Courts of Cambodia (ECCC), the tribunal created to address crimes in Cambodia, has recognized this in its judgments, as well. Prosecutor v. Kaing Guck Eav alias Duch (Duch), Case No. 001/18-07-2007/ECCC/TC, *Judgment* (July 26, 2010). This is logical because crimes against humanity, unlike war crimes, can be committed in peacetime, meaning that the civilian/combatant distinction does not apply.

§ 5.4.2 The Crimes

Unlike predecessor tribunals, the ICC is a permanent court operating in real time. Moreover, with the link to armed conflict explicitly severed by the text of Article 7, it is now clear that crimes against humanity may occur in times of relative peace. Thus, not only have crimes against humanity emerged as a pivotal offense, but they have also been alleged in all the situations referred to the Court to date. In situations involving armed conflict, crimes against humanity charges often track the war crimes charges or target persecution or sexual violence. In other situations, crimes against humanity may be the only charges that can be brought, due to the absence of armed conflict (at least at the outset of the referral), and the implausibility of alleging genocide.

The situations now before the ICC can be subdivided into three general categories: (1) situations and cases in which crimes against humanity have been committed during armed conflict (*e.g.*, Afghanistan, Central African Republic, the Democratic Republic of the Congo, Georgia, Sudan, and Uganda); (2) situations in which allegations of genocide have surfaced, but crimes against humanity may provide a "safer" and more winnable alternative for the prosecution (given the difficulty of establishing the *dolus specialis* for genocide) or may capture other harms more expressly, such as sexual violence, persecution, or torture (*e.g.*, Sudan and Bangladesh/Myanmar, as well as, potentially, Ukraine); and (3) situations in which cases involving only crimes against humanity have been brought or are envisaged (*e.g.*, Côte d'Ivoire, Kenya, Philippines, and Venezuela).

The crimes against humanity charged to date have included murder, extermination, torture, deportation or forcible transfer, rape, forced pregnancy, persecution, sexual slavery, and other inhumane acts, among others. The ICC, even with the small number of final judgments achieved to date, is thus generating significant and important jurisprudence setting out the elements for each of these crimes. Of particular significance, the *Ntaganda* and *Ongwen* decisions recognized sexual violence during wartime as a crime against humanity. Prosecutor v. Bosco Ntaganda, Case No. ICC-01/04-02/06, *Judgment* (TC VI, July 8, 2019). *Ongwen* added convictions for forced pregnancy under Article 7(1)(g) and forced marriage as other inhumane acts under Article 7(1)(k). Prosecutor v. Dominic Ongwen, Case No. ICC-02/04-01/15, *Trial Judgment* (TC IX, Feb. 4, 2021).

IV. WAR CRIMES

§ 5-5 ELABORATING THE DEFINITION

The war crimes provisions of Article 8 in the Rome Statute are extensive and detailed, and their negotiation was protracted. They are based upon the existing codifications of the laws and customs of war, including the four Geneva Conventions of 1949, Additional Protocols I and II to the Geneva Conventions, and the Hague Convention of 1907.

The Rome Statute is much more detailed than predecessor instruments, making it a more complete codification of offenses against the laws of war, but also expressly excluding certain profoundly serious threats to international peace and security, including the use of nuclear weapons. It divides the crimes into those committed during international armed conflict (IAC) and non-international armed conflict (NIAC), following the traditional (if often criticized) approach. Paragraphs (a) and (b) of Article 8(2) list the crimes applicable in international armed conflict, including, *inter alia,* grave breaches of the 1949 Geneva Conventions and Protocol I. Paragraphs (c) and (e) list offenses in non-international armed conflict, the addition of which was seen as an important success. They include Common Article 3 of the Geneva Conventions, as well as many provisions of Protocol II, which a significant number of delegations opposed during the Statute's negotiation. Because some delegations were concerned during the negotiations about potential war crimes liability, they inserted Article 124 into the Statute, permitting a 7-year "opt-out" for States in respect of war crimes allegedly committed by their nationals or on their territory. Only two States have invoked Article 124, France and Colombia. France withdrew its declaration early, in 2008, and Colombia's expired.

In 2015, the ICC's Assembly of States Parties adopted an amendment to delete Article 124 from the Rome Statute. As of this writing, only 19 States have ratified this Amendment, meaning that it has not yet entered into effect for all States, and will not do so until seven-eighths of all States Parties have ratified it. Art. 121(4).

The elements of the fifty-three war crimes listed in the Statute are not self-explanatory, and as was the case for crimes against humanity, the Elements of Crimes do not add much in the way of additional detail. Thus, it will be up to the judiciary to interpret the provisions of Article 8 in accordance with Articles 21 and 22, which set out the methodology to be employed by the Court in interpreting the Statute. Finally, while there have not as yet been any amendments to either Articles 6 (genocide) or 7 (crimes against humanity), there have been four amendments to the war crimes provisions of the Statute. These have not yet been widely ratified.

§ 5-6 INTERPRETATION BY THE COURT

Article 8(1) provides that the "Court shall have jurisdiction in respect of war crimes in particular when committed as part of a plan or policy or as part of a large-scale commission of such crimes." This provision was a compromise between States that wanted Article 8 to contain more context elements, along the lines of Article 7 on crimes against humanity, such as a requirement that there be a plan or policy to commit war crimes for them to be justiciable and States that wanted no context elements at all (other than the existence of an armed conflict). As a result, there is thus no *formal* contextual requirement that the crimes be committed pursuant to a policy or that they reach a particular scale. Prosecutor v. Jean-Pierre Bemba Gombo, Case

No. ICC-01/05-01/08, *Decision Confirming the Charges under Article 61(7)(1) and (b)*, ¶ 211 (PTC II, June 15, 2009). Rather, this provision is seen as a form of practical guidance to the Court.

That said, the Prosecutor has dismissed war crimes allegations on the basis of *gravity* (not jurisdiction *ratione materiae*) with respect to alleged war crimes referred to it resulting from an Israeli Defense Forces (IDF) attack on an eight-vessel humanitarian aid flotilla bound for the Gaza Strip in 2010. While finding that there was a reasonable basis to believe that war crimes were committed on board a Comorian-registered vessel, the *Mavi Marmara*, during the IDF's interception of the flotilla, which resulted in the deaths of ten passengers, it found that "the potential cases that would likely arise from an investigation of the flotilla incident would not be of sufficient gravity to justify further action by the Court," pursuant to the criteria for admissibility in Article 17(1)(d) of the Rome Statute, as well as the requirements of Article 8(1). INT'L CRIM. CT. OFF. OF THE PROSECUTOR, SITUATION ON REGISTERED VESSELS OF COMOROS, GREECE AND CAMBODIA, ARTICLE 53(1) REPORT, ¶ 24 (Nov. 6, 2014).

Thus, the only context element included in the war crimes provisions of the Statute is that the crime must be committed "in armed conflict," meaning that, in each case, the conduct must take place in the context of and be associated with an armed conflict, and the perpetrator must be aware of factual circumstances that established the existence of the armed conflict (but need not know whether it is an

IAC or a NIAC). INT'L CRIM. CT., ELEMENTS OF CRIMES, *Introduction to Article 8, War Crimes* (2013). Relying on the *Tadić* case decided by the ICTY, the ICC's case law has consistently defined IACs as arising "whenever there is a resort to armed force between States." Prosecutor v. Bosco Ntaganda, Case No. ICC-01/04-02/06, *Judgment*, ¶ 700 (TC VI, July 8, 2019). Conversely, NIACs exist in case of "protected armed violence between governmental authorities and organized armed groups or between such groups within a State." *Id.* ¶ 701. Determining whether a conflict is international rather than non-international is a factual determination to be made by the Trial Chamber, *id.* ¶ 702, and can be an important issue as certain offenses that can be charged in an IAC cannot be charged in a NIAC.

The ICC has heard many important war crimes cases in its early years, including its very first trial that found Thomas Lubanga Dyilo guilty of conscripting and enlisting children under the age of fifteen into armed forces or groups and using them to participate actively in hostilities in non-international armed conflict under Article 8(e)(vii) of the Statute. It also convicted Ahmad Al Mahdi of the war crime of intentionally directing attacks against religious and historic buildings under Article 8(2)(e)(iv), based upon his attacks upon religious shrines and a mosque in Timbuktu, which was an important case both for its emphasis on the need to protect cultural property and heritage in war, and because Al Mahdi admitted his guilt. Prosecutor v. Ahmad Al Faqi Al Mahdi, Case No. ICC-01/12-01/15, *Judgment and Sentence* (TC VIII, Sept. 27, 2016). Finally, in the *Ntaganda* case, which has been cited throughout this Chapter, in addition to crimes against humanity counts, the Prosecutor charged the accused of killing, rape, sexual slavery, pillage, ordering the displacement of the civilian population, attacking protected objects, and destroying the adversary's property as war crimes. This case represented the first successful conviction of an accused at the ICC for sexual and gender-based violence. Ongoing investigations and trials in the Afghanistan, Sudan, and Ukraine situations will presumably lead to more war crimes cases and judgments in the future.

V. AGGRESSION

§ 5-7 ELABORATING THE DEFINITION

The judgment of the Nuremberg Tribunal declared aggression to be "not only an international crime; [but] the supreme international crime differing only from other war crimes in that it contains within itself the accumulated evil of the whole." International Military Tribunal (Nuremberg), Judgment and Sentence (October 1, 1946) *reprinted in* 41 AM. J. INT'L L. 172 (1947). This prohibition on aggression was incorporated in Article 2(4) of the U.N. Charter and codified in 1974 by the General Assembly in Resolution 3314, which set out a list of seven acts a State might commit that would be considered "acts of aggression." Aggression was included, undefined, in article 16 of the Draft Code of Crimes Against the Peace and Security of Mankind, which was elaborated by the U.N. International Law

Commission, but it was not included in the Statutes of either the ICTY or the ICTR.

Criminalizing aggression in the Rome Statute proved difficult. Although the preamble of the Statute reaffirms the illegality of aggression in principle, the negotiations over its inclusion threatened to derail the Rome Conference. Ultimately, based on a proposal from Germany and the urging of the non-aligned States, Article 5(1)(d) of the Statute included aggression as one of the crimes within the ICC's jurisdiction, but left it undefined. Article 5(2) provides that the Court will exercise jurisdiction over aggression once the Statute is amended to include a definition of the crime and the "conditions under which" the Court would exercise jurisdiction over it. The negotiators did not reserve an article in the Statute for the definition, but provided, in Resolution F of the Diplomatic Conference's Final Act, that a Preparatory Commission would be established, one task of which would be to "prepare proposals for a provision on aggression," including the definition, the Elements of Crimes, and the exercise of jurisdiction thereover. The Preparatory Commission thereupon created a Working Group on the Crime of Aggression, which immediately began discussions on the drafting of a text that could be adopted at the first ICC Review Conference, to be held, according to Article 123(1), seven years after the Statute entered into force.

Following the Statute's entry into force in July 2002, the Assembly of States Parties established a Special Working Group on the Crime of Aggression

(SWGCA), which met from 2003 to 2009. The most significant obstacles to adoption of a definition were: (1) the concern of some States that lawful uses of force would be made criminal under the Statute if aggression was criminalized in the Statute; (2) an insistence on the part of some States that the Security Council should determine whether aggression cases could be prosecuted; and (3) the view that the Court should not have the power to exercise jurisdiction over the crime of aggression if the defendant's State of nationality had not ratified the aggression amendments.

When the Review Conference convened in Kampala, Uganda, on June 1, 2010, delegates took up the definition proposed by the SWGCA as Article 8 *bis* of the Statute, as well as proposed articles on the triggering mechanism and the exercise of the Court's jurisdiction. Delegates readily agreed that if the Security Council were to refer the case under Article 13(b) of the Statute, the ICC would exercise its jurisdiction over aggression in the same manner as it did for other crimes. This was proposed as Article 15 *ter* of the Statute. With respect to a State Party referral or *proprio motu* investigation, however, they struggled to find a compromise and it was only in the final hours of the conference, in a reprise of the Rome Conference, that a final text was adopted.

The definition adopted in Article 8 *bis* tracks General Assembly Resolution 3314, with important additional language requiring that the act must "by its character, gravity and scale," constitute a "manifest violation of the U.N. Charter." To assuage concerns of the United States, "Understandings" were adopted at the Kampala Review Conference which emphasized that the definition adopted was "for the purpose of [the Rome] statute only," (Annex III, Understanding 4), and that aggression was the "most serious and dangerous form of the illegal use of force," (Understanding 6), and that a "manifest violation," required that all three components (character, gravity and scale) be present. (Understanding 7).

In terms of jurisdiction, Article 15 *bis*(4), which applies in case of a State referral or *proprio motu* investigation, provides that jurisdiction exists only if the act of aggression has been committed "by a State Party," unless that State Party has previously declared it does not accept that jurisdiction. In addition, under Article 15 *bis*(5), non-States Parties are excluded from the jurisdiction of the Court over the crime of aggression.

§ 5-8 ACTIVATION AND ENTRY INTO FORCE

During the Kampala negotiations, provisos were added to Articles 15 *bis* and *ter* providing that the amendments would not enter into force until at least thirty States Parties had ratified them *and* States had taken a decision after January 1, 2017 to activate them. On December 14, 2017, the ICC Assembly of States Parties adopted Resolution ICC-ASP/16/Res. 5 on the activation of the jurisdiction of the Court over the crime of aggression, and on July 17, 2018, the jurisdiction of the ICC over the crime of aggression was activated. As of this writing, 45 States have ratified the aggression amendments, and no States have lodged a declaration opting out of the aggression regime under Article 15 *bis*(4) of the Statute.

The crime of aggression, as envisaged by the Rome Statute, is a leadership crime. Article 8 *bis*(1) provides that the crime can only be committed "by a person in a position effectively to exercise control over or to direct the political or military action of a State." Furthermore, it only applies to interstate conflicts.

There have not been any investigations or prosecutions of the crime of aggression to date. The restriction of the crime of aggression to offenses committed only by ICC States Parties under Article 15 *bis*(5) has meant that in the current situation involving the Russian Federation's invasion of Ukraine, although the ICC has jurisdiction over genocide, crimes against humanity and war crimes, by virtue of Ukraine's acceptance of the same, the ICC cannot hear a case against a Russian national in respect of the crime of aggression. There have been proposals to "fix" this jurisdictional carve out in the Statute for the crime of aggression, to bring it into line with the jurisdictional regime governing the other crimes.

Selected Sources and Additional Reading

THE LEGISLATIVE HISTORY OF THE INTERNATIONAL CRIMINAL COURT (M. Cherif Bassiouni & William A. Schabas, eds., 2d ed. 2016).

M. CHERIF BASSIOUNI, CRIMES AGAINST HUMANITY: HISTORICAL EVOLUTION AND CONTEMPORARY APPLICATION (2d ed. 2010).

FANNY BENEDETTI, KARINE BONNEAU & JOHN L. WASHBURN, NEGOTIATING THE INTERNATIONAL CRIMINAL COURT 39 (2014).

ANTONIO CASSESE, INTERNATIONAL CRIMINAL LAW (3d ed. 2013).

THE ELGAR COMPANION TO THE INTERNATIONAL CRIMINAL COURT (Margaret M. Deguzman & Valerie Oosterveld, eds., 2020).

MARK DRUMBL, REIMAGING CHILD SOLDIERS IN INTERNATIONAL LAW AND POLICY (2012).

EVE LA HAYE, WAR CRIMES IN INTERNAL ARMED CONFLICTS (2010).

THE CRIME OF AGGRESSION (Claus Kreß & Stefan Barriga, eds., 2017).

LEILA NADYA SADAT, THE INTERNATIONAL CRIMINAL COURT AND THE TRANSFORMATION OF INTERNATIONAL LAW: JUSTICE FOR THE NEW MILLENNIUM (2002).

WILLIAM SCHABAS, GENOCIDE IN INTERNATIONAL LAW: THE CRIME OF CRIMES (2d ed., 2009).

CARSTEN STAHN, THE LAW AND PRACTICE OF THE INTERNATIONAL CRIMINAL COURT (2015).

GERHARD WERLE & FLORIAN JEßBERGER, PRINCIPLES OF INTERNATIONAL CRIMINAL LAW (2014).

Patrick J. Keenan, *Doctrinal Innovation in International Criminal Law: Harms, Victims, and the Evolution of the Law,* 42 PENN. J. INT'L. L. 407 (2020).

Marco Longobardo, *Everything is Relative, Even Gravity: Remarks on the Assessment of Gravity in ICC Preliminary Examinations, and the Mavi Marmara Affair,* 14 J. INT'L. CRIM. J. 1011 (2016).

David Luban, *A Theory of Crimes Against Humanity,* 29 YALE J. INT'L. L. 85 (2004).

Theodor Meron, *The Humanization of Humanitarian Law,* 94 AM. J. INT'L. L. 239 (2000).

Guénal Mettraux, *The Definition of Crimes Against Humanity and the Question of a "Policy" Element, in* FORGING A CONVENTION FOR CRIMES AGAINST HUMANITY 142 (Leila N. Sadat ed., 2011).

Valerie Oosterveld, *The Definition of Gender in the Rome Statute of the International Criminal Court: A Step Forward or Back for International Criminal Justice,* 18 HARV. HUM. RTS. J. 55 (2005).

Bernard H. Oxman & Diane Marie Amann, Prosecutor v. Akayesu, 93 AM. J. INT'L. L. 195 (1999).

Leila Nadya Sadat, *Crimes Against Humanity in the Modern Age,* 107 AM. J. INT'L. L. 334 (2013).

Jennifer Trahan, *The Rome Statute's Amendment on the Crime of Aggression: Negotiations at the Kampala Review Conference,* 11 INT'L. CRIM. L. REV. 49 (2011).

Jennifer Tridgell, Prosecutor v. Ntaganda: *The End of Impunity for Sexual Violence Against Child Soldiers?,* 23 AUS. INT'L. L. J. 153 (2017).

CHAPTER 6

MODES OF LIABILITY AND DEFENSES

I. INTRODUCTION

The International Criminal Court was created to help end impunity for those who commit the most serious crimes that concern the international community. Central to this mission is the requirement of individual criminal responsibility. This notion has long been a part of international criminal law. The Nuremberg Tribunal held that international crimes are "committed by men, not by abstract entities," and that only individuals can be punished for them. Equally true, however, is the fact that the kinds of atrocities the ICC was created to address are not committed by individuals acting alone; they are committed by individuals acting within groups. This Chapter outlines the basic modes of individual criminal responsibility that allow courts to hold individuals accountable for what are often the acts of many persons.

Modes of liability are ways to connect individuals to crimes. They allow courts to determine the legal responsibility of individuals when multiple people contribute to a harmful outcome. The law does not necessarily treat the getaway driver the same as the bank robber, or the person who provides a weapon to the killer the same as the person who pulls the trigger. In the context of large-scale international atrocities, it can be difficult to sort out the roles and responsibilities of commanders in charge of troops that abused civilians, the abusive troops themselves, and the civilian leaders who directed those troops, for example. Legally-defined modes of liability are a way to do that.

Thus, in every case before the ICC, Prosecutors must not only prove the underlying offense—such as murder or rape—but must also prove what the individual accused did to incur liability. If the accused is the person who pulled the trigger and killed a civilian, liability can be simple to establish. It is more complicated when the accused is the commander of that person. This Chapter provides a detailed overview of the modes of liability used by the ICC. Each has elements that must be proven by the prosecution, just as with every other facet of a case.

The Rome Statute provides in Article 25(1) that the ICC has "jurisdiction over natural persons," and in Article 25(2) that persons who commit crimes covered by the Statute "shall be individually responsible" for their actions. Under basic concepts of criminal law, most crimes require that the individual charged commit some action (or omission) with the appropriate intent. The action is sometimes called the "objective element," or *actus reus*; the mental state is sometimes called the "subjective" or "mental element" or *mens rea*. It is only people whose actions meet both criteria who may be held criminally responsible for their wrongdoing. This ensures that those who commit an accidental wrong, for example, are not held accountable in the same way as those who do harm intentionally, or to ensure that those who possess evil intentions, but never act on them, are not treated the same as people whose bad intentions lead them to commit harm. Prosecutor v. William Samoei Ruto and Joshua Arap Sang, Case No. ICC-01/09-01/11, *Decision on the Confirmation of Charges*, ¶ 333 (PTC II, Jan. 23, 2012).

As discussed in Chapter 5, crimes are made up of elements: those facts that must be proven to convict a person of a crime. This Chapter provides an overview of the different ways that defendants can participate in crimes, known as modes of liability. This Chapter also provides an overview of the defenses available to those charged with crimes. Defenses provide the legal grounds to exclude liability for some reason.

II. THE BASICS: KNOWLEDGE AND INTENT

Criminal responsibility is reserved for those who commit acts that are defined as unlawful while having the requisite mental state. For U.S.-trained lawyers it is important to remember that the ICC's cases sometimes describe the *mens rea* requirement in terms that are different from the way the concept is typically described in the U.S. system. The term *dolus directus* in the first degree refers to the intent to undertake the illegal act when the harmful results were desired or anticipated by the perpetrator. For example, this could be when a person wishes to end the life of another and does something—like shoot him or her—that the perpetrator knows will kill the victim. *Dolus directus* in the second degree "does not require that the suspect has the actual intent or will to bring about the material elements of the crime, but that he or she is aware that those elements will be the almost inevitable outcome of his acts or omissions." Prosecutor v. Jean-Pierre Bemba Gombo, Case No. ICC-01/05-01/08, *Decision Pursuant to Article 61(7)(a) and (b)*, ¶ 359 (PTC II, June 15, 2009). For example, this might apply when a someone bombs a building with the desire to kill a particular person but is aware the building is inhabited by others who would also be killed by the bomb.

In contrast to some legal systems, the early case law of the Court suggests that ICC does not permit convictions based on reckless conduct; that is, when the defendant knows that his or her conduct might cause the result but the result is not inevitable in the ordinary course of events. It is not clear whether this view might evolve with the passage of time.

§ 6-1 MENTAL ELEMENT (*MENS REA*)

Article 30(1) of the Rome Statute states that, "unless otherwise provided," persons are criminally responsible "only if the material elements are committed with intent and knowledge." According to Article 30(2)(a), "a person has intent" with respect to specified conduct when that person "means to engage in the conduct." This amounts to *dolus directus* in the first degree and captures circumstances in which the action was purposeful and willful.

With respect to consequences, the mental element can be satisfied in two ways. Article 30(2)(b) states that a person has intent with respect to a consequence when the "person means to cause that consequence." This amounts to *dolus directus* in the second degree. Article 30(2)(b) also states that the intent requirement can be satisfied if the person "is aware that it will occur in the ordinary course of events."

§ 6-2 ACTUS REUS

It is a basic premise of criminal law that the law does not penalize guilty thoughts. An act or omission is also required. Sometimes this is an easy task. The person who intentionally kills someone with a gun is criminally responsible for his or her conduct. But determining who, beyond the principal, should be criminally responsible for a crime can be much more difficult. What about the person who gave the weapon to the shooter, or the person who drove the shooter to the crime scene? Similarly, the person who provides the alarm codes to a burglar but did not actually break into the business might be treated differently from the person who actually broke in or the person who received the stolen property after the break-in. In international law, the principal to a crime is sometimes referred to having direct liability or responsibility: the one who engaged in the unlawful act. Those having indirect liability or responsibility are responsible for the crime even if they were not the physical perpetrator.

The Rome Statute provides a number of means by which a defendant can satisfy the *actus reus* requirement. Individuals are liable for crimes that they physically commit, order, assist others to commit, and attempt to commit. People can be guilty of crimes that they do not physically commit if they are part of a group of people that includes members who commit the illegal acts. In addition, people can sometimes be guilty of crimes that they incite others to commit. Part III describes each of these different modes of participation.

III. MODES OF PARTICIPATION IN CRIMES

What particularly complicates international criminal law is that large-scale international crimes are almost always planned and executed by groups of people, each of whom might play a different role in bringing about the harm. The Rome Statute attempts to account for this reality by specifying a number of ways that an individual might work with others to cause harm, contribute to a common plan to do so, or otherwise be part of a group whose members commit crimes. Modes of participation are the legal links between particular individual defendants and situations in which a number of people might have participated. Article 28 covers command or superior responsibility. That issue is addressed later in this Chapter.

Article 25, on "individual criminal responsibility," sets forth most modes of participation. Article 25(3)(a) covers individuals who "commit" the crime; that is, those who are directly liable for the crime. Article 25(3)(b) covers individuals who solicit, order, or induce the commission of the crime, which is another form of direct liability. Article 25(3)(c)–(e) set forth additional modes of criminal participation.

Article 25(3)(f) provides that people who attempt a crime, with the requisite *mens rea*, can be guilty even if the crime is not actually committed. Although some of the Court's early decisions suggested that Article 25(3) contained a "hierarchy" of seriousness, later decisions of the Court have rejected that analysis, except perhaps as to aiding and abetting liability. Prosecutor v. Germain Katanga, Case No. ICC-01/04-01/07, *Judgment Pursuant to Article 74*, ¶ 1364 (TC II, Mar. 7, 2014).

§ 6-3 COMMISSION AND CO-PERPETRATION

When the defendant is the physical perpetrator of the crime, liability is straightforward. Article 25(3)(a) provides that a person who "commits" the crime is "criminally responsible" for it. In many cases, that person is the one who physically carries out the criminal act. If the defendant killed or raped another person, the defendant committed the act and criminal liability is uncomplicated. Usually, however, international atrocities are much more complicated. To account for this, Article 25(3)(a) provides that those who act "jointly with another" or "through another person" may also be criminally responsible for a crime.

Direct co-perpetration is when the defendant acts "jointly with" other persons to commit the crime. Although the exact contours of this can be difficult to discern, the ICC has provided some guidance. In *Prosecutor v. Lubanga*, the ICC addressed the issue of direct co-perpetration. First, there must be an "agreement" between the perpetrators "which led to the commission" of a crime in the ICC's jurisdiction. This agreement can be "express or implied, previously arranged or materializing extemporaneously." Second, there must be a "virtual certainty" that the implementation of the agreement would result in the commission of crimes in the ordinary course of events, even if the plan itself had other, non-criminal goals. Third, to be guilty, the defendant's actions must have made a sufficient contribution to the crime. Prosecutor v. Thomas Lubanga Dyilo, Case No. ICC-01/04-01/06, *Trial Judgment*, ¶¶ 445–447 (TC I, Dec. 1, 2014). The defendant must also have had "the power to frustrate the commission of the crime" by withholding his or her "essential contribution within the framework of the agreement."

Indirect co-perpetration occurs when a defendant might act both "jointly with" and "through" another person. To be guilty on this theory, the ICC requires that four elements be proved, two objective and two subjective. The objective, or *actus reus* elements are that there must be "an agreement or common plan" involving the accused and other persons to engage in conduct which, "in the ordinary course of events," would result in the commission of the crimes, and that the defendant must have control over "a person or persons who execute the material elements of the crimes by subjugating the will of the direct perpetrators." Prosecutor v. Dominic Ongwen, Case No. ICC-02/04-01/15, *Trial Judgment*, ¶ 2787 (TC IX, Feb. 4, 2021). The subjective, or *mens rea*, elements are that the defendant "must have meant to engage in the conduct which constituted his or her essential contribution[,]" and the defendant either "intended the material elements of the crime or [must] have been aware that the implementation of the agreement between the co-perpetrators would in the ordinary course of events result in execution of the material elements of the crimes." *Id.* ¶ 2788. Several judges of the Court, and many scholars, have argued forcefully that the theory of indirect co-perpetration, which is based upon the theory of the "control of the crime" found in German law and the writings of Claude Roxin, has been improperly imported into the Court's legal framework. Prosecutor v. Bosco Ntaganda, Case No. ICC-01/04-02/06, *Judgment: Separate Opinion of Judge Howard Morrison,* ¶ 3 (AC, Mar. 3, 2021).

§ 6-4 ORDERING, SOLICITING, INDUCING

Liability for ordering an offense is premised on the idea that fighting forces, including well-organized armies and irregular forces—typically have a hierarchy. There are those who make plans and give orders, and those who carry them out. The prohibition on ordering a crime is a way to hold commanders legally responsible for their orders when they know that those orders will be obeyed and are likely to result in the commission of a crime. Soliciting and inducing liability are premised on other forms of psychological influence that have a similar effect.

Liability for ordering an offense is different from superior (or command) responsibility. Article 28 of the ICC Statute, discussed more fully later in this Chapter, creates a separate form of liability for commanders. Ordering an offense criminalizes *doing* something—namely, giving an order that results in the commission of a crime. Only if the superior gives an order (and the other conditions are met) can the superior be guilty on order liability. In contrast, the doctrine of superior responsibility criminalizes *failing to do* something—namely, failing to prevent subordinates from committing crimes. Liability is premised on the failure to prevent troops from committing crimes, not on giving illegal orders.

Under Article 25(3)(b), a person can be guilty of a crime if he or she "orders, solicits or induces" its commission, provided that the crime "in fact occurs or is attempted." Ordering, soliciting, and inducing liability are part of a category the ICC describes as "instigating," which means "prompting another person to commit a crime" by exerting "psychological influence on another person" which results in the commission of the crime. Prosecutor v. Jean-Pierre Bemba Gombo, Case No. ICC-01/05-01/08, *Judgment Pursuant to Article 74*, ¶ 73 (TC VII, Oct. 19, 2016).

§ 6.4.1 Ordering

The early jurisprudence of the Court suggests that ordering liability has four elements, a conclusion that is consistent with the jurisprudence of the ICTY. Prosecutor v. Sylvestre Mudacumura, Case No. ICC-01/04-01/12, *Decision on the Prosecutor's Application under Article 58*, ¶ 63 (PTC II, July 13, 2012). First, the defendant must occupy "a position of authority."

That is, the defendant must have the power to give orders to the person who received them and committed the offense. Second, the defendant must "instruct another person in any form" to do one of two things, either commit a crime (that actually occurs or is attempted) or to do something "in the execution of which a crime is carried out." If no crime is committed despite the defendant's order, the defendant is not criminally liable. It is also not necessary for the defendant to give order directly to the physical perpetrator. Giving an order through an intermediary can still result in criminal liability.

The third element goes to the relationship between the order and the offense. The defendant's order must have had "a direct effect on the commission or attempted commission of the crime." International criminal tribunals are not unanimous regarding the relationship between the order and the offense. For example, in *Prosecutor v. Aleksovski*, the International Criminal Tribunal for the former Yugoslavia required proof of a direct and substantial effect on the commission of the crime, while the ICC has only required proof of a direct effect. Prosecutor v. Zlatko Aleksovski, Case No. IT-95-14/1, *Judgment*, ¶ 6 (T.C., June 25, 1999). Fourth and finally, the defendant must be "at least aware that the crime will be committed in the ordinary course of events as a consequence of the execution or implementation of the order." Prosecutor v. Sylvestre Mudacumura, Case No. ICC-01/04-01/12, *Decision on the Prosecutor's Application under Article 58*, ¶ 63 (PTC II, July 13, 2012).

§ 6.4.2 Soliciting and Inducing

In contrast to ordering liability, soliciting and inducing liability does "not require the perpetrator to hold a position of authority vis-à-vis the physical perpetrator." Prosecutor v. Al Hassan Ag Abdoul Aziz Ag Mohamed Ag Mahmoud, Case No. ICC-01/12-01/18, *Decision on the Prosecutor's Application for the Issuance of a Warrant of Arrest*, ¶ 184 (PTC I, May 22, 2018). Article 25(3)(b) also provides for liability for a person who "solicits or induces" someone to commit a crime (provided the crime actually occurs). To establish soliciting liability, the Prosecutor must show that the defendant "asks or urges the physical perpetrator to commit the criminal act." Prosecutor v. Jean-Pierre Bemba Gombo, Case No. ICC-01/05-01/08, *Judgment Pursuant to Article 74*, ¶ 75 (TC VII, Oct. 19, 2016). To establish inducing liability, the Prosecutor must prove that the defendant exerted "influence over the physical perpetrator, either by strong reasoning, persuasion or conduct implying the prompting of the commission of the offense." *Id.*, at ¶ 76.

The mental element for soliciting and inducing is the same. The Prosecutor must show that the defendant either "meant to" solicit or induce the physical perpetrator to commit the offense, or that the defendant "was aware" that the offense "would be committed in the ordinary course of events as a consequence of the realization of his or her act or omission." *Id.*, at ¶ 82.

§ 6-5 AIDING, ABETTING, ASSISTING

Accessory liability is a way to hold a defendant criminally liable for the actions of others if the defendant's actions help bring about the commission of the crime. Article 25(3)(c) provides that a defendant who "aids, abets or otherwise assists" in the commission or attempt of a crime can be held criminally responsible for the underlying crime or attempt. The ICC has interpreted this provision to cover a broad range of conduct. It covers assistance that occurs before the crime, such as help with the crime's planning or execution. It also covers assistance that happens after a crime, especially if the physical perpetrator knows that he or she can count on getting help after the crime. Prosecutor v. Jean-Pierre Bemba Gombo, Case No. ICC-01/05-01/08, *Judgment*, ¶ 20 (AC, Mar. 8, 2018). What matters is to determine, based on the unique facts of the situation, whether and to what extent the defendant's assistance influenced the commission of the crime. *Id.*, at ¶ 18.

To establish liability under Article 25(3)(c), the Prosecutor must first show that the defendant's assistance "facilitates or furthers the commission of the crime." *Id.* The ICC requires that the defendant's assistance furthers the commission of a crime, not that the assistance helps any specific person (including the physical perpetrator). Second, the Prosecutor must show that the defendant provided assistance for "the purpose of facilitating the commission of" a crime. The defendant need not know "all the details" of the crime or "all the factual circumstances in which it is committed." *Id.*, at ¶ 21.

Aiding and abetting liability has two *mens rea* requirements. Article 25(3)(c) requires that the act of aiding and abetting must have been done for "the purpose of facilitating the commission or attempted commission" of the crime. This heightened *mens rea* requirement means that, with respect to the act of assistance, the defendant must "have lent his or her assistance with the aim of facilitating the offense." Prosecutor v. Jean-Pierre Bemba Gombo, Case No. ICC-01/05-01/08, *Judgment Pursuant to Article 74*, ¶ 97 (TC VII, Oct. 19, 2016). In addition, the defendant's *mens rea* regarding the underlying crime matters. Aiding and abetting liability requires that the defendant "must at least be aware that the perpetrator's offense will occur in the ordinary course of events." *Id.*, at ¶ 98. The jurisprudence of previous *ad hoc* tribunals has not been consistent with respect to the elements of aiding and abetting liability.

§ 6-6 COMMON PURPOSE

Even though international atrocity crimes are often carried out by groups, the Rome Statute does not provide for collective responsibility or punishment. Only individuals may be charged with crimes, and no provision of the Statute permits punishment merely for belonging to any organization. But the Statute establishes a form of liability designed to encompass those who work with others to commit atrocities. Although the Rome Statute language could have been interpreted as a form of joint criminal enterprise liability, as is the case with Article 25(3)(a), the judges of the Court have developed a unique approach to common purpose liability at the ICC, different from that taken at the *ad hoc* criminal tribunals.

Article 25(3)(d) provides that defendants who contribute in "any other way" to the commission of a crime "by a group of persons acting with a common purpose" may be punished. Common purpose liability requires the Prosecutor to prove several elements. First, the Prosecutor must show that the underlying crime was committed. Unlike other forms of accessory liability, common purpose liability is not available for mere attempt. Second, the Prosecutor must show that the crime was committed "by a group of persons acting with a common purpose." Prosecutor v. Ahmad Al Faqi Al Mahdi, Case No. ICC-01/12-01/15, *Decision on the Confirmation of Charges*, ¶ 27 (PTC I, Mar. 24, 2016). Third, the Prosecutor must show that the defendant "provides a contribution to the commission" of the crime.

Common purpose has a double *mens rea* requirement, on which Trial Chamber II elaborated extensively in its judgment in the case of *Prosecutor v. Katanga*. Common purpose liability requires that the defendant's contributory acts be "intentional." It also requires that the defendant's contribution be made either (i) "with the aim of furthering the criminal activity or criminal purpose of the group," or (ii) "in the knowledge" that the group intended to commit the crime. It is not required that the defendant shared the group's intention to commit a crime. Prosecutor v. Germain Katanga, Case No. ICC-01/04-01/07, *Judgment Pursuant to Article 74 of the Statute*, ¶ 1638 (TC II, Mar. 7, 2014). But the defendant must at least "be aware that the intention existed when engaging in the conduct which constituted his or her contribution." *Id.*, at ¶ 1641.

In addition to these elements, common purpose liability requires the consideration of a number of other factors. The group at issue need not be a formal organization. Instead, the Statute requires only a "group of persons acting with a common purpose." *Id.*, at ¶ 1626. The Prosecutor is not required to prove that the common purpose "was previously arranged or formulated." Instead, the common purpose "may materialize extemporaneously and be inferred from the subsequent concerted action" of the group." *Id.* Of course, the prosecution must show that the persons who committed the crime belong to the group and that they and the defendant shared the common purpose. *Id.*, at ¶ 1628.The group need not exist merely for criminal purposes. If the group exists for political or other reasons and its actions also involve criminal conduct, it may constitute a group under the Statute. *Id.*, at ¶ 1627.

The universe of criminal acts for which the accessory may be charged is limited by the intentions of the group and the foreseeability of the underlying crime. The crime for which the defendant is charged as an accessory must have formed part of the common purpose. If the crime was an opportunistic criminal act done by a member of the group outside the common purpose, the accessory cannot be held criminally liable. *Id.*, at ¶ 1630. Only crimes "which the group harbored the intention to commit" and "falling within the ordinary course of events" can be attributed to the accessory. *Id.*

The accessory's contribution to the crime must be "significant," meaning that it is enough to "influence the commission of the crime." *Id.*, at ¶ 1632. The defendant's contribution need not have been outcome-determinative. Instead, it is enough if the defendant's contribution had "a bearing on the occurrence of the crime and/or the matter of its commission." *Id.* Further, the defendant cannot be convicted based on common purpose liability for making contributions to the group generally but not to the commission of the crime. *Id.* The defendant's contribution, however, need not have been made directly to the physical perpetrator. What matters is whether the contribution significantly influenced the commission of the crime, not whether the defendant was directly connected to the physical perpetrator. On this issue, as with several issues regarding modes of liability, there has been significant disagreement among the ICC's judges. For example, in *Prosecutor v. Ntaganda*, although the Appeals Chamber concluded that Ntaganda has been properly convicted, the judges disagreed on the theory of liability. Three judges wrote separate opinions addressing liability issues. Prosecutor v. Bosco Ntaganda, Case No. ICC-01/04-02/06, *Judgment: Separate Opinions of Howard Morrison, Chile Eboe-Osuji, and Luz Del Carmen Ibáñez Carranza* (AC, Mar. 30, 2021). The issue is likely to remain unsettled until the Court arrives at a coherent theory accepted by judges and used by prosecutors.

§ 6-7 INCITEMENT

Article 25(3)(e) establishes criminal liability for "directly and publicly" inciting others to commit genocide. Incitement liability is not available for any other crime. This prohibition on direct and public incitement to genocide comes directly from the 1948 Convention on the Prevention and Punishment of the Crime of Genocide, which includes incitement as a mode of responsibility for genocide. The ICC has not confronted any cases involving charges of incitement to genocide, but previous international criminal tribunals included the same prohibition and addressed the crime. Incitement to genocide does not require that a genocide actually take place.

Incitement to genocide is a way of encouraging or persuading someone to commit genocide. In *Prosecutor v. Akayesu*, the ICTR detailed the elements of incitement to genocide. Prosecutor v. Jean-Paul Akayesu, Case No. ICTR-96-4, *Judgment* (TC I, Sept. 2, 1998). The Prosecutor must first prove that the defendant encouraged or persuaded another person to commit genocide. Next the Prosecutor must prove that the acts of encouragement were public. This means that the incitement must have happened "in a public place" or "to members of the general public by such means as the mass media. *Id.*, at ¶ 556. Third, the Prosecutor must prove that the incitement was direct, which depends on the "culture" and "specific circumstances" of the place where the crimes occurred. *Id.*, at ¶ 558. What matters most to this determination is whether those people hearing the inciting messages immediately understood what the messages meant. *Id.*

The mental element of direct and public incitement to genocide requires proof that the defendant had the specific intent to commit genocide. *Id.*, at ¶ 560. In addition, the general *mens rea* requirement found in Article 30(2) also applies and requires that the defendant meant to engage in the inciting conduct.

Incitement can be proven in many ways. The inciting messages can take the form of speeches made in person or broadcast on the radio, on television, or by some other means. The messages can be in written material distributed at public gatherings or made available publicly. They can take the form of threats, encouragement, or other provocations. *Id.*, at ¶ 559. As of this writing, incitement has not yet been charged at the ICC.

§ 6-8 ATTEMPT

The Rome Statute recognizes attempt as a form of inchoate liability, which means that the defendant can be criminally liable even when the crime is not completed. The goal of punishing attempt is not to criminalize guilty thoughts or reckless behavior. Instead, it is to ensure that those with criminal intent who take substantial steps toward committing a crime do not escape punishment when the crime does not occur for reasons having nothing to do with the defendant.

Article 25(3)(f) provides for liability when a person attempts to commit a crime "by taking action that commences its execution by means of a substantial step," but the crime "does not occur because of circumstances independent of the person's intentions." Attempt liability requires that the defendant's actions "be adequate to bring about" the crime in question. Prosecutor v. Abdallah Banda Abakaer Nourain, Case No. ICC-02/05-03/09, *Corrigendum of the Decision on the Confirmation of Charges*, ¶ 96 (PTC I, Mar. 7, 2011).

The ICC considers attempt "a crime in which the objective elements are incomplete, while the subjective elements are complete." Prosecutor v. Germain Katanga and Mathieu Ngudjolo Chui, Case No. ICC-01/04-01/07, *Decision on the Confirmation of Charges*, ¶ 460 (PTC I, Sept. 30, 2008). This means that the mental element for attempt liability is the same as that required for the underlying crime. If the defendant is charged with attempted murder, then the Prosecutor must prove that the defendant had the *mens rea* required for a murder conviction.

A person is not guilty of attempt if the person "completely and voluntarily gave up the criminal purpose" by either abandoning the attempt to commit the crime, or by taking actions that prevent "the completion of the crime." This provision protects from liability the person who changes his or her mind but does not protect those who do not succeed in their attempt for reasons having nothing to do with them. For example, in *Prosecutor v. Banda*, a Pre-Trial Chamber of the Court confirmed attempt charges when the defendant attacked a group of victims. Several of the victims were killed and several more were injured. The Pre-Trial Chamber found that the injured victims were still alive not because the defendant abandoned the attempt to kill them, but because prompt medical attention was the kind of intervening event that was completely independent of the defendant's intention, which was to kill all of the victims. Prosecutor v. Abdallah Banda Abakaer Nourain, Case No. ICC-02/05-03/09, Corrigendum *of the Decision on the Confirmation of Charges*, ¶¶ 98–100 (PTC I, Mar. 7, 2011).

IV. RESPONSIBILITY OF COMMANDERS AND OTHER SUPERIORS

The responsibility of military commanders to control their subordinates was firmly established in international law well before the advent of the ICC. In perhaps the most notorious case, Japanese General Tomoyuki Yamashita was held criminally responsible by an American military tribunal in Manila for the murders, rapes, and other abuses committed by his troops during their occupation of the Philippines in World War II. The tribunal found that General Yamashita had failed in his duties as commander because he either permitted his troops to abuse civilians or had known about the abuses and failed to take the steps necessary to prevent or punish them. Trial of General Tomoyuki Yamashita, Law Reports of the Trials of War Criminals, United Nations War Crimes Commission, vol. IV (1948), pp. 34–35. The essence of the crime is the failure of command responsibility by failing to "provide effective control" of the troops as required by law. *Id.*, at 35. Yamashita sought habeas corpus relief in the U.S. Supreme Court, arguing that the U.S. military commission had improperly convicted him. The Supreme Court rejected his claims, over the dissents of Justices Rutledge and Murphy, who argued that the commission had improperly applied the law of command responsibility. *In re Yamashita*, 327 U.S. 1 (Feb. 4, 1946).

Superior responsibility is a different mode of liability than that for ordering offenses. Superior responsibility holds a commander or other superiors responsible for their failure to control their troops; it is a crime of omission. In contrast, ordering liability is premised on an action: the issuing of illegal orders. One of the foundational notions of superior responsibility is the superior-subordinate relationship. In the military, superiors have the power and responsibility to issue lawful orders and discipline troops. Their subordinates are required, in most instances, to comply with those orders. Superior responsibility, as a mode of liability, requires the existence of superior-subordinate relationship. Although the concept of superior responsibility originated with military commanders, it can now be applied to non-military superiors as well. This means that civilians who have a superior-subordinate relationship with individuals who commit crimes can also face criminal liability for their subordinates' crimes, even absent a formal military hierarchy.

Superior responsibility is a form of vicarious liability, as it holds commanders responsible for the crimes of their subordinates. For example, if the subordinates committed rape and murder, then the superior could be convicted of those crimes even though he or she was not the physical perpetrator. Superior responsibility does not create a strict liability regime. Commanders are not automatically liable every time their subordinates commit a crime. Instead, it is a crime of omission, requiring proof that the commander failed to do something within his or her power. For these reasons, establishing superior responsibility requires that crimes resulted from the defendant's failure to take all necessary and reasonable measures within his or her power to prevent, repress, or address them. Nonetheless, a superior may not avoid liability by remaining willfully blind to the actions of his or her subordinates. Prosecutor v. Zejnil Delalic, et al., Case No. IT-96-21, *Judgment*, ¶ 387 (TC, Nov. 16, 1998).

Article 28 sets out two modes of command and superior responsibility: for military commanders in 28(a), and for persons who are not in the military but have a superior-subordinate relationship in 28(b). Command and Superior responsibility have received substantial judicial attention at the ICC, and although its boundaries are likely still not entirely fixed, the Statute and cases provide substantial guidance. Article 28(a) establishes the possibility of criminal liability for military commanders and persons "effectively acting as a military commander" when the commander fails "to exercise control properly" over his or her forces.

The first step is to prove that the defendant is either a military commander or someone "effectively acting" as one. Military commanders are persons who "have command responsibility within the armed forces, irrespective of their rank or level." Prosecutor v. Jean-Pierre Bemba Gombo, Case No. ICC-01/05-01/08, *Decision Pursuant to Article 61(7)(a) and (b)*, ¶ 408 (PTC II, June 15, 2009). This can include low-ranking individuals with only a few troops under their command, or people at the very top of the military hierarchy. People "effectively acting as a military commander" are people without the formal, legal power to command troops, but who nonetheless "exercise effective control over a group of persons through a chain of command." *Id.*, at ¶ 409. This can include people who control paramilitary police units, rebel groups, militias, or similar armed groups.

The second step is to show that the physical perpetrator (or perpetrators) of the underlying crimes was either under the defendant's "effective command and control[,]" or under his or her "effective authority." This requirement is essential because superior responsibility is available only when the defendant has the legal power to act to control his or her underlings. Absent this power, there can be no superior responsibility (though there could be liability as a co-perpetrator or accomplice).

The terms "effective command and control" and "effective authority and control" convey the same thing; "command" applies to military commanders while "authority" applies to non-military persons acting as commanders. The concept of "effective control" means that the defendant must have the ability to prevent and punish the offenses or to submit the offenses to competent authorities to address. It is a greater power than simply the ability to "exercise influence" over troops. Prosecutor v. Jean-Pierre Bemba Gombo, Case No. ICC-01/05-01/08, *Decision Pursuant to Article 61(7)(a) and (b)*, ¶ 415 (PTC II, June 15, 2009).

Whether such effective control exists is a matter of fact; it is determined by the evidence and circumstances in the particular case. Effective control has temporal and geographic components; specifically, it must have existed at the time and in the place that the criminal conduct occurred. The ICC has identified several factors to guide this determination, all taken from the jurisprudence of the *ad hoc* international criminal tribunals. The factors include:

> (i) the official position of the suspect; (ii) his power to issue or give orders; (iii) the capacity to ensure compliance with the orders issued; (i.e., ensure that they would be executed); (iv) his position within the military structure and the actual tasks that he carried out; (v) the capacity to order forces or units under his command, whether under his immediate command or at a lower levels, to engage in hostilities; (vi) the capacity to re-subordinate units or make changes to command structure; (vii) the power to promote, replace, remove or discipline any member of the forces; and (viii) the authority to

send forces where hostilities take place and withdraw them at any given moment.

Id., at ¶ 417.

The mental element for superior responsibility comes from Article 28(a)(i) and asks whether the commander "knew, or owing to the circumstances at the time, should have known" that his or her forces were committing or about to commit crimes. The Statute thus creates two different ways to establish the requisite *mens rea*: by showing that the defendant "knew" or that the defendant "should have known."

The "knew" standard means that the defendant must have had actual knowledge of the underlying offenses. knowledge can be proven with either direct or circumstantial evidence, but it cannot be presumed. To make this determination, the ICC considers a number of factors, including the number, location, and scope of the illegal acts, whether they were widespread, how long they lasted, the troops involved, the available means of communications, the superior's role in the hierarchy, and the fighting unit's reporting and monitoring mechanisms. Prosecutor v. Jean-Pierre Bemba Gombo, Case No. ICC-01/05-01/08, *Decision Pursuant to Article 61(7)(a) and (b)*, ¶¶ 430–431 (PTC II, June 15, 2009).

The "should have known" standard applies when a superior is negligent in his or her duties; namely, the failure to take all reasonable and necessary measures to acquire information about the conduct of subordinates. In this circumstance, the failure to fulfill the obligation to adequately monitor troops is the linchpin of the analysis. To make this determination, the Court considers whether there was general information about the conduct of subordinates that should have put the superior on notice of their misdeeds, or if there had been previous incidents of criminal activity that went unpunished. *Id.*, at ¶¶ 432–434.

Because superior responsibility is potentially a very broad theory of liability, the early case law of the ICC has found that there to be evidence to "specifically identify what a commander should have done *in concreto.*" Prosecutor v. Jean-Pierre Bemba Gombo, Case No. ICC-01/05-01/08, *Judgment*, ¶ 7 (AC, June 7, 2018). This standard is context-dependent; what is reasonable and necessary in one situation might be unreasonable in another. What is reasonable will depend on the commander's level of authority and the measures available at the time and place of the underlying criminal acts. Commanders are not required to take "each and every possible measure at his or her disposal;" requiring this would amount to punishing a commander "for not having done something he or she had no power to do." *Id.*, at ¶¶ 167, 169.

Under the test in *Bemba*, whether the measures were appropriate should not be judged with the benefit of hindsight. Instead, the standard is whether the measures were those that were available at the moment and were such that a "reasonably diligent commander in comparable circumstances" would have adopted them. *Id.*, at ¶ 170. According to a

Majority, commanders may undertake a "cost/benefit analysis when deciding which measures to take, bearing in mind their overall responsibility to prevent and repress crimes by their subordinates." *Id.* They may consider, for example, the impact of such measures on their operations and choose those that are the least disruptive. Despite the ruling in *Bemba*, however, the issue is not definitively settled. In *Bemba* itself, the Appeals Chamber was bitterly divided over the issue of the steps a commander must take to avoid liability with Judges Monagang and Hofmański taking issue with the Majority's approach. Indeed, even though they joined the majority opinion and reversed Bemba's convictions, Judges Van den Wyngaert and Morrison issued a separate opinion on the issue of command responsibility.

V. OTHER MODES OF PARTICIPATION IN INTERNATIONAL CRIMINAL LAW

While the modes of liability recognized in the Rome Statute are the only modes of liability available in the ICC, they are not the only modes of liability recognized in international criminal law. Indeed, perhaps in time, the jurisprudence of the Court may bring the Rome Statute more closely in line with the modes of liability jurisprudence of the *ad hoc* international criminal tribunals. In addition to those mentioned, there are two modes of participation that may be familiar to students of international criminal law. Joint Criminal Enterprise (JCE) is a mode of liability developed by the ICTY and the ICTR. This mode of liability has not been recognized by the ICC, which instead has relied on co-perpetration and common plan liability to reach the conduct that might otherwise be addressed by JCE, but could be incorporated in Article 25(3)(d) as some scholars have argued.

Conspiracy, itself an inchoate crime, is another mode of criminal participation that may be familiar to many students and lawyers. The Rome Statute does not recognize conspiracy as a form of criminal participation (or an inchoate crime), relying instead on other forms of liability to punish those who participate in crimes committed by groups of people.

§ 6-9 JOINT CRIMINAL ENTERPRISE

The ICTY Appeals Chamber developed the concept of JCE in *Prosecutor v. Tadić*. In the first trial before the ICTY, the defendant had been convicted of a variety of charges relating primarily to crimes he participated in at the Omarska prison camp. Tadić was acquitted, however, on murder charges stemming from an incident in which a small group of armed men, including Tadić, entered the village of Jaskići and apparently shot five victims. The evidence was that the victims were alive when Tadić's group entered the village and had been shot dead by the time Tadić's group left. The Trial Chamber acquitted Tadić of these charges because there was no evidence that he personally shot any of the victims. The Appeals Chamber reversed. In the decision reversing the acquittal, the Appeals Chamber developed the doctrine of JCE. Prosecutor

v. Duško Tadić, Case No. IT-94-1, *Judgment* (AC, July 15, 1999).

After a thorough examination of the history of charging individuals for their participation in the crimes of groups of people, the Appeals Chamber recognized three forms of JCE available in customary international law: basic (JCE I), systemic (JCE II), and extended (JCE III). Each form addresses different levels of participation and defendants with different intentions. In each scenario, the defendant did not physically perpetrate the crime. The point of JCE is to determine the criminal liability of a defendant who participates in the plan or takes other steps but does not physically commit the unlawful act.

Basic JCE (I) covers those cases in which the defendant and the other co-perpetrators have a common plan, and all share the same criminal intention. The plan need not be explicit or agreed to in advance. Instead, there must be evidence to support the inference that there was a common plan, and that one of the common plan's participants must have actually perpetrated the crime under it. The defendant must have played at least some role in the common plan. Under the basic form of JCE, each participant who contributed to the common plan and had the intention to commit the crime can be held responsible for the actions of all members of the group. For example, basic JCE would apply in a case in which the defendant and several others planned to kill someone, and each member of the group played a different role in carrying out that common plan.

Systemic JCE (II) is appropriate in cases in which there is an organized system of abuse, such as a concentration camp or other system of mistreatment. Systemic JCE requires a common plan, but it need not be proven explicitly. Instead, the existence of the system can be sufficient proof of the plan. When the defendant knows about the system of ill-treatment and continues to operate within it by contributing to the system, the mental element is satisfied. While the defendant must contribute to the common plan, it need not be essential to the overall system of abuse. For example, systemic JCE would fit the case of a concentration camp guard who knew about the system of abuse and continued to do his or her work, even if the guard never personally abused anyone, because the guard prevented the prisoners from escaping.

Finally, the extended form of JCE (III) is the third category and has been the most controversial. This category covers cases in which one of the perpetrators commits a crime that, while outside the common plan, was nonetheless a foreseeable consequence of it. Under the extended form of JCE, if the defendant intended to participate in the group and to contribute to the common plan, he or she can be liable for unintended but foreseeable crimes committed by other members of the group. This would apply in cases in which the group planned to remove members of one ethnic group from a town through force and, while doing so, people were killed or abused. Even when the killing or abuse was not part of the common plan, that result was a natural and foreseeable consequence of it. Therefore, if the defendant intentionally contributed to the common plan, he or she can be guilty of these extended crimes if they were foreseeable even if unplanned.

All three categories require the existence of a common plan involving a plurality of persons and the participation of the defendant. What differentiates them is the mental element. With basic JCE I, the defendant must share the intention to perpetrate the crime. With systemic JCE II, the defendant must have personal knowledge of the system of abuse (or the resulting harms) and the intent to contribute to the system. Extended JCE III requires the defendant to intend to participate in or further the purpose of the group and willingly take the risk that extended crimes would occur. The defendant need not intend to commit the extended crimes, and those crimes need not be part of the common plan in which the defendant intentionally participates. The magnitude of the defendant's contribution to the joint criminal enterprise has been controversial. In general, there is no requirement that the defendant make a "substantial" contribution. Prosecutor v. Miroslav Kvočka, et al., Case No. IT-98-30/1, *Judgment*, ¶¶ 96–97 (AC, Feb. 28, 2005). However, "the significance of the accused's contribution" can be relevant to whether the accused "shared the intent to pursue the common purpose." *Id.*, at ¶ 97. The fact that a defendant can be convicted for crimes that he or she neither committed nor intended, as is possible with extended JCE, explains the continued controversy regarding that category in particular, although it was particularly useful in cases involving sexual and gender-based violence where establishing a prior intent or order to commit those crimes was not possible.

The ICC has referred to various forms of JCE in its jurisprudence but has never applied it or indicated that any of the modes of liability established by the Rome Statute are direct parallels to any form of JCE. In *Prosecutor v. Lubanga*, the Pre-Trial Chamber considered some of the normative and doctrinal similarities between some forms of JCE and co-perpetration before rejecting the JCE approach as a useful analogue for co-perpetration. Prosecutor v. Thomas Lubanga Dyilo, Case No. ICC-01/04-01/06, *Decision on the Confirmation of Charges*, ¶¶ 329–330 (PTC I, Jan. 29, 2007). It is not clear whether the Court will continue on this course in its future case law, and some scholars have argued that Article 25(3)(d) incorporates JCE I and II.

§ 6-10 CONSPIRACY

Conspiracy liability is well known to common law systems but is not widely established in other legal systems. The Rome Statute does not provide for conspiracy liability and the ICC has not established it through its case law.

Conspiracy is a way to hold individuals legally accountable for the actions of a group. Under U.S. law, the crime of conspiracy requires that two or more persons agree to commit an illegal act or to do something lawful using an illegal means. The key to the concept of conspiracy is the defendants' agreement to commit the crime, which itself is a criminal act, whether or not the agreement is consummated. The agreement is required, but it need not be explicit or long-lived. The *mens rea* requirement is satisfied by the defendant's intention to fulfill the agreement. Most jurisdictions require the defendant to commit at least one act in furtherance of the conspiracy. Thus, if there is an agreement and the defendant commits an overt act to achieve the objective, the defendant can be convicted of conspiracy even if the objective is not achieved.

In the U.S. legal system, conspiracy is an inchoate crime, which means that it is complete and can be prosecuted when the agreement is complete, and an overt act has been committed. In many jurisdictions, the defendants can be held responsible for the foreseeable results of the conspiracy, even if they do not personally commit the crimes, or intend for them to happen.

The ICC has not applied conspiracy liability in any of its cases, relying instead on accomplice, co-perpetration, or common plan liability. Indeed, in a concurring opinion, a Trial Chamber judge noted that the Rome Statute's drafters had rejected conspiracy as a mode of liability and that it was not available to the ICC. Prosecutor v. Mathieu Ngudjolo Chui, Case No. ICC-01/04-02/12, *Judgment Pursuant to Article 74, Concurring Opinion of Judge Christine Van den Wyngaert*, ¶ 15 (TC II, Dec. 18, 2012).

VI. GROUNDS FOR EXCLUDING CRIMINAL RESPONSIBILITY AND MITIGATING FACTORS

In most domestic criminal law systems, defenses are facts or circumstances that may preclude conviction under the right conditions. Many domestic systems recognize justifications or excuses. Justifications are those factors that entirely negate liability. Finding an act to have been justified means that the act was not criminal under the circumstances. This might include when a person who used violence either acted in self defense or was a law enforcement official with the legal authority to act as he or she did. Excuses are those factors that negate the culpability of the individual defendant. These might include the fact that he or she suffers from a mental disease or defect or committed the act under duress.

The Rome Statute does not specify defenses or explicitly distinguish between justifications and excuses, choosing instead the more neutral phrase "grounds for excluding criminal responsibility." These are mainly codified in Article 31 but also included in other parts of the Statute. Mitigating factors are facts or circumstances that may be used to support a lesser punishment, and Article 78 gives judges the discretion to consider "the individual circumstances of the convicted person" when setting the sentence, permitting the consideration of evidence in mitigation of punishment.

If a defendant is convicted, Rule 145 of the Court's Rules of Procedure and Evidence (RPE) provides more detailed rules regarding the factors that the Court should consider, both in terms of mitigation and aggravation, in the determination of a sentence. In mitigation, for example, the Court should consider the same factors that might constitute a reason to exclude criminal responsibility if those factors fall short of the high standard for excluding responsibility entirely.

§ 6-11 AGE

The age of a defendant can operate as both as defense and as evidence in mitigation of punishment. Article 26 provides that the ICC has no jurisdiction "over any person who was under the age of 18 at the time of the" alleged offenses. Thus, persons who committed crimes as juveniles may not be charged.

The ICC has also considered age as a mitigating factor, as required by RPE 145(1)(c). Article 78 gives sentencing judges wide discretion in determining the sentence for a convicted person, and age has played a role in this consideration in some cases. For example, in *Prosecutor v. Ongwen*, the Trial Chamber considered whether and how to give weight to the fact that the defendant was forcibly conscripted when he was just nine years old and forced to live with the Lord's Resistance Army (LRA). Ongwen became part of the LRA and eventually began to commit atrocities against civilians alongside the LRA's other members. Indeed, he became one of the LRA's most feared commanders until he was eventually arrested, tried before the ICC, and convicted of various crimes against humanity.

At sentencing, Ongwen's attorneys argued that what he had suffered as a child should mitigate his punishment, even if he was legally responsible for the crimes he committed after the age of 18. After considering both Ongwen's own history and the atrocities for which he had been convicted, the Trial Chamber concluded that it would give "a certain weight" in sentencing to several age-related factors, including Ongwen's "abduction as a child, the interruption of his education, the killing of his parents, [and] his socialization in the extremely violent environment of the LRA." Prosecutor v. Dominic Ongwen, Case No. ICC-02/04-01/15, *Sentence, Trial Judgment*, ¶ 87 (TC IX, May 6, 2021).

§ 6-12 MENTAL DISEASE OR DEFECT

Mental disease or defect can make it impossible to form the appropriate mental state, an essential element of criminal liability. Article 31(1)(a) provides that a person is not "criminally responsible if, at the time of that person's conduct" the person "suffers from a mental disease or defect that destroys that person's capacity to appreciate the nature of his or her conduct, or capacity to control his or her conduct to conform" to the law.

The ICC's mental disease or defect ground for excluding responsibility applies only if the incapacity or mental disease or defect affected the defendant at the time of the criminal conduct. If the defendant began to suffer from a mental disease or defect following the commission of the crime, the defense would not be available.

Article 31(1)(a) of the Rome Statute provides two grounds for excluding liability. First, a defendant can be relieved of liability if, at the time of the crime, the defendant did not appreciate the unlawfulness or nature of his or her conduct because of a mental disease or defect. Thus, for example, defendants who believe that they are killing an animal when they are actually killing a person would not be criminally responsible, if it can be established that this false belief arose from a mental disease or defect. It would also potentially be a mistake of fact that excludes criminal responsibility under Article 32(1). The other ground for excluding liability is if the defendant's mental disease or defect "destroys" their ability to control their conduct and act within the law. For example, a defendant whose mental disease or defect was so severe that he or she had no impulse control could be relieved of liability for criminal conduct.

A successful defense under Article 31(1)(a) requires that there be a finding of mental disease or defect. The first case that required the ICC to confront the issue directly was particularly complicated. In *Prosecutor v. Ongwen*, the defendant argued that because of the extensive trauma he had suffered as a child soldier (and due to other reasons), he suffered from a mental disease or defect that should exclude liability. Trial Chamber IX was required to consider evidence from the defense and prosecution regarding Ongwen's mental disease or defects and their effect, if any, on the commission of the crimes with which he was charged. Prosecutor v. Dominic Ongwen, Case No. ICC-02/04-01/15, *Trial Judgment*, ¶¶ 2450–2580 (TC IX, Feb. 4, 2021). It is not enough for the defendant to make general allegations relating to mental health. Instead, the Court must determine, based on all of the evidence and expert testimony, that a particular mental disease or defect affected the defendant at the time of the criminal conduct. *Id.*, at ¶¶ 2452–2453. Importantly, the early jurisprudence of the Court has found that even with respect to a defense raised by the accused, the burden of proof never shifts to the defense. When finding "the absence of any grounds excluding criminal responsibility" is necessary for a conviction—such as when the defense raises an issue under Article 31(1)(a)—the burden remains on the Prosecutor to show that the defendant is guilty beyond a reasonable doubt. *Id.*, at ¶ 231. Because of the unique facts in *Ongwen*, it is possible that the ICC's treatment of these issues may continue to evolve.

§ 6-13 INTOXICATION

Article 31(1)(b) excludes liability for a person whose intoxication is enough to destroy their "capacity to appreciate the unlawfulness or nature of his or her conduct, or capacity to control his or her conduct to conform to the requirements of the law." Based upon the language in the Statute, an intoxication defense will be successful only if the defendant shows that the level of intoxication was so high that his or her capacity was diminished as much as would be necessary for a mental disease or defect defense under Article 31(1)(a). Moreover, the intoxication defense is not available to defendants who "became voluntarily intoxicated" knowing, or disregarding "the risk, that, as a result of the intoxication, he or she was likely to engage" in criminal conduct. Thus, the intoxication defense is unlikely to be available in most cases.

The Statute neither limits the intoxication defense to specific intoxicants, nor excludes any intoxicants from consideration. Thus, based on the language of the Statute, those who used alcohol or illicit drugs, or presumably even misused prescription drugs, would have the defense available under appropriate circumstances.

§ 6-14 SELF DEFENSE

Self defense can be a ground to exclude criminal liability. In general, self defense is premised on the notion that a person who is not the aggressor in a violent encounter is not required to simply suffer the violence. People are justified in responding to protect themselves, their family, and sometimes their property. Article 31(1)(c) establishes a complex self-defense regime that imposes different legal requirements for different situations.

First, the law provides a defense from criminal responsibility for a person who "acts reasonably to defend himself or another person" against "an imminent and unlawful use of force." The defense is only available for people whose response is done "in a manner proportionate to the degree of danger to the person or the other person" who is being protected. This means, for example, that lethal force would not be an acceptable response to a minor or remote threat. But it could be justifiable, and therefore excluded from liability, in the face of imminent, deadly force.

Second, the Statute provides a separate rule for defendants charged with war crimes who wish to rely on self defense. In those cases, self defense may be justified if the person acts reasonably to defend "himself or herself or another person or . . . property which is essential for the survival of the person or another person or property which is essential for accomplishing a military mission." Thus, unlike in the general case, in a war crimes prosecution, the defense of essential property is a valid ground for responding with force that would otherwise not be lawful.

Both cases feature two important limitations. Self defense requires that a defendant seeking to avoid criminal responsibility must have acted "reasonably" when he or she acted against the threat. This means that the defendant's response must have been fair and appropriate given the nature of the threat and the circumstances prevailing at the time. If the response was disproportionate or otherwise unreasonable, self defense is not a viable defense. In addition, the Statute provides that "the fact that the person was involved in a defensive operation conducted by forces shall not in itself constitute a ground for excluding criminal responsibility." Thus, forces may not avoid criminal responsibility for their crimes by asserting self defense every time they are attacked.

§ 6-15 DURESS

The *ad hoc* international criminal tribunals did not have defense provisions written into their Statutes and struggled particularly with the concept of duress. For example, in *Prosecutor v. Erdemovic*, the ICTY held that, under customary international law, duress "does not afford a complete defense" to charges of killing a person as a crime against humanity or a war crime. Prosecutor v. Dražen Erdemović, Case No. IT-96-22, *Judgment*, ¶ 19 (AC, Oct. 7, 1997).

The Rome Statute, in contrast, expressly provides that a defendant who committed crimes only under duress can avoid criminal responsibility for his or her actions. At its most basic, the duress defense allows a defendant to avoid criminal responsibility when the defendant reasonably believes that the only way to avoid an imminent threat is to do something that would itself violate the law, and the defendant's actions were actually the result of the duress caused by the imminent threat and not some other reason. Under the Rome Statute, the threat that causes the defendant's duress can come from other persons or from "circumstances beyond that person's control." Art. 31(1)(d) (i & ii).

Article 31(1)(d) provides a duress defense if three conditions are met. First, the allegedly criminal conduct must have been "caused by duress resulting from a threat of imminent death or of continuing or imminent serious bodily harm against that person or another person." This requires that duress actually be the cause of the defendant's conduct. It also requires that the threat be sufficiently serious to justify the defendant's conduct. Only a threat of "imminent death" to self or another, or "continuing or imminent serious bodily harm" against self or another are sufficient. This means the threatened harm "must be either to be killed immediately ('imminent death'), or to suffer serious bodily harm immediately or in an ongoing manner ('continuing or imminent serious bodily harm')." Prosecutor v. Dominic Ongwen, Case No. ICC-02/04-01/15, *Trial Judgment*, ¶ 2582 (TC IX, Feb. 4, 2021). The duress defense is not available for abstract danger or risk that a bad situation might occur some day. If, for example, the threatened bodily harm is not going to happen soon enough, the defense would not be available.

Second, the person asserting the duress defense must have acted necessarily and reasonably to avoid the threat. Defendants are not required to take every possible action to avoid a threat before responding, but their actions must be reasonable. If, for example, others facing the same threatened harm did not respond by committing violent acts, that fact would be relevant to determining if the defendant's response to the alleged duress was reasonable or necessary.

Third, the defendant must not have intended "to cause a greater harm than the one sought to be avoided." The ICC has held that this "is a subjective element," which means that "it is not required that the person actually avoided the greater harm, only that he/she intended to do so."

In *Prosecutor v. Ongwen*, the only case to consider the duress defense thus far, the Trial Chamber considered and eventually rejected Ongwen's duress defense. In making its decision, the Court considered all the circumstances confronting Ongwen at the time he alleged to have been under duress. Among the factors that were relevant to the decision were the fact that Ongwen had a realistic possibility of leaving the situation, that he did not face death or serious bodily harm when he disobeyed those individuals whom he alleged were threatening him, and that he committed some crimes entirely in private, away from those he alleged were causing his duress. Prosecutor v. Dominic Ongwen, Case No. ICC-02/04-01/15, *Trial Judgment*, ¶¶ 2668–2671 (TC IX, Feb. 4, 2021).

§ 6-16 SUPERIOR ORDERS

A defense of obedience to superior orders might arise if a defendant claimed that he or she committed illegal acts because of the orders of a superior officer or other official. Under the Rome Statute, such a defense will only very rarely be available. Article 33 provides that a person who commits an offense on the order of a superior or other official is not relieved of criminal responsibility unless "(a) [t]he person was under a legal obligation to obey orders of the Government or the superior in question; (b) [t]he person did not know that the order was unlawful; and (c) [t]he order was not manifestly unlawful." All three of these conditions must be present, and, as a matter of law, "orders to commit genocide or crimes against humanity are manifestly unlawful."

Article 32 must be read alongside Article 33 which sets out the defense of superior orders. Pursuant to Article 32, a mistake of law may be a ground for excluding liability if that mistake was the reason the defendant did not know the order was unlawful. Article 32 does not otherwise affect the requirements of the superior orders defense: defendants would still be required to show that they were legally required to obey the order, and that the order was not manifestly unlawful.

§ 6-17 MISTAKE

Article 32 provides that, in most circumstances, mistakes as to fact or law are not grounds for excluding criminal liability. Article 32(1) states that a "mistake of fact shall be a ground for excluding criminal responsibility only if it negates the mental element required by the crime."

Article 32(2) addresses mistakes of law. A mistake of law as "to whether a particular type of conduct is a crime within the jurisdiction of the Court" is not grounds for excluding liability. A mistake of law may be "a ground for excluding criminal responsibility if it negates the mental element" of a crime. (Or, as described above, if it negates one of the elements in Article 32.)

§ 6-18 OFFICIAL STATUS

As already detailed in Chapter 2, Section VIII, Article 27 of the Rome Statute provides that Heads of State and other Government officials are not immune under the Statute. This provision was required because, as a general matter under international law, a head of state is immune from the jurisdiction of the domestic courts of another State for his or her official actions. Thus, one State may not prosecute the head of another State for something that person did while exercising the powers of his or her office, at least during the time they are still in office, and possibly thereafter.

When former Chilean President Augusto Pinochet was arrested on the territory of the U.K. in 1998 at the behest of Spanish officials seeking to prosecute him for torture, the U.K. courts were forced to address the issue of head of state immunity. The U.K.'s House of Lords initially held that Pinochet did not have immunity from arrest for the crime of torture after he left office for two reasons: his immunity from personal jurisdiction ended when he left office, and that there was no immunity from subject matter jurisdiction for the crime of torture as that cannot be a state function. That decision was set aside due to a procedural issue; however, in a subsequent decision, the House of Lords again denied immunity. Regina v. Bow Street Metropolitan Stipendiary Magistrate and Others, *Ex Parte* Pinochet Ugarte (No. 3), 1 A.C. 147 (1999).

As noted in Chapter 2, the ICC is different from domestic jurisdictions, but head of state immunity is still controversial. Like the International Military Tribunals at Nuremberg and Tokyo, and the subsequent *ad hoc* international criminal tribunals, the ICC does not recognize head of state immunity. The ICC has jurisdiction over all persons, even heads of state, regardless of the immunities that the person may have under domestic law or in another international court.

This provision of the Rome Statute and the ICC's application of it remain controversial. Because Article 27(1) states that official capacity does not exempt a person from criminal liability, the Rome Statute does not recognize head-of-state immunity from jurisdiction. Moreover, in a series of decisions in the case of *Prosecutor v. Al-Bashir*, the ICC has held that this means the ICC also does not recognize immunity from arrest. The ICC has long sought to arrest Omar Al-Bashir, the former president of Sudan, so he could be prosecuted for alleged crimes against humanity, genocide, and war crimes. In Prosecutor v. Omar Hassan Ahmad Al-Bashir, Case No. ICC-02/05-01/09, *Judgment*, ¶ 1 (AC, May 6, 2019), the Appeals Chamber stated that head of state immunity from prosecution "has never been recognized in international law as a bar to the jurisdiction of an international court."

§ 6-19 *TU QUOQUE*

Many students of international law will be familiar with the *tu quoque* defense. The essence of the *tu quoque* defense is that it is improper to prosecute a defendant for committing the same actions as his or her adversaries when those adversaries are not being prosecuted. *Tu quoque*, meaning "you also," was most famously raised as a defense by Karl Doenitz, the commander of the German navy during World War II, at the Nuremberg Tribunals. Doenitz argued that prosecuting him for engaging in unrestricted submarine warfare in the same way as the Allied navies had done was improper. The Nuremberg Tribunal rejected the defense and convicted Doenitz but imposed a much lighter sentence than those imposed on other defendants. Despite this example, the *tu quoque* defense is neither widely recognized in international law, nor codified in the Rome Statute.

§ 6-20 *NE BIS IN IDEM* (DOUBLE JEOPARDY)

As noted in Chapter 2, § 2.12.3, the ICC has provisions that address the issue of double jeopardy using the Latin term *ne bis in idem*, which means "not again about the same." The basic concept is that a defendant may not be prosecuted twice for the same conduct by the same sovereign. This protection is very important in domestic legal systems to prevent prosecutors from abusing their power by, for example, re-prosecuting an individual after an acquittal in the hope of convicting him or her on a second attempt. The defense is not widely applicable in international law because it only protects against re-prosecution by the same sovereign. In theory (but not widely seen in practice) two States could prosecute the same individual for the same conduct. When the Rome Statute was negotiated, a robust provision on *ne bis in idem* was inserted to respond to human rights concerns about potential defendants facing multiple prosecutions in several jurisdictions. The Court's early case law on this provision is set out in Chapter 2, § 2.12.3.

Selected Sources and Additional Reading

ELEMENTS OF GENOCIDE (Paul Behrens & Ralph Henham eds., 2013).

MODES OF LIABILITY IN INTERNATIONAL CRIMINAL LAW (Jérôme de Hemptinne, Robert Roth, Elies van Sliedregt, Marjolein Cupido, Manuel J. Ventura, Lachezar Yanev eds., 2019).

NEHA JAIN, PERPETRATORS AND ACCESSORIES IN INTERNATIONAL CRIMINAL LAW: INDIVIDUAL MODES OF RESPONSIBILITY FOR COLLECTIVE CRIMES (2014).

WAYNE R. LAFAVE, CRIMINAL LAW (6th ed. 2017).

WAYNE LAFAVE, SUBSTANTIVE CRIMINAL LAW (3d ed. 2018).

JORDAN J. PAUST, M. CHERIF BASSIOUNI, MICHAEL SCHARF, JIMMY GURULE, LEILA SADAT & BRUCE ZAGARIS, INTERNATIONAL CRIMINAL LAW: CASES AND MATERIALS (3d ed. 2007).

BETH VAN SCHAACK & RONALD C. SLYE, INTERNATIONAL CRIMINAL LAW AND ITS ENFORCEMENT (4th ed. 2020).

ELIES VAN SLIEDREGT, INDIVIDUAL CRIMINAL RESPONSIBILITY IN INTERNATIONAL LAW (2012).

Marjolein Cupido, *Common Purpose Liability Versus Joint Perpetration: A Practical View on the ICC's Hierarchy of Liability Theories*, 29 LEIDEN J. INT'L L. 897 (2016).

Alison Marston Danner & Jenny S. Martinez, *Guilty Associations: Joint Criminal Enterprise, Command*

Responsibility, and the Development of International Criminal Law, 93 CAL. L. REV. 75 (2005).

Sarah Finnin, *Mental Elements under Article 30 of the Rome Statute of the International Criminal Court: A Comparative Analysis*, 61 INT'L & COMP. L. Q. 325 (2012).

Oona Hathaway, et al., *Aiding and Abetting in International Criminal Law*, 104 CORNELL L. REV. 1593, 1609 (2009).

Jens David Ohlin, *Second-Order Linking Principles: Combining Vertical and Horizontal Modes of Liability*, 25 LEIDEN J. INT'L L. 771 (2012).

Susana SáCouto, Leila Nadya Sadat & Patricia Viseur Sellers, *Collective Criminality and Sexual Violence: Fixing a Failed Approach,* 40 LEIDEN J. INT'L L. 207 (2019).

Johan D. Van der Vyver, *The International Criminal Court and the Concept of Mens Rea in International Criminal Law*, 12 U. MIA. INT'L & COMP. L. REV. 57 (2004).

Leila Nadya Sadat & Jarrod M. Jolly, *Seven Canons of ICC Treaty Interpretation: Making Sense of Article 25's Rorschach Blot*, 27 LEIDEN J. INT'L. L. 755 (2014).

Liana Minkova, *A New Approach to Criminal Responsibility? Discussing the Separate Opinions on Indirect Co-Perpetration in the* Ntaganda *Appeals Judgment*, OPINIO JURIS (Aug. 4, 2021), http://opinio juris.org/2021/04/08/a-new-approach-to-criminal-responsibility-discussing-the-separate-opinions-on-indirect-co-perpetration-in-the-ntaganda-appeals-judgment/.

Elies van Sliedregt, *The ICC* Ntaganda *Appeals Judgment: The End of Indirect Co-perpetration?*, JUST SEC. (May 14, 2021), https://www.justsecurity.org/76136/the-icc-ntaganda-appeals-judgment-the-end-of-indirect-co-perpetration/.

CHAPTER 7

PRELIMINARY EXAMINATIONS AND INVESTIGATIONS

I. INTRODUCTION

Pursuant to the Rome Statute, a situation can be referred to the ICC by a State Party, the Security Council, or the Prosecutor on his or her own initiative, acting *proprio motu*. Art. 13. The referral process is covered in Chapter 2. This Chapter addresses a separate issue—what happens next? How does the Prosecutor decide whether to begin an investigation and eventually bring charges?

The ICC has its own vocabulary to describe the matters that come before it. As noted in Chapter 1, a "situation" is a group of possible crimes that are linked by geography and time. A "case" refers to the full list of charges against an individual defendant that the Prosecutor will pursue before the Court. "Crimes" are the specific charges against individual defendants and are contained in Articles 5–8 *bis* of the Rome Statute. For example, the situation in the Democratic Republic of Congo produced six cases against individual defendants who were charged with a wide range of crimes.

Each year the Office of the Prosecutor receives hundreds of communications under Article 15 of the Rome Statute. These communications cover a wide range of alleged crimes. For example, in 2022 the Office of the Prosecutor ("OTP") received communications regarding possible crimes committed against migrants in Libya, alleged war crimes committed in Syria by Iran, and alleged crimes associated with Russia's occupation of Crimea.

The OTP conducts an initial assessment of all communications, which filters out crimes that are manifestly outside the jurisdiction of the Court. For example, in 2020 the OTP received 813 communications. Of these, the Prosecutor determined that 612 were manifestly outside the ICC's jurisdiction, 104 were linked to a situation already under preliminary investigation, and 71 were linked to an investigation or prosecution. That left 26 communications warranting further analysis. INT'L CRIM CT. OFF. OF THE PROSECUTOR, REPORT ON PRELIMINARY EXAMINATION ACTIVITIES (Dec. 14, 2020).

The OTP then conducts a preliminary examination of the remaining communications to determine if the allegations meet the legal criteria necessary for prosecution. If the Prosecutor determines, after the preliminary examination, that the information meets the necessary criteria, the Prosecutor moves on to an investigation, during which he or she identifies the individual defendants to be charged, as well as the crimes for which each defendant will be charged.

II. THE PRELIMINARY EXAMINATION

When the Office of the Prosecutor receives an Article 15 communication, a referral of a situation from a State Party or the Security Council, or a declaration accepting the jurisdiction of the Court by a non-State Party to the Rome Statute, it follows a procedure that draws on the Rome Statute, the Regulations of the Court, and the Rules of Evidence and Procedure, the practice of which has been codified in the Prosecutor's 2013 *Policy Paper on Preliminary Examinations*. INT'L CRIM. CT. OFF. OF THE PROSECUTOR, POLICY PAPER ON PRELIMINARY EXAMINATIONS (Nov. 2013).

The first step is the initiation of a preliminary examination. The term "preliminary examination" appears only once in the Rome Statute, in Article 15(6), but it has become an important formal stage in a case. Although Article 15(1) refers to the Prosecutor's own power to initiate an investigation, not to referrals from States Parties or the Security Council, in practice, the Prosecutor undertakes a preliminary examination in all cases.

The Prosecutor's task at the preliminary examination stage is to determine if there is a "reasonable basis to proceed with an investigation" into the situation. Art. 15(2). To make this determination, the Prosecutor must consider whether the alleged crime is within the jurisdiction of the Court, whether the case would be admissible under Article 17 of the Statute (including consideration of the gravity of the alleged crimes), and whether bringing a case would serve the interests of justice. Art. 53(1)(a)–(c).

As noted in the Prosecutor's *Policy Paper on Preliminary Examinations*, the standard of proof for a preliminary examination is "reasonable basis." INT'L CRIM. CT. OFF. OF THE PROSECUTOR, POLICY

PAPER ON PRELIMINARY EXAMINATIONS, ¶ 5 (Nov. 2013). This means that the Prosecutor will move forward after a preliminary examination only if the available information provides a reasonable basis to conclude that a crime within the jurisdiction of the ICC has been committed.

The Prosecutor uses a four-phase process to assess possible cases. Phase one involves assessing the communications and other information that the Office of the Prosecutor is constantly receiving. The goal of this phase is to eliminate cases that are manifestly outside the ICC's jurisdiction and mandate or are already subject to prosecution in the ICC or elsewhere. The formal preliminary examination begins in phase two, which focuses on jurisdiction issues. Phase three focuses on admissibility, and phase four focuses on the interests of justice.

§ 7-1 JURISDICTION

After completing phase one, the Prosecutor moves to phase two to consider jurisdiction issues. For genocide, crimes against humanity, and war crimes, the Rome Statute requires the Prosecutor to consider two different types of jurisdiction: jurisdiction *ratione temporis* (or temporal jurisdiction), and subject matter jurisdiction. Additionally, during this phase, other limiting factors must also be considered. The jurisdiction regime for the crime of aggression is unique and addressed separately below.

Jurisdiction *ratione temporis* is the period of time during which the alleged criminal acts must have occurred to allow the ICC to consider the case. The Rome Statute entered into force on July 1, 2002, and limits the ICC's jurisdiction to acts occurring on or after that date. Art. 11(1). This date is the earliest possible date on which the acts may have occurred. But jurisdiction *ratione temporis* also depends on other factors. If a State joined the Rome Statute at a later date, it is that later date that sets the date parameters in cases involving that State. Art. 11(2). If the referral comes from the Security Council, the date parameters can be set in the referral. Finally, if a non-State Party accepts jurisdiction pursuant to Art. 12(3), the date parameters can be set in the declaration in which jurisdiction was accepted. (Although obviously different from jurisdiction *ratione temporis*, it is important to note that crimes within the jurisdiction of the ICC are not "subject to any statute of limitation" as long as the jurisdictional requirements are met. Art. 29.)

Subject matter jurisdiction refers to the notion that the ICC has power to adjudicate only specific kinds of cases. We address the subject matter jurisdiction of the Court in Chapters 2 and 5. As set forth in Chapter 2, there are other preconditions to the exercise of jurisdiction as well.

§ 7-2 ADMISSIBILITY

After jurisdiction, the Prosecutor must consider the admissibility of any cases that might arise from the situation. Art. 17. Whether a case is admissible turns on complementarity, gravity, and whether the case has been tried before, either in another jurisdiction or at the Court.

Part of the admissibility analysis is whether the allegations are of sufficient gravity to justify further action by the ICC. Art. 18(1)(d). The analysis at this stage is done with respect to the gravity of the situation, not to specific cases (because none have yet been identified). Situation in the Republic of Kenya, Case No. ICC-01/09, *Decision Pursuant to Article 15 of the Rome Statute on the Authorization of an Investigation into the Situation in the Republic of Kenya*, ¶ 58 (PTC II, Mar. 31, 2010).

§ 7-3 INTERESTS OF JUSTICE

As noted in Chapter 2, even if the Prosecutor concludes that the ICC has jurisdiction over an admissible and sufficiently grave situation, Article 53(1)(c) of the Rome Statute requires the Prosecutor to consider whether there are "substantial reasons to believe that an investigation would not serve the interests of justice." The Prosecutor is not required to demonstrate that the interests of justice would be served by an investigation. Instead, if the other criteria are met, the Prosecutor will proceed with an investigation, unless there are substantial reasons to believe that the interests of justice would not be served by an investigation.

This is a countervailing consideration to allow for some degree of Prosecutorial discretion, and it is meant to permit a Prosecutor to decline to move forward with an otherwise-viable case if bringing the case would not be in the interests of justice. Among the factors that are relevant to this analysis are "the gravity of the crimes" and "the interests of the victims." Situation in the Islamic Republic of Afghanistan, Case No. ICC-02/17, *Judgment on the Appeal Against the Decision on the Authorization of an Investigation into the Situation in the Islamic Republic of Afghanistan*, ¶ 49 (AC, Mar. 5, 2020).

The Prosecutor's 2007 Policy *Paper on the Interests of Justice* describes and guides his or her consideration of the issue. In it, the Prosecutor makes clear that the "interests of justice" consideration is an "exceptional" factor, and that there is a presumption in favor of prosecution where the other criteria are satisfied. INT'L CRIM. CT. OFF. OF THE PROSECUTOR, POLICY PAPER THE INTERESTS OF JUSTICE 1 (Sept. 2007). In addition, the Prosecutor distinguishes between the interests of justice, which he or she must consider, and the interests of peace, which should be considered by other institutions.

III. FROM PRELIMINARY EXAMINATION TO INVESTIGATION

The ICC system balances prosecutorial discretion, robust oversight from the Court, and due respect for States Parties and the U.N. Security Council. After the Office of the Prosecutor completes a preliminary examination, there are additional steps to take before the commencement of an investigation. How a case moves from preliminary examination to investigation depends on how the case comes to the attention of the ICC.

The Rome Statute includes no time limits for preliminary examinations. The situation in Colombia, for example, was under preliminary examination from 2004 until October 2021 when Prosecutor Khan closed it. INT'L CRIM CT. OFF. OF THE PROSECUTOR, REPORT ON PRELIMINARY EXAMINATION ACTIVITIES, ¶ 105 (Dec. 14, 2020). It is possible that the ICC could act to address the issue of delays, although delay may serve to remind a State Party that the situation is being examined by prosecutorial authorities and deter future crimes. The Independent Expert Review (IER) discussed in Chapter 1, § 1-19, suggested that slow, lengthy, or delayed preliminary examinations could undermine confidence in the Court. The IER suggested several ways to address this, including hiring more staff, creating new positions, or reallocating authority within the OTP, and adopting internal processes to avoid delays. Although some of these recommendations have been implemented by the ICC, the issue of unwarranted delay remains a significant concern.

§ 7-4 STATE PARTY OR SECURITY COUNCIL REFERRAL

In a situation arising from a referral from a State Party or the Security Council, if the Prosecutor decides to move forward after the preliminary examination, he or she can do so directly. Indeed, the Appeals Chamber has written that the Rome Statute "reflects an expectation that the Prosecutor will proceed to investigate referred situations, while allowing the Prosecutor not to proceed in limited circumstances" set out in the Statute. Situation in the Islamic Republic of Afghanistan, Case No. ICC-02/17, *Judgment on the Appeal Against the Decision on the Authorization of an Investigation into the Situation in the Islamic Republic of Afghanistan*, ¶ 29 (AC, Mar. 5, 2020).

If the Prosecutor decides not to move forward, he or she must report the decision to the referring State or the Security Council, which may then request that the Pre-Trial Chamber review the Prosecutor's decision not to proceed. The Pre-Trial Chamber can either affirm the Prosecutor's decision, or ask him or her to reconsider, after which the Prosecutor can either affirm the original decision or reverse the decision and open the investigation. Art. 53(3)(a). The Pre-Trial Chamber may also, on its own initiative, review the Prosecutor's decision not to proceed if this decision is based only on the Prosecutor's conclusion that the case is of insufficient gravity or not in the interests of justice. Art. 53(3)(b).

§ 7-5 PROSECUTOR'S *PROPRIO MOTU* POWERS

In a situation arising from the Prosecutor's own power to initiate a case, the Prosecutor must request authorization from the Pre-Trial Chamber before beginning an investigation. Art. 15(3). The Prosecutor's request is governed by the *Regulations of the Court*, an internal document setting out the processes for the Court's work. The *Regulations* require the request for authorization to specify the crimes the Prosecutor believes have been or are being committed, as well as the factual basis for this belief. INT'L CRIM. CT., REGULATIONS OF THE COURT, Doc. No. ICC-BD/01-05-16, Reg. 49(1)(a) (2018). The request must also declare why the Prosecutor believes the alleged crimes fall within the jurisdiction of the Court. The statement of facts must be detailed, including where the alleged crimes took place, when and for how long, and a description of who was involved. The *Regulations* also suggest, but do not require, that the request include a chronology of the events, detailed maps, and a glossary of names, places, and institutions affected or involved. *Id.*, Reg. 49(3).

For example, the request for authorization to open investigation into the situation in Kenya to look into post-election violence was accompanied by more than three dozen annexes. These contained detailed maps of the locations of violent acts, specific dates of the alleged crimes, reports by institutions and other sources in Kenya about the causes and consequences of the violence, and many other matters. Situation in the Republic of Kenya, Case No. ICC-01/09, *Request for Authorization of an Investigation Pursuant to Article 15* (PTC II, Nov. 26, 2009).

In addition to considering the Prosecutor's request, the Pre-Trial Chamber also considers representations from victims at this stage as well. Art. 15(3). Ordinarily the Office of the Prosecutor would provide notice to victims about the opportunity to share their views with the Pre-Trial Chamber. However, in exceptional circumstances, the Prosecutor has the discretion to make the request for authorization under seal and *ex parte*, so that only the Pre-Trial Chamber is aware of the potential for an investigation. This extraordinary step can be taken only when necessary to protect the lives of victims or to protect the integrity of the investigation. Situation in the Republic of Burundi, Case No. ICC-01/17, *Public Redacted Version of "Decision Pursuant to Article 15 of the Rome Statute on the Authorization of an Investigation into the Situation in the Republic of Burundi,"* ¶ 11 (PTC III, Nov. 9, 2017).

IV. INVESTIGATIONS

The Prosecutor must gather all the necessary evidence and identify potential defendants before initiating a prosecution. After the Prosecutor decides or is given the authorization to move forward with an investigation, the first step is to assemble a unified team to conduct the investigation. In 2021, the OTP published a policy paper on situation completion noting that its "overall aim in carrying out investigations and prosecutions is to represent as much as possible the true extent of the criminality which has occurred within a given situation. . . to ensure, jointly with the relevant national jurisdictions, that the most serious crimes committed in each situation do not go unpunished." INT'L CRIM. CT. OFF. OF THE PROSECUTOR, POLICY ON SITUATION COMPLEMENT ¶ 21 (June 2021).

Investigations are complex. Prosecutors must identify and secure relevant evidence, identify individual defendants, engage with victims and witnesses, and evaluate jurisdictional and other legal issues. Prosecutors develop a case hypothesis to help focus the investigation on the cases that most clearly indicate the scale of the crimes and their impact on victims. The Prosecutor is required to investigate exonerating and incriminating evidence equally and respect the legal rights of potential defendants. Art. 54(1). During the investigation, the Prosecutor must be sensitive to the interests and circumstances of victims and other witnesses. The Prosecutor must also pay special attention to crimes involving sexual violence, gender-based violence, or crimes against children. Art. 54(2).

During the investigation the Prosecutor may conduct investigations on the territory of States that give their approval to do so. States Parties are under a treaty obligation to cooperate with the Court in its investigations and prosecutions. Art. 86. If a State Party does not cooperate, the Court may make a finding to that effect and transmit it to the Assembly of States Parties, or, if the referral originated there, to the Security Council. Art. 87.

The Court has the authority to authorize the Prosecutor to investigate a case within the territory of a State Party without that State's consent if the Court concludes that the State Party is unable to comply with a request for cooperation because of the unavailability of any authority of its judicial system to execute the request. Art. 57(3)(d).

Non-States Parties to the Rome Statute are not obligated by treaty or customary law to cooperate but may do so in response to requests from the Court. In a situation arising from a referral from the Security

Council, the Security Council may order States to cooperate with investigations. For example, in 2005 the Security Council referred the situation in Darfur to the ICC. Included in the Security Council resolution was an order that the government of Sudan and all other Parties to the conflict to "cooperate fully with and provide any necessary assistance to the Court and the Prosecutor." U.N. Security Council, Resolution 1593, S/RES/1593, (Mar. 31, 2005), ¶ 2. As noted in Chapter 4, *supra,* the Security Council also urged, but did not require, other non-States Parties to the Rome Statute to cooperate with the ICC.

The investigation may produce evidence of many potential crimes and defendants. To select specific cases to pursue, the Prosecutor identifies the most serious crimes committed within the situation. Regulations of the Office of the Prosecutor, Reg. 33. When the Prosecutor has completed enough of the investigation to identify defendants and specific charges and has concluded that there is evidence to prove that crimes within the jurisdiction of the Court were committed, he or she may request the Pre-Trial Chamber to issue an arrest warrant or a summons to appear. Art. 58. Arrest warrants are issued only after the Pre-Trial Chamber is satisfied that there are reasonable grounds to believe that a crime within the jurisdiction of the Court was committed, and that arrest is necessary to ensure the person's appearance at trial or to prevent the person from endangering the investigation or committing further crimes.

If an arrest warrant is not necessary to ensure the appearance of the accused, the Prosecutor may seek a summons to appear from the Pre-Trial Chamber. The summons requires the appearance of the accused, but does not authorize other States to arrest him or her. Instead, it is used when there are reasons to believe that the accused will appear on his or her own. Art. 58(7).

V. INFORMATION AND EVIDENCE

Throughout the investigative stages of a case, the sources of information on which the Prosecutor bases his or her decisions can change throughout the process. The Rules of Evidence do not apply at this stage. The Prosecutor may, and often must, rely on information that would not be admissible as evidence at trial.

§ 7-6 INTRODUCTION

Initially, any person, organization, or State can submit a report to the Prosecutor about possible crimes. These communications, as they are called, can form the basis of a preliminary examination, which can lead to an investigation. The Prosecutor may also receive referrals from States Parties or the Security Council. Based on this information, the Prosecutor conducts an initial assessment of all the information in his or her possession. The goal is to analyze the information and weigh the seriousness of the underlying allegations to filter out those allegations that are outside the Court's jurisdiction or mandate.

At the preliminary examination stage, the Prosecutor does not have investigative powers; he or she cannot compel assistance or require the production of evidence. Instead, the Prosecutor relies on the information received through communications or from other sources, such as reports from non-governmental organizations or organs of the United Nations, stories from the news media, or reports from governments. At this stage, the information is gathered not for use in court proceedings, but to help the Prosecutor determine if it is appropriate to open an investigation based on the criteria described above.

§ 7-7 INVESTIGATIONS AND EXCULPATORY EVIDENCE

Prosecutors can face a dilemma when investigating a case. Under the Rome Statute, they are required to disclose exculpatory information to defendants. The Prosecutor has the obligation to provide the accused with any evidence which "shows or tends to show the innocence of the accused, or to mitigate the guilt of the accused, or which may affect the credibility of prosecution evidence." Art. 67(2). The Prosecutor must make such a disclosure "as soon as practicable," including during the investigation phase of the proceedings.

Prosecutors also face the reality that in many cases, victims and witnesses may be justifiably reluctant or frightened to share their stories with investigators for fear of reprisal or other threats. Victims and witnesses often agree to provide information about possible crimes only if they can be certain that they can do so safely. They may face threats to their lives or families for providing information to the Prosecutor and can be faced with the dilemma of either reporting suspected atrocities and risking harm or staying silent in order to be safe. Article 54(3)(e) gives the Prosecutor a way to address this problem. Prosecutors may make an agreement with a witness, organization, or other source of information "not to disclose, at any stage of the proceedings" any information that is (a) obtained on condition of confidentiality and (b) used solely to generate new evidence. This allows Prosecutors to gather evidence in secret to use to develop the case, while shielding the identities of the persons or groups who provided the lead evidence.

The power to obtain lead evidence confidentially can come into conflict with the obligation to disclose exculpatory evidence. In *Prosecutor v. Lubanga*, the Court confronted this issue. The Prosecutor had obtained substantial lead evidence from individuals, organs of the U.N., and elsewhere on the condition that the evidence remain confidential. Lubanga argued that it was impossible for his trial to be fair because the Prosecutor had not disclosed to him potentially exculpatory evidence that he needed to prepare for trial. The Prosecutor maintained that he was bound to respect the confidentiality agreements with sources and that, because those sources would not agree to the release of the evidence, he could not disclose it to Lubanga.

The Trial Chamber sided with Lubanga and issued a stay of proceedings. The Appeals Chamber upheld the stay, holding that the Prosecutor's confidentiality agreements did not prevent the Prosecutor from disclosing the evidence to the Court for the purpose of determining if the evidence was exculpatory. The Appeals Chamber also held that when the Office of the Prosecutor used its authority to gather evidence under confidentiality agreements, the Prosecutor must apply the confidentiality provisions in a way that would allow a court to resolve the tension between confidentiality and disclosure. Prosecutor v. Thomas Lubanga Dyilo, Case No. ICC-01/04-01/06, *Judgment on the Appeal of the Prosecutor Against the Decision of Trial Chamber I Entitled "Decision on the Consequences of Non-disclosure of Exculpatory Materials Covered by Article 54(3)(e) Agreements"* (AC, Oct. 21, 2008). The result of these proceedings is that when the Prosecutor exercises his or her authority under Article 54(3)(e), he or she must do so with the disclosure obligations in mind.

§ 7-8 SUFFICIENCY OF THE EVIDENCE

Under the Rome Statute, the objective of the preliminary examination is to determine if the information available constitutes "a reasonable basis for an investigation." Art. 15(3). The Pre-Trial Chamber applies the same "reasonable basis" test when considering whether to authorize an investigation when such authorization is necessary. The Court has made it clear that the Pre-Trial Chamber's review at this stage is limited. It is not the Pre-Trial Chamber's task to consider all of the factors the Prosecutor considers, including the interests of justice, when considering the request for authorization. Instead, "the pre-trial chamber need only consider whether there is a reasonable factual basis to proceed with an investigation, in the sense of whether crimes have been committed, and whether potential case(s) arising from such investigation appear to fall within the Court's jurisdiction." Situation in the Islamic Republic of Afghanistan, Case No. ICC-02/17, *Judgment on the Appeal Against the Decision on the Authorization of an Investigation into the Situation in the Islamic Republic of Afghanistan*, ¶¶ 34–35 (AC, Mar. 5, 2020).

To obtain an arrest warrant, the Prosecutor's evidence must be sufficient to convince the Pre-Trial Chamber that there are "reasonable grounds to believe" the accused has committed a crime within the Court's jurisdiction and that the arrest is necessary. Art. 58(1). When the investigation has gone far enough that the Prosecutor is ready to charge individuals with specific crimes, the Prosecutor must seek confirmation of the charges from the Pre-Trial Chamber. At this stage, the Prosecutor's evidence must be enough to convince the Court that there are "substantial grounds to believe that the person has committed the crime charged." Art. 61(7).

§ 7-9 UNIQUE INVESTIGATIVE OPPORTUNITIES

Prosecutors sometimes encounter unique opportunities to obtain testimony or otherwise acquire important evidence in cases. These opportunities may relate to particularly vulnerable witnesses, including those who may not be available for trial due to health reasons, or fragile evidence. Article 56 provides that when the Prosecutor identifies such an opportunity, he or she may inform the Pre-Trial Chamber and seek the Court's assistance in obtaining or preserving the evidence. Unless ordered not to by the Court, the Prosecutor must also notify the accused of the relevant information. Art. 56(1)(c). The Statute provides the Pre-Trial Chamber with a range of tools to enable the Prosecutor to secure the evidence, including appointing an expert to assist the Prosecutor or making a record of the proceedings. Art. 56(2).

While she was investigating the situation that eventually resulted in the case against Dominic Ongwen, the Prosecutor made use of this power. After identifying seven women who were allegedly the victims of sexual or gender-based crimes, the Prosecutor argued that these witnesses might be intimidated and be unable or unwilling to testify later, and that a prolonged delay between experiencing sexual violence and testifying about it could cause them psychological harm. The Pre-Trial Chamber permitted the Prosecutor to call the witnesses during the investigation stage to preserve their testimony. The witnesses testified by video link from Uganda, with the Court sitting in The Hague, and were subject to cross-examination by the defense. Prosecutor v. Dominic Ongwen, Case No. ICC-02/04-01/15, *Decision on the Prosecution's Submissions on the Conduct of Proceedings Pursuant to Decision ICC-02/04-01/15-277* (PTC II, Mar. 27, 2016).

VI. STATE COOPERATION

Unlike domestic legal systems, the ICC does not have a police force that it can rely on to investigate cases, secure evidence, or apprehend suspects. Instead it must rely on State cooperation. States Parties to the Rome Statute are under a treaty obligation to cooperate with the Court in its investigations and prosecutions. While other States are not obligated under treaty or customary international law to cooperate with the ICC, many have been willing to do so on some matters.

The formal cooperation regime, set forth in Part 9 of the Rome Statute, is straightforward on paper but has been contentious in practice.

§ 7-10 GENERAL REQUIREMENTS

Article 86 requires all States Parties to "cooperate fully with the Court in its investigation and prosecution of crimes." This is a general requirement. Other provisions in Part 9 specify many of the ways that States must cooperate with the ICC, but the text of Article 86 suggests that the types of cooperation specified in the Statute are not the only possible forms of required cooperation. States Parties also must ensure that their domestic statutes contain procedures that allow States to fulfill their cooperation obligations. Art. 88.

States Parties may be asked to keep confidential the request for cooperation and the information offered in support of the request. The Court may, when requesting cooperation, require that the requested assistance be provided in a way that does not endanger the physical or psychological safety of victims, survivors, witnesses, or their families. Arts. 87(3) & (4).

The Court may refer States Parties that fail to cooperate fully with its requests to the Assembly of States Parties or to the Security Council, depending on the source of the referral.

States have customary and treaty law obligations beyond those to the ICC. Under the terms of the Rome Statute, the Court may not proceed with an arrest request which would require the State to violate its international law obligations with respect to state or diplomatic immunity of a person from a third State, unless that third State has waived immunity. Art. 98(1).

The Court may also request assistance from non-States Parties to the Rome Statute, through an *ad hoc* agreement or other understanding. Art. 87(5)(a). States are not required to comply with such requests. If a non-State Party enters into an *ad hoc* cooperation arrangement with the ICC and fails to fulfill its terms, the Court may refer the matter to the Assembly of States Parties or to the Security Council, depending on the source of the referral. Art. 87(5)(b).

§ 7-11 FORMS OF COOPERATION

States Parties may be asked to cooperate in arresting a suspect, ensuring the surrender of the suspect to the ICC, or assisting in locating and securing evidence. Non-States Parties may also be asked to assist in these ways, albeit through *ad hoc* arrangements described in Article 87.

§ 7.11.1 Securing Suspects

When it wants to secure a suspect in a case, the Court may request that any State in which that suspect is found arrest the person and surrender him or her to the ICC. States Parties are required by the Rome Statute to comply with such requests. Art. 89(1). Non-States Parties, however, are not required to do so.

Requests for arrest and surrender from the ICC can be challenged in the domestic courts of the arresting State if the suspect claims, pursuant to Article 20, that the case is improper because he or she has already been tried by another court. Art. 89(2). If the ICC has already found the case to be admissible—a decision that includes an analysis of whether domestic proceedings would bar ICC prosecution—the State receiving the request must comply with it. If the request for arrest comes before the ICC has ruled on admissibility, the State receiving the request may postpone the suspect's surrender to the ICC until it has ruled on admissibility.

Sometimes the ICC seeks a suspect who is also sought by prosecutors in a domestic court. When there are competing requests for the arrest of a suspect and the requesting State is a State Party to the Rome Statute, the ICC's request takes priority, but only if it has already ruled on admissibility and this admissibility decision took into account the requesting State's proceedings. Art. 90(2).

When the competing State is a non-State Party, the detaining State may surrender to the suspect to the competing State if it is under a treaty obligation to do so. If not, it should surrender the suspect to the ICC. Art. 90(4).

In urgent cases, the Court has the power to request the provisional arrest of a suspect even before the formal request for arrest and surrender can be processed. Art. 92.

§ 7.11.2 Securing Evidence

Prosecutors investigating crimes also need to secure evidence and must rely on State cooperation to do so. Article 93 of the Rome Statute spells out the various forms of cooperation that the Court may request of States Parties. States may be asked to assist in locating people or things, producing evidence, serving documents, executing searches and seizures, providing documents and records, and protecting witnesses. Art. 93(1). The Statute also expressly provides that States Parties must provide any "other type of assistance which is not prohibited by the law of the requested State." Art. 93(1)(*l*). States that receive requests that appear to be against their own laws must consult with the Court to resolve the situation. Art. 93(3). States are also permitted to deny a request for assistance if it concerns the production of documents or disclosure of evidence relating to national security. Art. 93(4).

§ 7-12 LACK OF COOPERATION IN PRACTICE

Despite the clear and broad cooperation requirements in the Rome Statute, States Parties have not always been willing to cooperate with the ICC. For example, many States Parties refused to comply with the ICC's request to arrest and surrender Omar Al-Bashir, former president of Sudan. The ICC has attempted to address this non-cooperation through the Assembly of States Parties and other methods.

The United States has sometimes erected substantial barriers to cooperation with the Court. It has done this by executing what it calls Article 98 agreements, based on Article 98 of the Rome Statute. These are bilateral agreements in which the signatories agree not to turn over the other State's nationals to the ICC or otherwise facilitate their arrest or surrender to the Court. The United States has executed dozens of these agreements with States—both States Parties and non-States Parties to the Rome Statute—since the ICC came into existence.

§ 7.12.1 Instances of Failure to Cooperate

Many States have not fully complied with their cooperation obligations under the Rome Statute. The most prominent example of State non-cooperation has been in the case of Omar Al-Bashir. The ICC issued arrest warrants in 2009 and 2010 for Al-Bashir, alleging that he had committed crimes against humanity in Darfur between 2003 and 2008. Prosecutor v. Omar Hassan Ahmad Al-Bashir, Case No. ICC-02/05-01/09, *Second Decision on the Prosecution's Application for a Warrant of Arrest* (PTC I, July 12, 2010). The case grew out of a referral from the Security Council about the situation in Darfur. U.N. Security Council, Resolution 1593, S/RES/1593 (Mar. 31, 2005). At the time the warrants were issued, Al-Bashir was the president of Sudan. Under the terms of the Rome Statute, States Parties were obligated to comply with the ICC's request to arrest him and surrender him to the Court. Despite the pending arrest warrants, Al-Bashir continued to travel—including to other States Parties—and remained at large until he was arrested in Sudan. Press Release, International Criminal Court, *Pre-Trial Chamber I informs the Security Council and the Assembly of States Parties about Omar Al-Bashir's visits to Kenya and Chad*, ICC-CPI-20100827-PR568 (Aug. 27, 2010). He has not been surrendered to the ICC to date.

The have been other instances of non-cooperation. Simone Gbagbo is the former first lady of Côte d'Ivoire and faced prosecution in the ICC for crimes against humanity arising out of post-election violence in 2010 and 2011. In 2012, the ICC issued an arrest warrant and requested her surrender, but Côte d'Ivoire refused. Prosecutor v. Simone Gbagbo, Case No. ICC-02/11-01/12, *Warrant of Arrest for Simone Gbagbo* (PTC III, Feb. 29, 2012). After facing arrest in the ICC, she was prosecuted in the domestic courts of Côte d'Ivoire. Gbagbo sought to have the ICC warrant dismissed, arguing that prosecuting her in the ICC would be illegal as she was being investigated or prosecuted for the same conduct in Côte d'Ivoire. The ICC eventually concluded that the conduct for which she was prosecuted in Côte d'Ivoire was different from the conduct under investigation in the ICC and upheld the arrest warrant. Prosecutor v. Simone Gbagbo, Case No. ICC-02/11-01/12, *Judgment* (AC, May 27, 2015). Nonetheless, the government refused to surrender her, and she was never brought to the ICC. After the acquittal of her husband, Laurent Gbagbo, on substantially similar evidence, the ICC vacated Simone Gbagbo's arrest warrant at the request of the Prosecutor. Prosecutor v. Simone Gbagbo, Case No. ICC-02/11-01/12, *Decision on Prosecutor's Request to Vacate Warrant of Arrest* (PTC II, July 19, 2021).

§ 7.12.2 Cooperation Issues and the United States

As discussed in greater detail in Chapter 10, the United States has only intermittently cooperated with the ICC. As a non-State Party, it is not under a treaty obligation to cooperate with the Court. The United States has pursued a series of Article 98 agreements. Article 98(2) of the Rome Statute provides that the ICC may not proceed with a request for surrender from a State that would require the State receiving the request to violate any of its international agreements by obtaining the consent of a sending State before surrendering the suspect.

Furthermore, when the ICC began investigating alleged violations of international criminal law that occurred during the conflict in Afghanistan, the United States signaled that it would not cooperate in any way with that investigation or any eventual prosecution, which has slowed the ICC's investigation.

a. Article 98 Agreements

Almost since the Court's inception, the United States has expressed reluctance to participate in the work of the ICC. Article 98 agreements are one way it has attempted to insulate itself from the ICC's jurisdiction. These agreements sometimes known as Bilateral Immunity Agreements, are based on Article 98(2), which the United States has argued prohibits the Court from requesting a State to surrender an individual to the ICC if the State has entered into an international agreement not to do so. (The Court takes the view that the BIAs only affect the relations of the two States *inter se,* not the relationship between the ICC State Party and the ICC).

States that have entered into Article 98 agreements with the United States pledge that they will not surrender U.S. persons to the ICC, in exchange for a promise from the United States to not send that State's nationals to the ICC without the State's consent. To date, the United States has executed over 100 such agreements with States around the world.

b. The United States and the Afghanistan Investigation

The ICC has received more than one hundred communications about alleged crimes in Afghanistan. In 2007, the Prosecutor made public that he was conducting a preliminary examination in Afghanistan. Because Afghanistan is a State Party to the Rome Statute, the ICC may exercise jurisdiction over crimes committed on its territory, regardless of the nationality of the perpetrators of those crimes. After considerable research and investigation, the Office of the Prosecutor concluded in 2016 that there was a reasonable basis to believe that war crimes and crimes against humanity had occurred in Afghanistan. It further reported that there was a reasonable basis to believe that war crimes of torture and related ill-treatment had been committed by U.S. military forces and in facilities operated by the C.I.A. INT'L CRIM CT. OFF. OF THE PROSECUTOR, REPORT ON PRELIMINARY EXAMINATION ACTIVITIES—2016 (Nov. 14, 2016).

After completing the preliminary examination, in 2017 the Prosecutor requested authorization from the Pre-Trial Chamber to open a formal investigation into alleged war crimes and crimes against humanity committed in Afghanistan since 2003. Situation in the Islamic Republic of Afghanistan, Case No. ICC-02/17, *Request for Authorization of an Investigation Pursuant to Article 15* (Nov. 20, 2017). The United States refused to cooperate with the investigation and in 2020, President Donald Trump signed an executive order imposing sanctions on the Prosecutor and other persons associated with the ICC. Executive Order 13928 (June 11, 2020).

Pre-Trial Chamber II rejected the Prosecutor's request for authorization to open an investigation into the situation in Afghanistan. It found that there was a reasonable basis to believe that crimes within the jurisdiction of the ICC had been committed, and that potential cases would be admissible. Situation in the Islamic Republic of Afghanistan, Case No. ICC-02/17, *Decision Pursuant to Article 15 of the Rome Statute on the Authorisation of an Investigation into the Situation in the Islamic Republic of Afghanistan*, ¶ 87 (PTC II, Apr. 12, 2019). However, it decided that opening an investigation was not in the interests of justice. It concluded that the likelihood of a successful investigation was low because of the unsettled situation in Afghanistan and the United States' stated refusal to cooperate, and that launching an investigation under these conditions would have diverted scarce resources away from investigations with a greater chance to result in viable cases. *Id.*, at ¶¶ 94–96.

The Appeals Chamber reversed this decision on March 5, 2020. Situation in the Islamic Republic of Afghanistan, Case No. ICC-02/17, *Judgment* (AC, Mar. 5, 2020). The State of Afghanistan then requested that the Prosecutor defer the investigation pursuant to Article 18(2), which provides that the ICC must defer to national courts when a State informs the ICC that it is investigating the case. The Prosecutor requested authorization from the Pre-Trial Chamber to resume the investigation, albeit in limited form. The Prosecutor stated that the investigation would focus only on crimes alleged committed by the Taliban and the Islamic State, not the United States or its coalition partners. Karim A.A. Khan KC, *Statement of the Prosecutor of the International Criminal Court, Karim A. A. Khan QC, following the application for an expedited order under article 18(2) seeking authorisation to resume investigations in the Situation in Afghanistan*, Statement of Sept. 27, 2021. On October 31, 2022, Pre-Trial Chamber II authorized the resumption of the investigation into the Afghanistan situation on the grounds that Afghanistan was not carrying out genuine investigations that warranted the Court's deferral of its own investigation. Situation in the Islamic Republic of Afghanistan, Case No. ICC-02/17, *Decision pursuant to article 18(2) of the Statute authorizing the Prosecution to resume investigation* (PTC II, Oct. 31, 2022).

§ 7-13 RESPONSES TO NON-COOPERATION

Article 87(7) is the main provision of the Rome Statute addressing non-cooperation by States Parties, while Article 87(5) addresses non-cooperation by non-States Parties. When a State Party fails to comply with a request to cooperate in violation of the Rome Statute, the Court may refer the matter to the Assembly of States Parties or the Security Council (if the matter originated there). The Rome Statute does not specify what action the Assembly of States Parties may take, if any, in response to such a referral.

The issue of non-cooperation is serious enough that, in 2011, the Assembly of States Parties adopted a resolution devoted to enhancing cooperation. Assembly of States Parties to the Rome Statue of the International Criminal Court, Resolution on Strengthening the International Criminal Court and the Assembly of States Parties, Resolution ICC-ASP/10/Res.5 (Dec. 21, 2011). As part of this resolution, the ASP adopted procedures relating to non-cooperation. These procedures describe a series of steps that range from informal negotiations between the ICC and the non-cooperating state, to referral to the U.N. Security Council.

The Rome Statute does not contain any provision providing coercive enforcement powers for the ICC. Its responses are limited to negotiating with States, issuing reports naming the non-cooperating States, referring issues to the Security Council, and the like. For example, in August 2010, the Court notified the Security Council that Chad, the Democratic Republic of Congo, Djibouti, Kenya, and Malawi had failed to cooperate in Al-Bashir's arrest. Those States had failed to arrest Al-Bashir when he was in their territory, violating their treaty obligations. Despite these appeals, to date the Security Council has not taken substantive action in response to non-cooperation.

Selected Sources and Additional Reading

NANCY A. COMBS, FACT-FINDING WITHOUT FACTS: THE UNCERTAIN EVIDENTIARY FOUNDATIONS OF INTERNATIONAL CRIMINAL CONVICTIONS (2010).

JORDAN J. PAUST, M. CHERIF BASSIOUNI, MICHAEL SCHARF, JIMMY GURULE, LEILA SADAT & BRUCE ZAGARIS, INTERNATIONAL CRIMINAL LAW: CASES AND MATERIALS (4th ed. 2013).

BETH VAN SCHAACK & RONALD C. SLYE, INTERNATIONAL CRIMINAL LAW AND ITS ENFORCEMENT (4th ed. 2020).

LAW AND PRACTICE OF THE INTERNATIONAL CRIMINAL COURT (Carsten Stahn ed., 2015).

Kai Ambos, *Confidential Investigations (Article 54(3)(E) ICC Statute) vs. Disclosure Obligations: The Lubanga Case and National Law*, 12 NEW CRIM. L. REV. 543 (2009).

Olympia Bekou, *Dealing with Non-Cooperation at the ICC: Towards a More Holistic Approach*, 19 INT'L CRIM. L. REV. 911 (2019).

David Bosco, *Discretion and State Influence at the International Criminal Court*, 111 AM. J. INT'L L. 395 (2017).

Paul Bradfield, *Preserving Vulnerable Evidence at the International Criminal Court—the Article 56 Milestone in* Ongwen, 19 INT'L CRIM. L. REV. 373 (2019).

Rosemary Grey and Sara Wharton, *Lifting the Curtain: Opening a Preliminary Examination at the International Criminal Court*, 16 J. INT'L CRIM. JUST. 593 (2018).

Alexa Koenig & Ulic Egan, *Power and Privilege: Investigating Sexual Violence with Digital Open Source Information,* 19 J. INT'L CRIM. JUST. 55 (2021).

Antoinette Pick-Jones, *Towards Permanently Delegitimizing Article 98 Agreements: Exercising the Jurisdiction of the International Criminal Court over American Citizens*, 93 N.Y.U. L. REV. 1779 (2018).

Carsten Stahn, *Damned If You Do, Damned If You Don't: Challenges and Critiques of Preliminary Examinations at the ICC*, 15 J. INT'L CRIM. JUST. 413 (2017).

INT'L CRIM. CT. OFF. OF THE PROSECUTOR, POLICY PAPER ON THE INTERESTS OF JUSTICE (Sept. 2007), https://www.icc-cpi.int/sites/default/files/ICCOTP InterestsOfJustice.pdf.

INT'L CRIM. CT. OFF. OF THE PROSECUTOR, POLICY PAPER ON PRELIMINARY EXAMINATIONS (Nov. 2013), https://www.icc-cpi.int/sites/default/files/iccdocs/otp/OTP-Policy_Paper_Preliminary_Examinations_2013-ENG.pdf.

INT'L CRIM. CT., REGULATIONS OF THE COURT, Doc. No. ICC-BD/01-05-16 (2018), https://www.icc-cpi.int/sites/default/files/Publications/Regulations-of-the-Court.pdf.

INT'L CRIM CT. OFF. OF THE PROSECUTOR, REPORT ON PRELIMINARY EXAMINATION ACTIVITIES (Dec. 14, 2020), https://www.icc-cpi.int/sites/default/files/itemsDocuments/2020-PE/2020-pe-report-eng.pdf.

INT'L CRIM. CT. OFF. OF THE PROSECUTOR, POLICY ON SITUATION COMPLETION (June 2021), https://www.

icc-cpi.int/sites/default/files/itemsDocuments/20210615-Situation-Completion-Policy-eng.pdf.

U.N. Security Council, Resolution 1593, S/RES/1593 (Mar. 31, 2005).

Press Release, International Criminal Court, *Pre-Trial Chamber I informs the Security Council and the Assembly of States Parties about Omar Al-Bashir's visits to Kenya and Chad*, ICC-CPI-20100827-PR568 (Aug. 27, 2010), https://www.icc-cpi.int/news/pre-trial-chamber-i-informs-security-council-and-assembly-states-parties-about-omar-al-bashirs.

CHAPTER 8

THE PRE-TRIAL, TRIAL, AND APPEALS PROCESSES

I. INTRODUCTION

The pre-trial, trial, and appeals processes at the International Criminal Court are different from similar processes at the *ad hoc* and hybrid tribunals. The pre-trial process begins with an arrest warrant or summons to appear against an accused. Next is the initial appearance of the accused before a Pre-Trial Chamber. What happens after that depends on how the case was initiated. In cases not referred to the Court by the U.N. Security Council, the case must proceed to the confirmation of charges by a Pre-Trial Chamber, but in cases referred by the Security Council this step is not required. The trial process consists of the trial itself and, if the accused is convicted, a sentencing hearing, followed by the pronouncement of the actual sentence by the Trial Chamber. The trial process concludes with reparations proceedings, which are also conducted by the Trial Chamber. Finally, the appeals process consists of interlocutory appeals and appeals launched after the trial proceedings. The Appeals Chamber is charged with overseeing the appellate proceedings, and a case is final when the Appeals Chamber has ruled on all appeals.

II. WARRANTS OF ARREST AND SUMMONSES TO APPEAR

After an investigation is initiated, a Pre-Trial Chamber may, at the Prosecutor's request, issue a warrant of arrest or a summons to appear if there are reasonable grounds to believe that the accused has committed a crime within the Court's jurisdiction.

§ 8-1 DIFFERENCES BETWEEN WARRANTS OF ARREST AND SUMMONSES TO APPEAR

Pursuant to the Rome Statute, an arrest warrant is issued against an accused to ensure that the person either appears at trial and does not endanger or obstruct the investigation or the court proceedings, or, where applicable, to prevent the person from continuing with the commission of that crime or a related crime. Art. 58(1)(b). Some of the most notable arrest warrants issued by the ICC were those directed towards the former president of Sudan, Omar Al-Bashir. Prosecutor v. Omar Hassan Ahmad Al-Bashir, Case No. ICC-02/05-01/09, *Second Decision on the Prosecution's Application for a Warrant of Arrest* (PTC I, July 12, 2010). The issues surrounding the Al-Bashir arrest warrant are addressed in Chapters 2 and 7. More recently, the ICC Prosecutor issued arrest warrants directed against the President of the Russian Federation, Vladimir Putin, and the Russian Minister for Children, Maria Lvova-Bulova.

A summons to appear is issued when the Pre-Trial Chamber believes that it is sufficient to ensure the suspect's appearance. Art. 58(7). Suspects subject to a summons appear voluntarily before the Court and are neither arrested nor held in detention. So far, the Court has issued warrants of arrest or summonses to appear in twenty-seven different cases. As of 2023, at least fifteen persons subject to arrest warrants are at large. The warrants relate to the situations in Côte d'Ivoire, Darfur, Sudan, the Democratic Republic of the Congo, Kenya, Libya, Russia, and Uganda.

If the Prosecutor requests the issuance of an arrest warrant or a summons to appear, he or she must provide the Pre-Trial Chamber the suspect's name, a description of the crimes the suspect is believed to have committed, and a brief summary of the facts alleged to constitute those crimes. In the case of a request for an arrest warrant, the Prosecutor must further provide reasons why it is necessary to arrest the person. Because ICC does not have its own police force, it must rely on State cooperation to arrest suspects. State cooperation is discussed in detail in Chapter 7.

§ 8-2 THE NON-APPLICABILITY OF STATUTES OF LIMITATION

Because the crimes within the Court's jurisdiction are the most serious crimes known to humanity, they are not subject to any statute of limitations under the Rome Statute. Art. 29. Thus, warrants of arrest do not automatically expire with the passage of a certain amount of time.

A warrant of arrest remains in effect "until otherwise ordered by the Court." Art. 58(4). In the case against Simone Gbagbo in the Côte d'Ivoire situation, a Pre-Trial Chamber granted the Prosecutor's request to vacate an outstanding arrest warrant against Gbagbo after her husband and another defendant were acquitted on evidence that would have formed the basis of the Prosecutor's case against her. Prosecutor v. Simone Gbagbo, Case No. ICC-02/11-01/12, *Decision on Prosecutor's Request to Vacate Warrant of Arrest* (PTC II, July 19, 2021).

§ 8-3 EXECUTING WARRANTS OF ARREST AND SUMMONSES TO APPEAR

After a Pre-Trial Chamber issues an arrest warrant, the warrant is transmitted to the State where the suspect is believed to be located. States Parties to the Rome Statute that receive a request for provisional arrest must immediately take steps to arrest the suspect. Art. 59. Non-States Parties may comply voluntarily. The issue of State cooperation is addressed in Chapter 7. After a person is arrested, he or she must be brought before a competent judicial authority in the State where the arrest took place. Art. 59(2). The custodial State determines whether the warrant was executed consistently with the suspect's due process rights.

Once an order of surrender is issued by the custodial State, the person is transferred to the at the ICC Detention Center in The Hague, Netherlands. The ICC Detention Center operates in conformity with international human rights standards and is routinely inspected by relevant inspection bodies. The ICC maintains that detainees are properly fed, provided with exercise opportunities, have access to computers, television, books, and magazines, and are allowed to call their defense counsel free of charge during business hours. In addition, all detainees may be visited by their families regularly. Persons convicted by the Court do not serve their sentences at the ICC Detention Center, as this facility is not designed for long-term imprisonment.

III. INITIAL APPEARANCE AND THE CONFIRMATION OF CHARGES

The suspect first appears before the Court shortly after his or her arrival to The Hague. During the suspect's first appearance, a panel of three Pre-Trial judges confirms the suspect's identity, ensures that the suspect understands the charges, and confirms the language in which the proceedings should be conducted. Although Article 64 states that the Trial Chamber is to determine the language or languages to be used at trial, in practice, the Pre-Trial Chambers make this determination at the accused's initial appearance.

Article 61(1) requires the Pre-Trial Chamber to hold a confirmation of charges hearing in the presence of the accused within a reasonable amount of time after the accused's initial appearance. The confirmation of charges procedure is an essential part of the ICC system. The hearing operates as a first check on the Prosecutor's power to unilaterally determine the charges in a case. The hearing allows Pre-Trial Chambers to have some influence on the process at a very early stage, which can promote prosecutorial fairness. The hearing also protects the due process rights of the accused. It allows the accused to challenge the charges well before trial and protects him or her from wrongful or unfounded charges. Furthermore, this hearing can contribute to judicial economy by promoting efficient trial preparation.

§ 8-4 THE BASICS OF THE CONFIRMATION OF CHARGES PROCESS

After the accused surrenders or voluntarily appears before the Court, the Pre-Trial Chamber must hold a confirmation of charges hearing. Article 61(7) requires the Prosecutor to prove to the Pre-Trial Chamber that there are "substantial grounds to believe that the person committed each of the crimes charged." The hearing is not a substitute for the trial. It is an early process that allows the Pre-Trial Chamber to confirm some, all, or none of the charges against the accused. The confirmation of the charges hearing is public, and the accused has a right to be present. After hearing from the Prosecutor, the defense, and the legal representative of victims, the Pre-Trial Chamber decides, usually within 60 days, if the "substantial grounds to believe" standard of Article 61(7) has been met.

Article 61(2) permits the accused person to waive his or her right to be present at the hearing. It also permits the Pre-Trial Chamber to go forward with the hearing in the absence of the accused person if he or she has fled or cannot be found after a reasonable search.

§ 8-5 POSSIBLE OUTCOMES OF THE CONFIRMATION OF CHARGES HEARING

After the confirmation of charges hearing, the Pre-Trial Chamber may do one of three things. Art. 61(7)(c). First, the Pre-Trial Chamber may decline to confirm the charges; in this case, the Prosecutor may still present a subsequent request for confirmation of the charges on the basis of additional evidence. Second, the Pre-Trial Chamber may adjourn the hearing and request the Prosecutor to conduct a further investigation, provide additional evidence, or amend the charges. Third, the Pre-Trial Chamber may confirm the charges and commit the case for trial. Article 61 permits the decision by a Pre-Trial Chamber confirming or declining to confirm charges against a particular subject to be appealed. If a Pre-Trial Chamber confirms charges against an accused, the President of the Court will constitute a Trial Chamber responsible for the trial phase of the proceedings.

§ 8-6 CONFIRMATION OF CHARGES AND THE RIGHTS OF THE ACCUSED

The Pre-Trial Chamber's decision to confirm the charges does not prejudge the accused's guilt. The primary purpose of the confirmation hearing is to safeguard the rights of the accused by preventing proceedings with insufficient legal basis from going forward. This is why the Prosecutor must satisfy the Pre-Trial Chamber that there is sufficient evidence to show that there are substantial grounds to believe that the person committed the crimes with which he or she is charged.

Pre-Trial Chambers have refused to confirm charges in some cases. For example, in *Prosecutor v. Mbarushimana*, the Pre-Trial Chamber declined to confirm the charges against the accused and did not commit the case to trial. The Prosecution's appeal was dismissed, and the accused was released from custody. Prosecutor v. Callixte Mbarushimana, Case No. ICC-01/04-01/10, *Decision on the Confirmation of the Charges and, in the Alternative, Against the Decision on the Prosecution's Request for Stay of Order to Release Callixte Mbarushimana and on the Victims' Request for Participation of 20 December 2011* (PTC I, Jan. 24, 2012).

IV. TRIAL

All ICC trials take place in The Hague unless the Trial Chamber judges decide to hold the trial elsewhere. So far, The Hague has been the location of every trial conducted by the ICC. Trials are held in public, and the accused must be present, unless the Trial Chamber determines that proceedings should be held in closed session to protect either the safety of victims and witnesses, or the confidentiality of evidentiary material. Arts. 64 & 68.

§ 8-7 THE ACCUSED HAS THE RIGHT TO PLEAD GUILTY OR NOT GUILTY

The Rome Statute requires the Trial Chamber to read the charges against the accused at the start of the trial and ask the accused if he or she understands such charges. Art. 64. The Trial Chamber then asks the accused to plead not guilty or admit guilt. If the accused pleads guilty, the Trial Chamber must ensure that he or she understands the consequences of such an admission of guilt, that the admission is voluntary and made after the accused has consulted with his or her attorney, and that the admission of guilt is supported by the facts of the case. If the Trial Chamber is satisfied that these conditions have been met, it may convict the accused; otherwise, the Trial Chamber will disregard the admission of guilt and will order that the trial be continued. Art. 65.

In *Prosecutor v. Al Mahdi*, the accused pleaded guilty to a war crime consisting of the destruction of historical and religious monuments. The Trial Chamber determined that Al Mahdi understood the nature and consequences of the admission, and that his admission was voluntarily made after sufficient consultation with defense counsel, and that it was supported by the facts of the case. The Trial Chamber thus found Al Mahdi guilty beyond a reasonable doubt and sentenced him to nine years of imprisonment. Prosecutor v. Ahmad Al Faqi Al Mahdi, Case No. ICC-01/12-01/15, *Judgment and Sentence* (TC VIII, Sept. 27, 2016).

§ 8-8 THE TRIAL PROCESS

At trial, the Prosecutor must present evidence to the Court to prove beyond a reasonable doubt that the accused is guilty. Art. 66. The Trial Chamber has the power to determine the admissibility of evidence. Art. 69; INT'L CRIM. CT., RULES OF PROCEDURE AND

EVIDENCE, Doc. No. ICC-PIOS-LT-03-004/19, Rule 63 (2019) (RPE). Evidence may include witness testimony, tangible objects, documents, or other material deemed relevant and admissible by the Trial Chamber. The Prosecutor must disclose to the defendant any evidence which may show that the defendant is innocent. Art. 67(2). Article 64(8) gives the Trial Chamber the authority to give directions regarding the conduct of the trial proceedings. Because the defendant is presumed innocent, art. 66, the Prosecutor presents his or her evidence first. After the Prosecutor has examined each prosecution witness, the defense has the opportunity to examine each witness. RPE 140.

Once the Prosecutor has presented all of his or her evidence, the accused has the opportunity, through defense counsel, to present his or her defense. The defendant may call new witnesses under the same conditions as witnesses called by the Prosecutor. *Id.*

Although Article 64 gives the Trial Chamber the power to "require" witnesses to appear before the Court, in reality the Court does not have the means to force witnesses to appear because it has no police force. Instead, the Court must rely on State cooperation to secure the presence of witnesses. Article 93(1)(e) provides that States Parties shall facilitate "the voluntary appearance of persons as witnesses. . . before the Court." The issue of State cooperation is addressed in Chapter 7.

Because of the difficulties associated with bringing witnesses to The Hague to appear before the Court, the ICC's *Rules of Procedure and Evidence* allow for witness testimony via video link. As provided in RPE 67, the technology chosen for video-link testimony must permit the witness to be examined by the Prosecutor, defense counsel, and the Chamber itself while the witness is testifying. The Trial Chamber, working with the Registry, must have ensured that the venue chosen for the video- or audio-link is "conducive to the giving of truthful and open testimony and to the safety, physical and psychological well-being, dignity and privacy of the witness." RPEs 67(1) & 67(3).

§ 8-9 VICTIMS' RIGHT TO PRESENT EVIDENCE

If the personal interests of the victims are affected, the Trial Chamber may allow their views and concerns to be presented by their legal representatives during the trial proceedings. In *Prosecutor v. Lubanga*, the Appeals Chamber granted victims the right to have access to lead evidence pertaining to the guilt or innocence of the accused, as well as the right to challenge the admissibility of evidence. Prosecutor v. Thomas Lubanga Dyilo, Case No. ICC-01/04-01/06, *Judgment on the Appeals of The Prosecutor and The Defence Against Trial Chamber I's Decision on Victims' Participation of 18 January 2008* (AC, July 11, 2008). Any exercise of this right by the victims must be consistent with the rights of the defense and the requirements of a fair trial under Article 67 of the Rome Statute. Victims also must comply with disclosure and notice obligations and must abide by the Court's protection orders. RPE 87. Chapter 9 addresses the rights of victims extensively.

V. JUDICIAL MANAGEMENT OF CHARGES IN PRE-TRIAL AND TRIAL PROCEEDINGS

Judicial management of charges during pre-trial and trial proceedings has been a contentious issue. Regulation 55 of the *Regulations of the Court* was adopted in 2004 and permits the Trial Chamber to change the legal characterization of the evidence against the defendant in order to better fit with the definitions of crimes or forms of participation available under the Rome Statute. INT'L CRIM. CT., REGULATIONS OF THE COURT, Doc. No. ICC-BD/01-05-16, Reg. 55 (2018) (Court Regulations). For example, if a defendant is charged with directly committing a crime, but the evidence presented shows only that he or she attempted to commit the crime or aided and abetted another person to commit the crime, the Court can convict the person of attempt or aiding and abetting, even if that was not the original charge. During the pre-trial process, Article 61(7)(c)(ii) provides that, at the end of the confirmation of charges hearing, the Pre-Trial Chamber can request that the Prosecutor amend "a charge because the evidence submitted appears to establish a different crime within the jurisdiction of the Court."

The Court's authority to regulate or modify the charges comes with important limitations. The Trial Chamber's power under Regulation 55 is limited in several ways. First, a change to the legal characterization of the facts may not exceed the facts and circumstances described in the charges (and any amendments to the charges). Court Regulations, Reg. 55(1). Furthermore, Regulation 55(2) requires judges to notify the parties of such changes and to give the parties the opportunity to present oral or written submissions in response. Regulation 55(3) provides additional protections to the defense by requiring judges to ensure that the defense is afforded adequate time to effectively prepare and, if necessary, to present additional evidence. During the pre-trial process, the Pre-Trial Chamber's authority to modify the charges is cabined by the requirements of fairness. Despite this, the issue of the management or amendment of charges by the Court has proven controversial.

§ 8-10 THE MANAGEMENT OF CHARGES IN PRE-TRIAL PROCEEDINGS

Pre-Trial Chambers have struggled to determine the Court's role in shaping the appropriate charges against the accused. Article 61(7) regulates the confirmation of charges process and delineates the Pre-Trial Chamber's options at and after the hearing. However, despite the language of Article 61(7), Pre-Trial Chambers in the cases against Thomas Lubanga Dyilo and Jean-Pierre Bemba Gombo issued decisions that were not fully consistent with the express language.

In *Lubanga*, the Pre-Trial Chamber amended the charges against Lubanga at the close of the confirmation hearing; it neither requested that the Prosecutor do so, nor did it adjourn the hearing.

Prosecutor v. Thomas Lubanga Dyilo, Case No. ICC-01/04-01/06, *Decision on the Confirmation of Charges*, ¶¶ 200–204 (PTC I, Jan. 29, 2007). In the document laying out the charges, the Prosecutor had alleged that the conflict was one not of an international character; however, the Pre-Trial Chamber concluded that the conflict was of an international character. *Id.* ¶¶ 200, 204. The Pre-Trial Chamber declined to adjourn the proceedings before amending the charges, as Article 61(7)(c) requires. *Id.* ¶¶ 202–203. Ultimately, the Appeals Chamber held that, while the Pre-Trial Chamber's legal re-characterization of the facts was not inconsistent with the Rome Statute, a re-characterization must not exceed the facts contained in the charges or amendments thereto. Prosecutor v. Thomas Lubanga Dyilo, Case No. ICC-01/04-01/06, *Judgment on the Appeals of Mr Lubanga Dyilo and the Prosecutor against the Decision of Trial Chamber I of 14 July 2009 entitled "Decision giving notice to the parties and participants that the legal characterization of the facts may be subject to change in accordance with Regulation 55(2) of the Regulations of the Court,"* ¶ 37 (AC, Dec. 8, 2009).

In *Bemba*, the Pre-Trial Chamber declined to confirm certain charges presented by the Prosecutor, despite finding that there was sufficient evidence to support them. Prosecutor v. Jean-Pierre Bemba Gombo, Case No. ICC-01/05-01/08, *Decision Pursuant to Article 61(7)(a) and (b) of the Rome Statute on the Charges of the Prosecutor Against Jean-Pierre Bemba Gombo* (PTC II, June 15, 2009). Instead, the Pre-Trial Chamber determined that some of the charges were not warranted as a matter of fairness and expeditiousness because they amounted to cumulative charging. *Id.* ¶¶ 72 & 202. When the Prosecutor filed an interlocutory appeal of the decision declining to confirm certain charges, the *Bemba* Pre-Trial Chamber acknowledged the express language of Article 61(7) but held that it could not be bound to a "literal" reading of the Rome Statute. The Pre-Trial Chamber thus rejected the interlocutory appeal and held that its decision to decline the charges was based on its "inherent powers" to conduct fair and expeditious proceedings. Prosecutor v. Jean-Pierre Bemba Gombo, Case No. ICC-01/05-01/08, *Decision on the Prosecutor's Application for Leave to Appeal the "Decision Pursuant to Article 61(7)(a) and (b) of the Rome Statute on the Charges of the Prosecutor Against Jean-Pierre Bemba Gombo,"* ¶ 52 (PTC II, Sept. 18, 2009).

§ 8-11 THE MANAGEMENT OF CHARGES IN TRIAL PROCEEDINGS

In *Prosecutor v. Lubanga*, the Trial Chamber decided that it had the authority to change the legal characterization of the charges against the defendant during an ongoing trial, even if the re-characterized charges exceed the facts and circumstances of the charges confirmed by the Pre-Trial Chamber. Prosecutor v. Thomas Lubanga Dyilo, Case No. ICC-01/04-01/06, *Decision Giving Notice to the Parties and Participants that the Legal Characterization of the Facts May Be Subject to Change in Accordance with Regulation 55(2) of the Regulations of the Court* (TC I, July 14, 2009).

The *Lubanga* Trial Chamber majority reached this conclusion by parsing the provisions of Regulation 55. The Trial Chamber distinguished re-characterization under Regulation 55(1), which happens after the trial, from that under Regulation 55(2), which may happen at any time during the trial. It held that Regulation 55(2) does not limit permissible re-characterizations to the facts and circumstances described in the charges. Thus, a re-characterization during the trial under Regulation 55(2) is permitted to exceed the factual scope of the charges. Prosecutor v. Thomas Lubanga Dyilo, Case No. ICC-01/04-01/06, *Decision Giving Notice to the Parties and Participants that the Legal Characterization of the Facts May Be Subject to Change in Accordance with Regulation 55(2) of the Regulations of the Court,* ¶¶ 27–32 (TC I, July 14, 2009). The Trial Chamber later clarified that the additional facts must "have come to light during the trial and build a unity, from the procedural point of view, with the course of events described in the charges." Prosecutor v. Thomas Lubanga Dyilo, Case No. ICC-01/04-01/06, *Clarification and Further Guidance to Parties and Participants in Relation to the "Decision Giving Notice to the Parties and Participants that the Legal Characterisation of the Facts May be Subject to Change in Accordance with Regulation 55(2) of the Regulations of the Court,"* ¶ 8 (TC I, Aug. 27, 2009).

The Trial Chamber's decision in *Lubanga* was reversed by the Appeals Chamber, which held that the Trial Chamber's justification for permitting a change to the legal characterization of the facts was "extremely thin." Prosecutor v. Thomas Lubanga Dyilo, Case No. ICC-01/04-01/06, *Judgment on the Appeals of Mr. Lubanga Dyilo and the Prosecutor against the Decision of Trial Chamber I of 14 July 2009 entitled "Decision giving notice to the parties and participants that the legal characterization of the facts may be subject to change in accordance with Regulation 55(2) of the Regulations of the Court,"* ¶ 109 (AC, Dec. 8, 2009).

In a later case, *Prosecutor v. Katanga*, the Trial Chamber notified the parties six months after the closing arguments that it would consider a re-characterization of the charges under Regulation 55 to modify the mode of liability under which Katanga was originally charged. Prosecutor v. Germain Katanga and Mathieu Ngudjolo Chui, Case No. ICC-01/04-01/07, *Decision on the Implementation of Regulation 55 of the Regulations of the Court and Severing the Charges against the Accused Persons*, ¶¶ 44–47 (TC II, Nov. 21, 2012). Katanga appealed, arguing that the Trial Chamber erred in permitting the re-characterization so late in the proceedings, but the Appeals Chamber rejected his argument. Prosecutor v. Germain Katanga, Case No. ICC-01/04-01/07, *Judgment on the Appeal of Mr. Germain Katanga against the Decision of Trial Chamber II of 21 November 2012 Entitled "Decision on the Implementation of Regulation 55 of the Regulations of the Court and Severing the Charges against the Accused Persons"* (AC, Mar. 27, 2013). The Trial Chamber subsequently convicted Katanga on five counts of a lesser mode of liability.

The Court's handling of the re-characterization of the facts in *Katanga* was controversial. *Katanga* suggests that the Trial Chamber will allow the legal re-characterization of facts at any time during the trial, even if the new characterization conflicts with what the Prosecutor relied on at the confirmation of charges hearing. This could permit the Prosecutor to change the mode of liability at any time before the end of the trial, even if the new mode of liability was not raised earlier. At the same time, the need to re-characterize the Prosecutor's chosen mode of liability has largely disappeared because the Pre-Trial Chambers have abandoned their earlier requirement that the Prosecutor choose a single mode of liability for the case in favor of permitting the Prosecutor to charge several different modes of liability. This is consistent with the practice of other international courts and tribunals and most national court systems and will make re-characterization of the facts to adjust the mode of liability unnecessary in the future.

VI. APPLICABLE PENALTIES AND SENTENCES

After the parties have presented all their evidence, the Prosecutor and defense counsel are invited to make their closing statements. After considering all the evidence, the Trial Chamber decides whether the defendant is guilty. There is no jury in the ICC system. The sentence is pronounced in public, in the presence of not only the accused, if possible, but also the victims or their legal representatives if they have taken part in the proceedings. The Trial Chamber may impose a prison sentence, as well as a fine or forfeiture of the proceeds, property, or assets derived from the crime. As detailed in Chapter 9, the Court may also order reparations to victims, including restitution, rehabilitation, and compensation. Such orders may be directed against a convicted person.

§ 8-12 CASE OUTCOMES AND PRISON SENTENCES

Sentences may be a term of years, with a maximum of 30 years. Art. 77. The Statute also permits a term of life imprisonment "when justified by the extreme gravity of the crime and the individual circumstances of the convicted person." *Id.* The Court may not impose a death sentence. Thus far, the Court has imposed sentences ranging from 9 years to 30 years. The Court has acquitted four defendants through 2022: Jean-Pierre Bemba Gombo, Charles Blé Goude, Laurent Gbagbo, and Mathieu Ngudjolo Chui.

In determining the appropriate sentence, the ICC will take mitigating evidence into account. For example, the Trial Chamber in *Prosecutor v. Ongwen* considered in mitigation the convicted person's status as a former child soldier when imposing a sentence of twenty-five years' imprisonment. Prosecutor v. Dominic Ongwen, Case No. ICC-02/04-01/15, *Sentence* (TC IX, May 6, 2021). The Appeals Chamber subsequently confirmed the Trial Chambers' approach in *Ongwen*, as well as the pronounced sentence. Prosecutor v. Dominic Ongwen, Case No. ICC-02/04-01/15, *Judgment on the Appeal of Mr. Dominic Ongwen Against the Decision of Trial Chamber IX of 6 May 2021 entitled "Sentence"* (AC, Dec. 15, 2022).

§ 8-13 SERVICE OF PRISON SENTENCES

As described in Chapter 3, under Article 103 of the Rome Statute, convicted persons serve their sentences in a State designated by the ICC from a list of States which have indicated their willingness to the Court to accept convicted persons. Although conditions of confinement are governed by the laws of the State where the sentence is served, they must be consistent with international human rights standards, as well as with imprisonment standards applicable to other prisoners convicted of similar offenses in the State of enforcement. For example, Lubanga and Katanga were both transferred to the Democratic Republic of Congo and finished serving their prison sentences in facilities there.

§ 8-14 REPARATION ORDERS

In addition to imprisonment, the ICC can also issue reparations orders against the convicted person and in favor of the victims. Under Article 75(2) of the Rome Statute, the Court can make a reparations order directly against a convicted person. Reparations proceedings typically start after the person is convicted. If the convicted person does not have resources, reparations are paid out of the Trust Fund for Victims, which is also charged with determining the size and scope of reparations. Chapter 9 provides a thorough discussion of ICC reparations.

VII. APPEALS AND REVISIONS OF JUDGMENTS

Both the Prosecutor and defense counsel may appeal against the decision of a Pre-Trial or Trial Chamber. Under Article 81, the Prosecutor may appeal against a conviction or acquittal on the grounds of procedural error, error of fact, or error of law. Similarly, under Article 81, both sides may appeal on other grounds that affect the fairness or reliability of the proceedings or the decision, particularly those related to the disproportion between the sentence and the crime. In addition, the legal representatives of the victims, the convicted person, or the owner of property adversely affected by an order for reparations to the victims may appeal against orders issued by both the Pre-Trial and Trial Chambers.

Article 83 permits the Appeals Chamber to order a new trial before a different Trial Chamber. The Appeals Chamber can also reverse or amend the decision or conviction. In cases of an acquittal, the accused is released immediately, unless there are exceptional circumstances. A convicted person generally remains in custody pending an appeal, unless otherwise ordered by the Trial Chamber. If a convicted person's time in custody exceeds the sentence of imprisonment imposed, the person is released. This happened in the case of Jean-Pierre Bemba Gombo, who was acquitted of substantive charges against him, but was sentenced to one year of imprisonment in 2018 for offenses committed against the administration of justice. He had already served several years in detention, and that time was counted toward the completion of the one-year sentence, so his sentence was considered to have been served. Prosecutor v. Jean-Pierre Bemba Gombo, Aimé Kilolo Musamba, Jean-Jacques Mangenda Kabongo, Fidèle Babala Wandu and Narcisse Arido, Case No. ICC-01/05-01/13, *Decision Re-sentencing Mr Jean-Pierre Bemba Gombo, Mr Aime Kilolo Musamba and Mr Jean-Jacques Mangenda Kabongo* (TC VII, Sept. 17, 2018).

Article 83 permits both the Prosecutor and the convicted person to apply to the Appeals Chamber to revise a conviction or sentence under several circumstances: (1) if new evidence has been discovered; (2) if it has been newly discovered that decisive evidence was false, forged, or falsified; or (3) if one or more judges has committed an act of serious misconduct to justify the removal of that judge from office. Article 83 also provides that a person who has been the victim of unlawful arrest or detention has the right to compensation. The Court can award such compensation if a grave and manifest miscarriage of justice is conclusively shown.

VIII. INTERLOCUTORY APPEALS

Article 82 lays out the conditions pursuant to which interlocutory appeals may be made to the Appeals Chamber. Parties have the right to launch interlocutory appeals with respect to decisions on jurisdiction or admissibility, decisions granting or denying release from custody, and decisions of the Pre-Trial Chamber regarding the preservation of evidence essential for the defense at trial. All other interlocutory appeals may be made only with the permission of the Pre-Trial or Trial Chamber that issued the relevant decision.

Under Article 82(1)(d), parties are permitted to appeal decisions which involve an issue that would significantly affect the fair and expeditious conduct of the proceedings or the outcome of the trial. Such appeals are only permitted if, in the opinion of the Pre-Trial or Trial Chamber, an immediate resolution by the Appeals Chamber would materially advance the proceedings.

As the Court's jurisprudence shows, the Pre-Trial Chambers have rejected a number of requests to file interlocutory appeals. *See, e.g.*, Situation in Uganda, Case No. ICC-02/04, *Decision on the Prosecutor's Application for Leave to Appeal in the Pre-Trial Chamber II's Decision on the Prosecutor's Applications for Warrants of Arrest under Article 58* (PTC II, Aug. 19, 2005); Situation in the Democratic Republic of the Congo, Case No. ICC-01/04, *Decision On The Prosecution's Application For Leave To Appeal The Chamber's Decision Of 17 January 2006 On The Applications For Participation In The Proceedings Of Vprs 1, Vprs 2, Vprs 3, Vprs 4, Vprs 5 And Vprs 6* (PTC I, Mar. 31, 2006).

Selected Sources and Additional Reading

T. MARKUS FUNK, VICTIMS' RIGHTS AND ADVOCACY AT THE INTERNATIONAL CRIMINAL COURT (2d ed. 2015).

WILLIAM A. SCHABAS, AN INTRODUCTION TO THE INTERNATIONAL CRIMINAL COURT (5th ed. 2017).

Margaux Dastugue, *The Faults in "Fair" Trials: An Evaluation of Regulation 55 at the International Criminal Court*, 48 VAND. J. TRANSNAT'L L. 273 (2015).

Jennifer Easterday, *Germain Katanga & Mathieu Ngudjolo Chui at the International Criminal Court: A Closer Look at Regulation 55 at the ICC*, INT'L JUST. MONITOR (May 28, 2013), https://www.ijmonitor.org/2013/05/a-closer-look-at-regulation-55-at-the-icc/.

Luke Moffett & Clara Sandoval, *Tilting at Windmills: Reparations and the International Criminal Court*, 34 LEIDEN J. INT'L L. 749 (2021).

How the Court Works, INT'L CRIM. CT., https://www.icc-cpi.int/about/how-the-court-works.

INT'L CRIM. CT., ARRESTING ICC SUSPECTS AT LARGE: WHY IT MATTERS, WHAT THE COURT DOES, WHAT STATES CAN DO (2019), https://www.icc-cpi.int/sites/default/files/bookletArrestsENG.pdf.

INT'L CRIM. CT., ICC DETENTION CENTRE, Doc. No. ICC-PIOS-FS-08-002/18_Eng (n.d.), https://www.icc-cpi.int/sites/default/files/Publications/DetentionCentreENG.pdf.

INT'L CRIM. CT., UNDERSTANDING THE INTERNATIONAL CRIMINAL COURT, Doc. No. ICC-PIOS-BK-05-009/20_Eng (2020), https://www.icc-cpi.int/sites/default/files/Publications/understanding-the-icc.pdf.

Press Release, International Criminal Court, *Al-Bashir Case: ICC Appeals Chamber confirms Jordan's non-cooperation but reverses the decision referring it to the ASP and UNSC* (May 6, 2019), https://www.icc-cpi.int/news/al-bashir-case-icc-appeals-chamber-confirms-jordans-non-cooperation-reverses-decision.

Press Release, International Criminal Court, *ICC Trial Chamber VIII declares Mr Al Mahdi guilty of the war crime of attacking historic and religious buildings in Timbuktu and sentences him to nine years' imprisonment* (Sept. 27, 2016), https://www.icc-cpi.int/news/icc-trial-chamber-viii-declares-mr-al-mahdi-guilty-war-crime-attacking-historic-and-religious.

Press Release, International Criminal Court, *Dominic Ongwen sentenced to 25 years of imprisonment* (May 6, 2021), https://www.icc-cpi.int/news/dominic-ongwen-sentenced-25-years-imprisonment.

Amy Senier, *The ICC Appeals Chamber Judgment on the Legal Characterisation Facts in* Prosecutor v. Lubanga*: A Commentary*, THE HAGUE JUSTICE PORTAL, http://haguejusticeportal.net/Docs/Commentaries%20PDF/Senier_Lubanga_EN.pdf.

WAR CRIMES RESEARCH OFFICE, INTERNATIONAL CRIMINAL COURT, LEGAL ANALYSIS AND EDUCATION PROJECT, DEFINING THE CASE AGAINST AN ACCUSED BEFORE THE INTERNATIONAL CRIMINAL COURT: WHOSE RESPONSIBILITY IS IT? (Nov. 2009), https://www.wcl.american.edu/wcl-american-edu/assets/WCRO_Report_on_Defining_Case_Nov2009.pdf.

WAR CRIMES RESEARCH OFFICE, INTERNATIONAL CRIMINAL COURT, LEGAL ANALYSIS AND EDUCATION

PROJECT, INTERLOCUTORY APPELLATE REVIEW OF EARLY DECISIONS BY THE INTERNATIONAL CRIMINAL COURT (Jan. 2008), https://www.icc-cpi.int/sites/default/files/RelatedRecords/CR2012_09480.PDF.

WAR CRIMES RESEARCH OFFICE, INTERNATIONAL CRIMINAL COURT, LEGAL ANALYSIS AND EDUCATION PROJECT, THE CONFIRMATION OF CHARGES PROCESS AT THE INTERNATIONAL CRIMINAL COURT: A CRITICAL ASSESSMENT AND RECOMMENDATIONS FOR CHANGE (Oct. 2015), https://www.legal-tools.org/doc/d8c2d5/pdf/.

WAR CRIMES RESEARCH OFFICE, INTERNATIONAL CRIMINAL COURT, INTERLOCUTORY APPELLATE REVIEW OF EARLY DECISIONS BY THE INTERNATIONAL CRIMINAL COURT (Jan. 2008), https://www.wcl.american.edu/wcl-american-edu/assets/wcro_report_on_interlocutory_appeals_january_2008.pdf.

Leili Bohlooli Zanjani, *The battle of interpretation between the ICC and Jordan in* The Prosecutor v. Al-Bashir *(2010) judgments*, LEIDENLAWBLOG (May 31, 2022), https://www.leidenlawblog.nl/articles/the-battle-of-interpretation-between-the-icc-and-jordan-in-the-prosecutor-v-al-bashir-2010-judgments.

CHAPTER 9

VICTIMS AND THE INTERNATIONAL CRIMINAL COURT

I. INTRODUCTION

Victims have a much more prominent role at the International Criminal Court than in domestic criminal proceedings in many countries. The Rome Statute provides victims with an explicit right to present their views and concerns throughout a case. The Statute and the Court's internal rules also require the Court to take a range of steps to ensure the safety of victims and witnesses during the proceedings. Victims can seek reparations from convicted perpetrators or from a special trust fund established by Article 79 of the Statute (the ICC's "Trust Fund for Victims" or "TFV"), which is set up to address any damage, loss, or injury suffered by victims. The ICC's Registry has, as required by the Rome Statute, also created a Victims and Witnesses Unit, which helps to coordinate victim participation in ICC proceedings. Through all these measures, the ICC provides a robust set of tools for victims to make their voices heard, be made as safe as possible throughout the proceedings, and receive at least some reparations for harms they experienced.

The Court uses the term "victim" in a technical manner, following the lead of the Rome Statute itself, to refer to those harmed by atrocity crimes and defined as victims under Rule 85 of the Court's *Rules of Procedure and Evidence*. At the same time, we recognize that those harmed by atrocity crimes are not passive or weak. Indeed, the ICC Trust Fund for Victims itself has observed that "the word 'victim' suggests a state of powerlessness. Our beneficiaries are far from that. They are survivors, active agents in the restoration of their dignity, empowered to lead fulfilling lives."

II. PARTICIPATION AT ICC PROCEEDINGS

The principal rules governing victim participation in proceedings are set forth in the Rome Statute, the Court's *Rules of Procedure and Evidence* ("RPE"), and the internal rules of the Office of the Prosecutor and the Registry. These provide a range of ways that victims can have their interests brought before the Court, apart from appearing as witnesses for the Prosecutor or the defense.

§ 9-1 THE BASIC RIGHT TO PARTICIPATE

Article 68(3) of the Statute provides that when victims' "personal interests" are affected, the Court must permit their "views and concerns" to be presented, and that the Court must consider them. The Statute requires the Court to ensure that the participation of victims is not "prejudicial to or inconsistent with" the defendant's rights and the general interest in a fair and impartial trial.

In the ICC system, "victims" are defined as natural persons who have suffered harm as a result of a crime within the Court's jurisdiction. They can also be organizations or institutions that have sustained direct harm to their property, provided that such property was either dedicated to religious, educational, or cultural purposes, or served as a monument or hospital. RPE 85(a) & (b). For example, in *Prosecutor v. Lubanga*, Trial Chamber I wrote that the victims were mostly former child soldiers, some of whom were still children. In addition, some of the victims were parents of former child soldiers and one victim was a school. Prosecutor v. Thomas Lubanga Dyilo, Case No. ICC-01/04-01/06, *Judgment Pursuant to Article 74 of the Statute*, ¶ 17 (TC I, March 14, 2012). The Rome Statute and the Rules of Procedure and Evidence do not define what constitutes "personal interests." This has been left to the Chambers to determine in each case. In the main, Chambers have considered whether a victim's legal interests would adversely be affected in the stage in which the victim sought to participate. The ways that individual people were affected by the defendant's crimes can require the disclosure of sensitive information, decisions about the eligibility of individual victims are typically taken based on evidence submitted confidentially. For example, in *Lubanga*, the Trial Chamber described the process by which victims were approved for participation, noting that the "case-by-case analysis" of each victim had been redacted. *Id.*, at ¶ 15 & n. 53.

To be permitted to participate in any proceedings, victims must apply to the Registrar and demonstrate that they meet the criteria set forth in Article 68(3). RPE 89(1). Applications to participate are shared with the Prosecutor and defense counsel and may be rejected if the Court concludes that the applicant does not meet the statutory criteria. Victims are permitted to choose a legal representative to represent their interests before the Court. RPE 90(1).

The Statute gives the Court the discretion to determine when victims' views and concerns will be presented to the Court. Article 68(3) allows the Court to do this at "stages of the proceedings" determined by the Court to be appropriate, "in a manner which is not prejudicial to or inconsistent with the rights of the accused and a fair and impartial trial." The term "stages of the proceedings" can even include the investigation or other parts of the process at which there are not formal proceedings in court. Situation in the Democratic Republic of the Congo, Case No. ICC-01/04, *Decision on the Applications for Participation in the Proceedings of VPRS 1, VPRS 2, VPRS 3, VPRS 4, VPRS 5 and VPRS 6* (PTC I, Jan. 17, 2006). In contrast, in another decision, the Court decided not to permit victims to participate in a status conference because the issues to be addressed appeared not to touch on their personal interests. Prosecutor v. Thomas Lubanga Dyilo, Case No. ICC-01/04-01/06, *Decision on the application for participation of victims a/0001/06 to a/0003/06 in the status conference of 5 September 2006*, ¶ 3 (PTC I, Sept. 4, 2006).

The *Rules of Procedure and Evidence* give effect to victims' basic right to participate by regulating the ways that victims can participate and ensuring that victims have the information they need to make their voices heard. The Court has recognized several points in cases in which it must notify victims to facilitate victim participation.

- *Jurisdiction or Admissibility*. Article 19 governs the process for challenging the jurisdiction of the Court or the admissibility of a case. Article 91(3) provides that victims may "submit their observations" to the Court in any proceedings to determine jurisdiction or admissibility.

- *Request to Authorize an Investigation*. Article 15, which governs investigations initiated pursuant to the Prosecutor's *proprio motu* powers, provides that victims may make "representations" to the Pre-Trial Chamber when it decides the Prosecutor's request for authorization of an investigation. Rule 92(2) requires the Court to notify victims of such a decision to allow them to participate.

- *Confirmation of the Charges*. Rule 92(3) requires the Court to notify victims of a confirmation of charges hearing, at which the Court decides whether to confirm the Prosecutor's charges against a defendant.

- *Appeals*. In *Prosecutor v. Lubanga*, the Court permitted victims to participate in interlocutory appeals to present their views and concerns. Prosecutor v. Thomas Lubanga Dyilo, Case No. ICC-01/04-01/06, *Decision, in limine, on Victim Participation in the appeals of the Prosecutor and the Defence against Trial Chamber I's Decision entitled "Decision on Victims' Participation,"* ¶ 1 (AC, May 16, 2008).

In addition to ensuring the participation of victims, the Rome Statute requires the ICC to consider their interests. Most broadly, Article 68(3) requires the Court to consider the "views and concerns" of the victims at any stage of the proceedings that is "determined to be appropriate by the Court." This is a general requirement designed to ensure that the views of victims are integrated into the entire process, as long as that can be done without prejudice to the defense.

There are also specific stages at which the interests of victims must be considered. For example, when determining whether to authorize a *proprio motu* investigation, Article 15(4) requires the Court to consider supporting material—which includes any representations submitted by victims—when considering the request. After the preliminary examination, the Prosecutor must consider the interests of the victims when determining whether to initiate an investigation. Art. 53(c).

§ 9-2 INFORMATION FOR VICTIMS

To participate meaningfully in legal proceedings, victims need basic information about the proceedings and the actions and arguments of the Prosecutor and the defense. RPE 92(5) requires the Registrar to inform victims of all proceedings before the Court and make available to them all pleadings or other documents submitted by the parties. Rule 92(6) requires the Registrar to inform victims any time the Court issues a decision in their case.

If the Prosecutor decides to seek authorization to initiate an investigation, he or she must inform the victims of this (unless doing so would pose a danger to the integrity of the investigation) so they are able to share their views with the Court. RPE 50(1). The Registrar must notify victims of any challenges to admissibility or jurisdiction to ensure they have the opportunity to communicate their concerns to the Court as provided in Article 19(3). RPE 59. Victims must also be notified of any decision by the Prosecutor not to initiate an investigation or proceed with a prosecution. RPE 92(2). Additionally, they are required to be notified if the Court decides to hold a hearing on confirmation of charges. RPE 92(3). All of these information-forcing rules have the effect of ensuring that victims have the information they need to exercise their rights under the Statute.

§ 9-3 PRACTICAL SUPPORT FOR VICTIM PARTICIPATION IN INVESTIGATIONS AND CASES

The Rome Statute gives victims the right to participate in proceedings. By definition they have been affected in some personal way by atrocity crimes and may be experiencing the effects of trauma, displacement, or other harms. And most people—whether they have been affected by atrocity crimes or not—do not know how to engage effectively with the International Criminal Court. For these reasons, the ICC engages in outreach to potential victims to better fulfill its statutory obligation to permit them to participate in proceedings.

The Registry is the unit of the ICC that works most directly with victims. It contains two units devoted to support for victims, the Victims Participation and Reparations Section ("VPRS") and the Office of Public Counsel for the Victims ("OPCV"). Together, these two units provide much of the assistance victims need to fully participate in the Court's work. The ICC collaborates with victims and affected communities not only to facilitate their participation in cases, but also in other ways, some of which are entirely separate from Court proceedings. These other types of support are addressed elsewhere in this Chapter.

The VPRS provides initial support for victims in Court proceedings. Victims must apply for official victim status to participate in Court proceedings, which requires them to complete a form in either English or French, languages that many victims may not speak. The VPRS can help victims complete the necessary paperwork so they can participate. The VPRS also helps victims navigate the reparations process, described more fully below, as well as assisting them in identifying appropriate legal representation. Finally, Registry staff can take victims and witnesses to the courtroom in advance, outline the way the courtroom functions, demonstrate courtroom technology, and allow victims and witnesses to experience what it will be like to participate in Court proceedings.

The OPCV is an official organ of the ICC, created pursuant to Rule 81 of the Regulations of the Court. The OPCV can provide a range of assistance to victims and can even go as far as representing victims throughout the proceedings. In other cases, it can provide support to legal representatives of victims, including legal research and advice. The OPCV may also, with Court permission, appear on behalf of victims for hearings or other proceedings.

When the Prosecutor indicates that he or she intends to request authorization to open an investigation, he or she will notify the Presidency and the Registry. The Registry then implements an outreach strategy to reach potential victims to inform them of the proceedings, their right to participate, and how to make their voices heard. The exact approach in a particular situation depends on the dynamics of that situation, but there are some common components. For example, in the situation in Bangladesh/Myanmar, the Registry reported that it had adopted a two-part strategy to engage potential victims. First it used an open approach, designed to reach as many victims as possible. The Registry made the victim representation form—a document that victims must submit to be permitted to participate in formal proceedings—available on the ICC website in the languages used in the situation countries. Similar information was also disseminated through social media. The Registry also used a targeted approach, the details of which the ICC has not made public. The targeted approach was designed to reach people in refugee camps or remote areas and other vulnerable populations who might not have access to the Internet or other means to learn about the proceedings.

After it receives applications from victims who wish to participate, the Registry organizes the applications into groups, including those who are obviously qualified to participate, those who obviously do not meet the criteria, and those whose applications are difficult to categorize. This information (in redacted form) is shared with the Court, the Prosecutor, and defense counsel. When the qualified victims have been identified, the Registry then helps to facilitate not only their legal representation, but also their eventual participation in proceedings.

In addition to this type of outreach, the ICC has also opened field offices in certain situation countries including the Central African Republic, Côte d'Ivoire, the Democratic Republic of Congo, Georgia, Mali, and Uganda. These offices allow potential victims to learn about the Court's proceedings, engage directly with ICC staff, and more effectively participate.

III. SUPPORT AND SAFETY OF VICTIMS AND WITNESSES

The safety of victims and witnesses is of paramount importance to the ICC. Victims and survivors are often deeply traumatized by the atrocities that give rise to ICC proceedings. They may not trust international institutions or have any experience engaging with them. Those with knowledge of atrocity crimes may justifiably fear for their safety if they provide evidence to the ICC. And the ICC's legitimacy depends, at least in part, on its ability to ensure that those willing to bear witness to atrocity crimes are kept safe and treated with dignity and respect. For those affected by atrocities, safety has two important dimensions: physical safety during and after Court proceedings and support for the effects of trauma on individuals and communities. As an institution the ICC is not able to fully guarantee either aspect of safety, but the Rome Statute and the Court's internal regulations obligate the ICC to account for the needs of victims and witnesses.

§ 9-4 SUPPORT FOR VICTIMS AND WITNESSES

The ICC supports the testimony of victims and witnesses in several ways. Even before witnesses testify before the ICC, they meet members of the Victims and Witnesses Unit (VWU) to make the necessary arrangements for travel, the costs for which are covered by the Court. This can include helping witnesses obtain passports or other necessary documents, purchasing appropriate courtroom clothing, and undergoing a basic medical examination to be certain that the witness is fit to travel. The VWU oversees the necessary security arrangements for witnesses to travel safely to and from the location of their testimony and can even help arrange childcare if needed.

Part of the preparation for facilitating victim and witness participation in ICC proceedings is a vulnerability assessment. Any party calling a witness who might be especially vulnerable to psychosocial or physical difficulties is required to notify the VWU so it can make arrangements to mitigate these issues. Witness vulnerability depends on a host of factors, but the ICC is particularly sensitive to issues that can come from age, disability, mental illness, the effects of sexual or gender-based trauma, the trauma associated with torture, and the effects of crimes on children. There is no universal formula for addressing these vulnerabilities; the VWU and other Court personnel manage these issues in ways that are specific to each witness and situation.

§ 9-5 SAFETY

The Rome Statute requires the Court to "take appropriate measures to protect the safety, physical and psychological well-being, dignity and privacy of victims and witnesses." Art. 68(1). The Court is required to pay special regard to age, gender, and the needs of those affected by sexual or gender violence or violence against children. There are a number of practical steps the Court takes to implement this mandate.

The Court has the discretion to permit witnesses or victims to give evidence *in camera* or remotely (using electronic means). Art. 68(2). The Court may implement protective measures to ensure the safety of persons at risk because of their testimony. RPE 87(1). For example, the Court may order that the witness's name be expunged from the Court's public records, that participants not disclose information about the witness to others, that testimony be presented through videoconference, that the witness be referred to using a pseudonym, or the proceedings take place *in camera*. RPE 87(3). The Court may also regulate the manner in which a witness is questioned or require that a psychologist, family member, or other support person attend the proceedings when the victim is testifying to help protect the victim's psychological well-being. RPE 88(2) & (5).

In addition to measures implemented for Court proceedings, the ICC can also facilitate other protective measures. The Court can, in extreme circumstances, arrange the permanent relocation of witnesses who can no longer live safely in their home communities on account of their testimony. In less extreme cases, the Court can arrange for other protective measures in the witness's home community to protect them.

IV. REPARATIONS

§ 9-6 GENERAL PRINCIPLES OF REPARATIONS

The Rome Statute gives the Court the power to order convicted defendants to provide reparations to victims. Art. 75(2). These reparations can be made either directly to victims, or "in respect" of victims. Reparations awards can include restitution, compensation, and rehabilitation. To determine appropriate reparations, the Court considers the views of defendants, victims, and others who might have an interest in the matter, including States. Art. 75(3). Reparations orders can be made upon request of victims or on the Court's own initiative. Art. 75(1).

Determining the appropriate scope of reparations is a difficult task. To make its determination, the Court may engage experts to help it assess the "extent of any damage, loss and injury to, or in respect of victims." RPE 98(2).

The reparations process has multiple steps. Article 75(1) requires the Court to establish principles relating to reparations, which are the basic rules for the reparations process. They determine who is liable for reparations, who may receive them, and how they must be implemented. These principles are general; that is, they are meant to serve as a guidepost for all cases. The Court has elaborated these principles and describes them as "general concepts" to be used, in a case-appropriate way, in future cases. The Appeals Chamber first laid out the principles for reparations in Prosecutor v. Thomas Lubanga Dyilo, Case No. ICC-01/04-01/06, *Order for Reparations (Amended)* (AC, Mar. 3, 2015). In its 2021 order in the case of *Prosecutor v. Ntaganda,* the Trial Chamber applied the principles set forth in *Lubanga* and added several more. Prosecutor v. Bosco Ntaganda, Case No. ICC-01/04-02/06, *Reparations Order,* ¶ 29 (TC VI, Mar. 8, 2021).

To impose reparations, the Court enters a reparations order, which sets rules for that specific case, considering the types of harm caused, the nature of the victims, and the convicted person's liability. This order must comply with the reparations principles.

The Trust Fund for Victims implements the reparations order by developing and administering specific mechanisms to deliver reparations to victims and affected communities. The TFV designs compensation schemes, rehabilitation or support programs, or other measures required to accomplish the mandate of the reparations order.

In *Prosecutor v. Ntaganda*, the Court issued its fourth reparations order. Prosecutor v. Bosco Ntaganda, Case No. ICC-01/04-02/06, *Reparations Order* (TC VI, Mar. 8, 2021). In this order it promulgated the reparations principles that would guide that case and future cases. The principles in *Ntaganda* built on and modified principles set forth in the previous reparations orders in *Lubanga*, *Katanga*, and *Al Madhi*.

The Court in *Ntaganda* identified five principles that must be followed in any reparations order. These pertain to the definition of victims, the concept of harm and causation, the specification of the types and modalities of reparations, the notion of liability, and the rights of the defense.

§ 9.6.1 Identifying Victims

Atrocity crimes can affect thousands of people and can affect victims in many different ways. The reparations principles are sufficiently flexible to permit each Chamber to craft reparations that are appropriate for those affected by the defendant's crimes. For example, in *Ntaganda*, Trial Chamber VI wrote that there could be between 2,500 and 100,000 victims affected by the crimes charged. Thus, in that case the first task in determining reparations was to either identify the victims or set the rules for later determining the identity of the victims, whether natural persons, organizations, or institutions.

Although the general reparations principles do not specify the mechanics by which victims are to be identified in each case, they do require the Chamber to engage with affected communities, attempt to cause no further harm when doing so, and be especially sensitive to gender issues, those affected by sexual violence, and child victims.

In *Ntaganda*, the Chamber recognized two categories of victims, direct and indirect. Direct victims are those whose harm is the result of the crime for which the defendant was convicted. Prosecutor v. Bosco Ntaganda, Case No. ICC-01/04-02/06, *Reparations Order*, ¶ 108 (TC VI, Mar. 8, 2021). Indirect victims are those who suffer harm as a result of the harm suffered by direct victims. Indirect victims can include family members of direct victims, those who attempted to prevent the crimes, those who were harmed when attempting to provide help to direct victims, or other people who were harmed by the offenses. *Id.*, at ¶¶ 124–128.

Importantly, in *Ntaganda*, Trial Chamber VI recognized the concept of intergenerational trauma in its discussion of harm or trauma. Intergenerational trauma describes the ways that traumatic events can be transmitted from one generation to the next. Traumatized parents or communities can unintentionally exhibit difficult behaviors or social dynamics, which can negatively affect future generations. By defining harm to include intergenerational trauma, the *Ntaganda* reparation principles effectively added future generations to the list of possible indirect victims. Prosecutor v. Bosco Ntaganda, Case No. ICC-01/04-02/06, *Reparations Order*, ¶ 73 (TC VI, Mar. 8, 2021). The Trial Chamber held that the notion of harm can include effects that are material, physical, psychological, moral, and psychosocial. Intergenerational harm—harms to future generations caused by the harm done to their parents, grandparents, or community—are also relevant. While individual harm must be personal to each victim, community-based harm can be demonstrated by what happens to communities after the atrocities for which the defendant was convicted. If communities disperse, disintegrate, or cease to function, these harms can be relevant and justify reparations. On appeal, the Appeals Chamber ordered the Trial Chamber to reconsider this part of its opinion, and that process was ongoing in late 2023. Thus, the concept and method of proof of intergenerational trauma is still in flux. Prosecutor v. Bosco Ntaganda, Case No. ICC-01/04-02/06, *Judgment on the appeals against the decision of Trial Chamber VI of 8 March 2021 entitled "Reparations Order,"* ¶1 (AC, Sept. 12, 2022).

Also, in *Ntaganda*, Trial Chamber VI identified yet another group of possible direct victims. As the crime of rape was one of several crimes for which Ntaganda was convicted, and the Court held that children born of rape can qualify as direct victims of the defendant's crimes. Prosecutor v. Bosco Ntaganda, Case No. ICC-01/04-02/06, *Reparations Order*, ¶¶ 120–123 (TC VI, Mar. 8, 2021).

§ 9.6.2 Causation, Standard of Proof, and Harm

The exact harm suffered by each victim, community, or category of victim will necessarily differ in each case. The reparations principles detail the causation standard and the types of harm that may be relevant. They leave the application of these principles in specific cases for each reparations order. The harm must stem from a crime for which the defendant was convicted, and there must be a causal nexus between the harm and the crime of conviction. Individuals and organizations that satisfy these criteria are considered eligible for reparations.

The ICC Trial Chambers have employed a but/for relationship between the crimes and the harms to establish causation. This means that those claiming reparations must show that but for the defendant's crimes, they would not have suffered harm. Further, in the *Lubanga* reparations order, the Appeals Chamber stated that reparations orders must apply a proximate cause standard to establish liability. This test examines whether it was reasonably foreseeable that the acts and conduct underlying the defendant's crimes would produce the victim's harms. The Court rejected the relevance of a break in causation between the defendant's crimes and the victim's harms, which means that even if there was an intervening event occurring after the defendant's crimes that the defendant could not have foreseen, the defendant may still be liable for the victim's harms, as long as those harms otherwise satisfy the standard. Prosecutor v. Lubanga, Case No. 01/04-

01/06-3129-AnxA, *Order for Reparations (Amended)*, ¶ 59 (AC, Mar. 3, 2015).

The standard of proof in reparations proceedings is the balance of probabilities. Prosecutor v. Thomas Lubanga Dyilo, Case No. ICC-01/04-01/06, *Judgment on the appeals against the decision of Trial Chamber VI of 8 March 2021 entitled "Reparations Order,"* ¶ 31 (AC, Sept. 12, 2022). Victims must demonstrate their identity, type of harm, and a causal link by a balance of probabilities. In *Ntaganda*, the Appeals Chamber affirmed Trial Chamber VI's conclusion that this can be done through official documents, statements from two credible witnesses, or other means. Prosecutor v. Bosco Ntaganda, Case No. ICC-01/04-02/06, *Reparations Order*, ¶¶ 136–138 (TC VI, Ar. 8, 2021); Prosecutor v. Bosco Ntaganda, Case No. ICC-01/04-02/06, *Judgment on the appeals against the decision of Trial Chamber VI of 8 March 2021 entitled "Reparations Order,"* ¶ 518 (AC, Sept. 12, 2022). Trial Chamber VI also set out different rules to allow child victims and victims of sexual violence to meet the standard of proof. For these victims, courts considering reparations may presume the harms once the victim demonstrates under the balance of probabilities standard that he or she is a victim of the crimes. Prosecutor v. Bosco Ntaganda, Case No. ICC-01/04-02/06, *Reparations Order*, ¶ 139 (TC VI, Ar. 8, 2021). This approach was affirmed by the Appeals Chamber. Prosecutor v. Bosco Ntaganda, Case No. ICC-01/04-02/06, *Judgment on the appeals against the decision of Trial Chamber VI of 8 March 2021 entitled "Reparations Order,"* ¶¶ 714–717 (AC, Sept. 12, 2022).

§ 9.6.3 Types and Modalities of Reparations

By adopting an inclusive concept of victims and a broad definition of harm, the Court's Chambers necessarily permit a wide range of types and modalities of reparations. RPE 97(1) permits the Court to award individual or collective reparations, and the categories are not mutually exclusive; courts may order either one or both if appropriate.

Individual reparations are directed to individuals in reflection of the harm they personally suffered. Collective reparations are goods or services that are distributed to communities on the basis of categories of persons who suffered a shared harm. These need not be made solely to existing or recognized community groups. Instead, they are meant to address similar harms suffered by similarly situated people.

In addition to these categories that directly correspond to the language of the Rome Statute, the Trial Chamber in *Prosecutor v. Ntaganda* described a third category of reparations: collective reparations with individualized components. Prosecutor v. Bosco Ntaganda, Case No. ICC-01/04-02/06, *Reparations Order*, ¶¶ 7–9 (TC VI, Ar. 8, 2021). These are reparations provided to individual members of a group that suffered a collective harm. They are meant to respond to the fact that individual people may experience the same harm in diverse ways and have different individual needs, even if the harm was suffered collectively.

Modalities of reparations are the distinct types of response to the harm suffered by victims. These can include monetary compensation or other economic relief, psychosocial rehabilitation, medical services, social assistance or job training, and other approaches that might be appropriate in a specific case.

Reparations must be determined and awarded in a way that is sensitive to local community dynamics. This means avoiding awarding reparations in a way that creates or exacerbates community tensions, and with due attention to gender dynamics and the need for equity. The Court requires reparations to be as prompt as practicable and proportionate to the loss or harm suffered. Victims with immediate medical or psychological needs, the elderly or those with disabilities, victims of sexual violence, former child soldiers, and children born of rape are given priority.

§ 9-7 LIABILITY ISSUES

The Rome Statute requires that reparations orders be made "directly against a convicted person." Art. 75(2). The convicted person's liability for reparations stems from his or her culpability for the crimes and must be proportionate to the harm caused. Any alleged responsibility of other persons, organizations, or states is irrelevant to this determination. Also, not relevant to the reparations decision are the convicted person's financial situation and the extent of funds available from the Trust Fund for Victims. Similarly, the mode of liability, gravity of the crimes, and other possible mitigating factors are irrelevant to the decision. The focus must remain on the extent of the harm caused and what it will cost to repair those harms. Thus, it is a victim-centered approach. It asks what it will take to repair the victims, not the proportion of harm attributable to the convicted person.

Because reparations are meant to repair harm done to the victims, they must not overcompensate victims. Moreover, reparations are not designed to further punish convicted persons, so they must not have a punitive aspect. The goal is solely to repair the harm caused. If the defendant does not have sufficient resources to pay for reparations, the TFV provides the funds.

§ 9-8 RIGHTS OF THE DEFENDANT AND IMPLEMENTATION OF THE REPARATIONS ORDER

Defendants have a right to fair and impartial reparation proceedings. The Court has not detailed what this requirement means in practice. The *Ntaganda* Reparations Order states that uncertainties as to the amount of reparations must be resolved in favor of the convicted person. The reparations principles require that reparations proceedings be public and transparent. (Of course, this requirement also ensures that victims have the information they need to fully participate in the process.)

Under the Rome Statute, States Parties are required to give effect to reparations orders. Art. 75(5). States must not prevent the enforcement of reparations orders or the implementation of reparations awards. Additionally, ICC reparations must not supplant each State's primary responsibility to address the harm suffered by victims.

Reparations orders are implemented through the TFV, which is charged with designing the program for victims and determining the exact nature and size of each modality of reparation.

V. TRUST FUND FOR VICTIMS

The TFV was created in 2002 by the Assembly of States Parties, as required by Article 74(1) of the Rome Statute. Although it is separate from the Court, the TFV works to implement reparations orders and other programs to address harm to victims. The TFV has two principal mandates: to administer reparations orders entered by the Court, and to provide other support for victims and communities affected by atrocity crimes. The TFV is led by an Executive Director and administered by a secretariat headquartered in the Hague. It is governed by a Board of Directors whose members represent five regions of the world and are elected by the Assembly of States Parties to 3-year terms.

Pursuant to the Rome Statute, the TFV is funded by monies collected through Court-ordered fines or forfeitures from convicted persons. Art. 79(2). It is also funded by voluntary contributions from States, individuals, corporations, and other organizations. It has devoted a significant amount of funds to the services it provides for victims, including more than

3.7 million Euros for assistance and support programs, in addition to more than 4.3 million Euros for reparations themselves.

§ 9-9 REPARATIONS

The TFV plans and administers reparations programs pursuant to orders entered by the Court. To date it has administered reparations orders in four cases: *Katanga*, *Lubanga*, *Al Mahdi*, and *Ntaganda*. Each of these cases featured a different reparations scheme directed toward different victims, all of which were implemented by the TFV. Before it can provide support, the TFV must first identify eligible victims. The rules for identifying victims are set in reparations orders, but the administration of the process is left to the TFV.

After identifying eligible victims and affected communities, the TFV has put in place a range of modalities of reparations. It has provided individual reparations to victims, such as in *Katanga*, when it provided symbolic payments of $ 250 to almost 300 individual victims. It has provided housing assistance, support for education through the payment of school fees, and funding for income-generating activities like starting small businesses or vocational training. It has also provided funding for individuals to purchase livestock or motorcycles, as well as support for medical and psychological rehabilitation.

In *Lubanga*, the TFV worked through implementing partners, which are social service organizations that work in and for the benefit of communities affected by the crimes for which Lubanga was convicted. Through collective reparations awards, the TFV can provide funding to these implementing partners. These groups organize the mechanisms by which individuals and affected communities can benefit from reparations programs. Services provided in this reparations model can include vocational training, support for schools, training for non-governmental organizations in peace and rehabilitation activities, and mental health services.

§ 9-10 NON-REPARATIONS ASSISTANCE

Part of the TFV's mandate is to provide assistance to victims and affected communities in countries with situations under examination or investigation by the ICC. These activities are funded only by voluntary contributions, not by fines or forfeitures. The activities are not tied to any particular case before the ICC, but to the entire situation. For this reason, they are open to a wider range of persons and communities, so long as they have been harmed in some way by atrocity crimes within the Court's jurisdiction. Furthermore, these crimes may have taken place at any point in the process, even before judicial proceedings begin.

Assistance programs can take the form of physical rehabilitation, psychological rehabilitation, and material support. Physical rehabilitation includes addressing the immediate medical needs stemming from violence, such as trauma surgery, reconstructive procedures, or the provision of prosthetic limbs, and ongoing medical needs, such as HIV/AIDS care. Psychological rehabilitation programs can take diverse forms, including counseling, providing information, and collaborating with entire communities to resolve disputes and rebuild more peacefully. Almost half of the TFV's distributions—all of which come from voluntary contributions and donations—have gone to such programs.

VI. OTHER ENGAGEMENT WITH AFFECTED COMMUNITIES

The ICC attempts to involve affected communities in its activities in multiple ways. In situations under investigation, the Registry actively engages with affected communities to make potential victims aware of the proceedings, provide information about how they might participate as victims, and support those who wish to participate. In addition to these situation-specific activities, the ICC also engages in more general outreach to raise awareness of its mandate and activities.

The ICC's general outreach activities are not specifically directed toward victims, but they are an important part of the ICC's efforts to raise awareness about its work and avenues for participation and engagement. These activities can include holding information sessions in situation countries, including sessions designed for particular groups such as women or religious leaders. They can also include outreach to legal professionals or scholars so they can advise others about the work of the ICC. Finally, these outreach efforts can include media engagement, including working with local and international journalists and others to provide information about the ICC's work and cases.

Selected Sources and Additional Reading

DOUGLAS GUILFOYLE, INTERNATIONAL CRIMINAL LAW (2016).

INT'L CRIM. CT., REGULATIONS OF THE COURT, Doc. No. ICC-BD/01-05-16 (2018), https://www.icc-cpi.int/sites/default/files/Publications/Regulations-of-the-Court.pdf.

INT'S CRIM. CT., REGULATIONS OF THE OFFICE OF THE PROSECUTOR, ICC Doc. No. ICC-BD/05-01-09 (2009), https://www.icc-cpi.int/sites/default/files/Publications/Regulations-of-the-Office-of-the-Prosecutor.pdf.

INT'L CRIM. CT., RULES OF PROCEDURE AND EVIDENCE, Doc No. ICC-PIOS-LT-03-004/19_Eng (2019), https://www.icc-cpi.int/sites/default/files/Publications/Rules-of-Procedure-and-Evidence.pdf.

INTERNATIONAL CRIMINAL COURT TRUST FUND FOR VICTIMS, 2020 ANNUAL REPORT (Sept. 2021), https://www.trustfundforvictims.org/sites/default/files/reports/TFV%20AnnualReport%202020_final.pdf.

INTERNATIONAL CRIMINAL COURT TRUST FUND FOR VICTIMS, NOW & INTO 2021 (Dec. 14, 2020), https://www.trustfundforvictims.org/sites/default/files/reports/TFV%20Event%20Report%2014%20Dec%202020%20-%20TFV%20Now%20and%20Into%202021.pdf.

INTERNATIONAL FEDERATION FOR HUMAN RIGHTS, VICTIMS AT THE CENTER OF JUSTICE FROM 1998 TO 2018: REFLECTIONS ON THE PROMISES AND THE REALITY OF VICTIM PARTICIPATION AT THE ICC (Dec. 2018), https://www.fidh.org/IMG/pdf/droitsdesvictimes730a_final.pdf.

Marina Lostal, *The* Ntaganda *Reparations Order: A Marked Step Towards a Victim-Centered Reparations Legal Framework at the ICC*, EJIL: TALK (May 24, 2021), https://www.ejiltalk.org/the-ntaganda-reparations-order-a-marked-step-towards-a-victim-centred-reparations-legal-framework-at-the-icc/.

WAR CRIMES RESEARCH OFFICE, INTERNATIONAL CRIMINAL COURT LEGAL ANALYSIS AND EDUCATION PROJECT, VICTIM PARTICIPATION BEFORE THE INTERNATIONAL CRIMINAL COURT (Nov. 2007), https://www.wcl.american.edu/wcl-american-edu/assets/wcro_report_on_victim_participation_december_2007.pdf.

CHAPTER 10

THE INTERNATIONAL CRIMINAL COURT AND THE UNITED STATES

I. INTRODUCTION

The United States has had an uneasy relationship to the International Criminal Court since its inception. The U.S. delegation participated extensively in the Rome Statute's negotiation and the Court represents a permanent embodiment of the Nuremberg ideal. Thus, it is unsurprising that a majority of Americans polled about the ICC support it. At the same time, many U.S. policymakers, politicians, and military leaders have been wary of an international court with criminal jurisdiction that might one day constrain the United States. Thus, the United States has not yet joined the Court, although it signed the Statute on December 31, 2000, the last day the treaty was open for signature. This brief Chapter surveys the involvement of the United States at the Rome Conference when the Statute was drafted, the positions of five presidential administrations, the incorporation of ICC law in the U.S. legal system, and the likely future of the U.S. relationship with the Court.

II. THE U.S. POSITION AT ROME

The United States has been a long-time supporter of the *ad hoc* international tribunals for the former Yugoslavia and Rwanda, and prior to the Rome Conference, former President Bill Clinton expressed general support for the establishment of a permanent international criminal court. Throughout the 1990s, the United States participated in the U.N. Preparatory Committee meetings that prepared the text of the ICC Statute for negotiation in Rome. However, as the negotiations progressed, statements made about the future court by U.S. officials reflected divisions between various government agencies and no unified position emerged. The view of the Department of State was largely positive. Conversely, the Department of Defense opposed the establishment of the Court, worrying that it could target American soldiers based overseas. The Department of Justice, meanwhile, was concerned that the creation of an international criminal court might disrupt domestic prosecutions, and the Treasury Department was adamant that an international criminal court should have jurisdiction over drug enforcement cases.

As the 1998 Rome Diplomatic Conference drew near, attacks on the soon-to-be-established court increased. Republican Senator Jesse Helms of North Carolina famously quipped that any international criminal tribunal would be "dead on arrival" in the United States unless Washington retained a veto over potential cases. At and before the Rome Conference, the United States did not join the group of like-minded States favoring the creation of the Court that included many of its traditional allies. Although many concessions were made towards the U.S. position during the negotiations, the defensive posture of the United States hardened as the Conference progressed. On the last day of the

Conference, the U.S. delegation submitted two amendments for consideration in an effort to delay adoption of the Statute. After these proposals were voted down, the White House instructed the U.S. delegation to request a written, recorded vote on the adoption of the Rome Statute. This resulted in a humiliating defeat for the United States as the delegates at the Rome Conference voted overwhelmingly to approve the Statute, as noted in Chapter 1.

Testifying before the Senate Foreign Relations Committee later that summer, the U.S. head of delegation, Ambassador David Scheffer, identified six objections to the Statute, three of which formed the crux of the Clinton Administration's opposition to the Court. First, he argued that the Statute permitted the exercise of jurisdiction over the nationals of non-States Parties. Second, the Statute created a Prosecutor that could, on his or her own authority (and with the consent of two judges), initiate investigations and prosecutions. Finally, the Statute did not clearly require an affirmative determination by the United Nations Security Council prior to bringing a complaint for aggression before the Court.

There were also less significant concerns, as well as complaints that the Statute was negotiated behind closed doors and without the involvement of the U.S. delegation (which was not correct), and that it was adopted against a backdrop of antagonism towards the United States. Despite these objections and what President Clinton labelled "significant flaws" in the treaty, the United States signed the Rome Statute. However, President Clinton recommended that his successor not submit the treaty to the U.S. Senate for ratification until U.S. concerns had been satisfied.

III. U.S. ATTITUDES TOWARDS THE COURT IN THE TWENTY-FIRST CENTURY

§ 10-1 THE BUSH ADMINISTRATION'S APPROACH TO THE COURT (2000–2008)

The U.S. position towards the ICC took a sharply hostile turn upon the election of George W. Bush in 2000. The newly inaugurated President repeatedly stated that becoming a party to the Court was not in the interests of the United States. Throughout his eight-year administration, U.S. policy became to "isolate and ignore" the Court so that it would, in the words of one former U.S. official, John Bolton, "wither and collapse." The stated goal of the 2002 National Security Strategy of the administration was to "protect Americans" from "the potential for investigations, inquiry, or prosecution by the International Criminal Court (ICC), whose jurisdiction does not extend to Americans and which we do not accept."

As noted earlier in Chapter 7, § 12, From 2002 until 2006, the United States entered into Bilateral Immunity Agreements (BIA) with more than 100 countries. These agreements relied on Article 98(1) of the ICC Statute, which provides that the ICC "may not proceed with a request to surrender or assistance which would require the requested State to act inconsistently with its obligations under international law." These Article 98 agreements meant that States agreed not to turn over the other State's nationals to the ICC, or otherwise work with the Court to facilitate the arrest or surrender of a suspect. The result was to grant immunity from ICC prosecution to U.S. citizens and allies accused of committing possible ICC crimes on the territory of a Rome Statute State Party. The United States sometimes punished States that refused to sign Article 98 agreements by withholding economic assistance.

The Bush Administration took the view that the Court should be prevented from becoming a constraint on the preventative use of U.S. military force. This led to the adoption of the American Service members' Protection Act of 2002 (ASPA), which protects members of the United States military from prosecution by the ICC and prohibits military aid to countries that are ICC States Parties. The ASPA does, however, permit the President to grant such aid at his or her discretion under the so-called "Dodd Amendment,", which was recently expanded to permit the United States to support the investigation of the ICC in respect of Russia's invasion of Ukraine. Additionally, in April of 2002, then Undersecretary of State for Arms Control and International Security John R. Bolton sent a letter to United Nations Secretary General Kofi Annan stating that the United States did "not intend to become a party to the treaty." The letter added that "[a]ccordingly the United States has no legal obligations arising from its signature." While popularly referred to as a "nullification" of the U.S. signature, or as "unsigning" the ICC Treaty, the U.S. signature remains "on the books" of the treaty depositary, but with an asterisk referencing the Bolton letter.

From this point until the end of Bush's term in 2009, the United States no longer participated in multilateral discussions regarding the ICC, including the meetings of the ICC's Assembly of States Parties. It further voiced its objections to the Court in the United Nations Security Council, arguing in discussions relating to Resolution 1422, which provides immunity to peacekeepers from ICC non-States Parties, that "[t]he ICC is not 'the law.' "

That said, toward the end of President Bush's second term, a softening in U.S. attitudes towards the ICC was evident. The rate of new Article 98 agreements slowed, and the President was making exemptions to APSA's provisions for an increasing number of States Parties to the Rome Statute. The United States also abstained from (rather than vetoed) the adoption of Security Council Resolution 1593 in 2005, which referred the Darfur situation to the ICC, largely due to pressure from the "Save Darfur" campaign. Even following the adoption of the Darfur Resolution, however, Anne Woods Patterson, U.S. Acting Permanent Representative to the United Nations, stated that the United States continued to hold fundamental objections to both the Court and the Rome Statute.

§ 10-2 THE OBAMA ADMINISTRATION'S APPROACH TO THE COURT (2009–2016)

The administration of President Barack Obama returned to the original policy of "cautious engagement" with the Court that was the hallmark of the Clinton years. At her January 2009 hearing on her confirmation as Secretary of State, Senator Hillary Rodham Clinton referenced U.S. policy towards the Court, noting that she would "end hostility towards the ICC, and look for opportunities to encourage effective ICC action in ways that promote U.S. interests by bringing war criminals to justice." One concrete measure of this policy change was the attendance of a high-level U.S. delegation at the 8th Session of the Assembly of States Parties in November of 2009.

In 2010, the National Security Strategy summarized the U.S. position towards the ICC as follows:

> From Nuremberg to Yugoslavia to Liberia, the United States has seen that the end of impunity and the promotion of justice are not just moral imperatives; they are stabilizing forces in international affairs. . . . . Although the United States is not at present a party to the Rome Statute of the International Criminal Court, and will always protect U.S. personnel, we are engaging with State Parties to the Rome Statute on issues of concern and are supporting the I.C.C.'s prosecution of those cases that advance U.S. interests and values, consistent with the requirements of U.S. law. The White House,

National Security Strategy of the United States of America (May 27, 2010), p. 48.

This policy was consistently voiced through both U.S. National Security Strategy statements and remarks given at the ICC's Assembly of States Parties (ASP). The United States stopped actively pursuing Article 98 agreements (the last such agreement was reportedly one with Montenegro in 2007), and actively assisted the Court with the arrests of Dominic Ongwen and Bosco Ntaganda (both of whom were transferred to the Court by U.S. embassies abroad). Although the United States still did not provide any direct financial support to the Court, per the restrictions of the ASPA, it aided governments pursuing ICC fugitives. This assistance included support for Ugandan efforts to capture Joseph Kony and other members of the Lord's Resistance Army.

While the Obama Administration did not propose joining the Court or sending a letter to the U.N. Secretary-General repudiating the 2002 Bolton letter, it did increase the focus on atrocity prevention, and many government agencies now have atrocity prevention and/or criminal investigation as at least part of their mandates. The Obama Administration created a new section in the criminal division of the Department of Justice that works to deny safe haven to human rights violators. In addition, many individuals have been deported from the United States on the basis of acts that might be characterized as ICC crimes.

§ 10-3 THE TRUMP ADMINISTRATION'S APPROACH TO THE COURT (2017–2020)

Before taking office in January 2016, candidate Donald Trump reportedly condemned the threatened mass withdrawal from the ICC by African states, opining that African leaders only wish to oppress the poor and accumulate wealth. The 2016 Republican National Platform, however, firmly rejected the Court, stating that it did not "accept the jurisdiction of the International Criminal Court" and supported "statutory protection for U.S. personnel and officials as they act abroad to meet our global security requirements."

As discussed earlier, in Chapter 7, in 2017, after having received more than 100 communications over the course of a decade, the ICC Prosecutor requested authorization to begin an investigation into the situation in Afghanistan, which included allegations against the Taliban, Afghan National Forces, and members of the Central Intelligence Agency regarding detainee mistreatment. The Trump Administration criticized the Afghanistan investigation, which largely targeted Taliban crimes, and began to ramp up rhetoric against the Prosecutor and her staff, refusing them visas to come to the United States and threatening them in public statements. In 2019, a Pre-Trial Chamber found that the Prosecutor could not commence an investigation regarding the actions of U.S. persons in Afghan territory (or anyone else), determining that the investigation would not be in the interests of justice, discussed in detail in Chapter 7, § 7-12.

The Appeals Chamber reversed and authorized the Prosecutor's investigation. The judgment found that the Prosecutor had jurisdiction to undertake an investigation into alleged war crimes occurring in the territory of Afghanistan since May 2003, including those allegedly committed by members of the U.S. armed forces and the CIA and Afghan national forces, as well as crimes against humanity and war crimes allegedly perpetrated by the Taliban and affiliated groups. Situation in the Islamic Republic of Afghanistan, Case No. ICC-02/17, *Judgment on the appeal against the decision on the authorisation of an investigation into the situation in the Islamic Republic of Afghanistan* (AC, Mar. 5, 2020).

In response, on June 11, 2020, President Donald Trump issued Executive Order 13928 declaring the ICC to be a threat to national security, and in September personally sanctioned Prosecutor Fatou Bensouda and a high-ranking member of her team, Phakiso Mochochko, pursuant to the order. Two lawsuits were filed against the sanctions, alleging them to be unconstitutional as improperly interfering with the constitutional rights of U.S. persons and dual nationals. Open Soc'y Justice Initiative et al. v. Trump et al., 510 F. Supp. 3d 198 (S.D.N.Y. 2021); Compl. for Dec. and Inj. Relief, Leila Sadat et al. v. Trump et al, (No. 21-CV-00416), 2021 WL 194155 (N.D. Cal. Jan. 15, 2021).

§ 10-4 THE BIDEN ADMINISTRATION'S APPROACH TO THE COURT (2021–)

The Biden Administration has once again reset the U.S. relationship with the Court. Less than three months after taking office, the Biden Administration repealed the sanctions imposed by the Trump Administration in response to the investigation into the situation in Afghanistan, settled the lawsuits that had been initiated against the U.S. government, and began reengaging with the Court. The advent of the war in Ukraine brought about a rare showing of bipartisan U.S. support for the ICC, including from prominent and formerly hostile members of Congress such as Senator Lindsay Graham. With the 2023 Consolidated Appropriations Act § 7073, Congress broadened the exception to the ASPA under the Act's Dodd Amendment for support in form of "rendering assistance to the International Criminal Court to assist with investigations and prosecutions of foreign nationals related to the situation in Ukraine, including to support victims and witnesses." 22 U.S.C. § 7433(a).

IV. THE STATUS OF ICC LAW IN THE UNITED STATES

§ 10-5 U.S. CASE LAW CITING TO THE ROME STATUTE

A survey in Westlaw's federal case law database showed that 60 different U.S. federal judicial cases, dated between 1999 and 2016, cited to the Rome Statute as an authoritative statement of customary international law. Fifty-two of these cases involved civil claims and eight involved criminal matters for non-ICC crimes.

On the civil side, discussion of the Rome Statute by U.S. courts occurred in a number of contexts, including the *mens rea* standard for aiding and abetting (*In re* South African Apartheid Litigation, 617 F. Supp. 2d 228, 257–62 (S.D.N.Y. 2009)), corporate liability (Kiobel v. Royal Dutch Petroleum Co., 621 F.3d 111 (2d Cir. 2010)), and the definition of crimes against humanity (Morales v. Brown, 2015 WL 6167451, at *7). One of the most interesting references to the Rome Statute is the 2013 District Court case of *Sexual Minorities Uganda v. Lively*, 960 F. Supp. 2d. 304 (D. Mass. 2013), *dismissed* 254 F. Supp. 3d 262 (D. Mass. 2017) on grounds of jurisdiction, *aff'd in part, app. dismissed in part*, 899 F.3d 24 (1st Cir. 2018), which held that the Alien Tort Statute furnished jurisdiction when a U.S. national aided and abetted in a crime against humanity. In this case, the conduct in question was the persecution of LGBTQ individuals in Uganda, actions the District Court had no difficulty finding constituted "a crime against humanity that unquestionably violates international norms." *Id.* at 316. In another interesting opinion, the D.C. Circuit Court of Appeals in *Simon v. Republic of Hungary* relied on the definition of genocide in the Rome Statute to support its reversal of a lower court decision in a case brought by Hungarian survivors of the Holocaust. Simon v. Republic of Hungary, 812 F.3d 127, 143 (D.C. Cir. 2016). Although the Rome Statute is not binding on the United States, the Fourth Circuit noted in 2011 that "this does not lessen its importance as an international treaty and, thus, a primary source of the law of nations." Aziz v. Alcolac, Inc., 658 F.3d 388, 400 (4th Cir. 2011). *See also* United States v. Mohammad, 398 F. Supp. 3d 1233, 1246 (U.S.C.M.C.R. 2019). Indeed, references to the Rome Statute in U.S. courts often buttress or support claims regarding the content of customary international law, particularly in Alien Tort Claims Act litigation.

On the criminal side, the D.C. Circuit in *Hamdan* looked to the Geneva Conventions, incorporated into the Rome Statute, for the definition of war crimes and regarding modes of liability for the commission of international crimes. Hamdan v. Rumsfeld, 344 F. Supp. 2d 152 (D.D.C. 2004), *rev'd* on other grounds, 415 F.3d 33 (D.C. Cir. 2005), *rev'd and remanded*, 548 U.S. 557 (2006). In another example, in *United States v. Al-Bahlul*, the Court of Military Commission Review referenced the ICC Statute in its analysis of common purpose and joint criminal enterprise liability. United States v. Al Bahlul, 820 F. Supp. 2d 1141, 1213–14 (U.S.C.M.C.R. 2011), *vac. on other grounds*, No. 11–1324, 2013 WL 297726 (D.C. Cir. Jan. 25, 2013), *reh'g en banc granted, vacated on other grounds* (Apr. 23, 2013).

§ 10-6 U.S. STATUTORY ANALOGUES TO ICC CRIMES

The three ICC crimes over which the Court can currently exercise inherent jurisdiction—war crimes, crimes against humanity, and genocide—are punishable in some fashion under U.S. law. U.S. federal, and to a lesser degree, state law codifies some of the crimes that conceptually relate to conduct proscribed in the Rome Statute. But this coverage is incomplete, and jurisdiction is often lacking. Regardless, the United States can prosecute a limited number of ICC crimes in federal courts, including genocide, torture, and some war crimes such as the recruitment or use of child soldiers. Other crimes might be prosecuted as "ordinary" offenses using statutory provisions on murder, rape, and so forth. Finally, military courts operating under the Uniform Code of Military Justice (UCMJ) may also have jurisdiction over some ICC war crimes, again, with substantial gaps in coverage. There is no equivalent in U.S. law to the crime of aggression.

There is no U.S. federal legislation on crimes against humanity, although Puerto Rico has a law criminalizing it, and legislation has been considered in the Senate on multiple occasions, most recently in 2023. Gaps in coverage regarding crimes against humanity could make prosecuting these types of crimes in U.S. courts particularly challenging. Under the ICC's "same person/same conduct" test for inadmissibility, discussed in Chapters 5, 7 and 8, existing U.S. law might be sufficient in many cases to permit the complementarity principle to deprive the Court of jurisdiction in cases being investigated or prosecuted by the United States, although it would depend upon the facts and circumstances of the particular case. However, there are considerable legal gaps in coverage, particularly as regards crimes against humanity, that could prevent U.S. courts from exercising criminal jurisdiction over U.S. and foreign nationals accused of committing ICC crimes. This is especially true given the presumption against extraterritoriality in the application of U.S. federal criminal law.

Under a series of U.S. Supreme Court decisions, including *United States v. Morrison*, 529 U.S. 598 (2000) and *Kiobel v. Royal Dutch Petroleum Co.*, 569 U.S. 108 (2013), U.S. courts employ a presumption against the extraterritorial application of U.S. law as a matter of statutory construction. Thus, unless Congress has evinced a clear intention otherwise, U.S. law is presumed to apply only to conduct occurring within the territorial jurisdiction of the United States. This presumption appears to have less force respecting criminal statutes, where vigorous extraterritorial enforcement of federal criminal law is more the rule than the exception (as shown by the *Noriega* prosecution, for example) and the federal courts have found that many federal crimes, either explicitly or through judicial interpretation, apply to acts abroad. As one federal court put it, criminal prohibitions "can have many obvious extraterritorial applications even if [they are] most readily and naturally deployed domestically." U.S. v. Abu Khatallah, 151 F. Supp. 3d 116 (D.C. Cir. 2015).

§ 10.6.1 Federal Statutes

The Genocide Convention Implementation Act of 1987, as amended, and the War Crimes Act of 1996, as amended, offer some specific possibilities of prosecution in U.S. federal courts for ICC crimes.

There are also federal statutes prohibiting torture, forced marriage, and the use of child soldiers. In addition, federal law prohibits murder, rape, and other crimes which may address conduct that also constitutes an international crime. The Justice for Victims of War Crimes Act expanded federal jurisdiction for war crimes committed within and outside U.S. territory. The War Crimes Rewards Expansion Act broadened the scope for the Department of State to offer rewards for information that would lead to convictions or transfer of foreign nationals accused of ICC crimes to a tribunal or the United States. Under Article 17 of the Rome Statute, which sets forth the principle of complementarity, the ICC must defer to genuine national investigations and prosecutions, provided that the proceedings are not intended to shield the accused from justice. This was interpreted broadly by the Court's Office of the Prosecutor in closing the situation involving the British in Iraq. INT'L CRIM CT. OFF. OF THE PROSECUTOR, SITUATION IN IRAQ/UK: FINAL REP., ¶¶ 280–293 (Dec. 9, 2020). The capacity of the United States to investigate and try individuals for atrocity crimes, regardless of how they are labelled, means that justice can be served in either civilian or military U.S. courts.

§ 10.6.2 State Law

At the state level, while most states criminalize terrorism, the case law is relatively sparse. No U.S. state directly criminalizes ICC crimes. One exception, although not a state, is Puerto Rico's statute on crimes against humanity. Searching the statutes and legislation of all fifty states for the terms of genocide, war crimes, and crimes against humanity yielded mostly "recognition" legislation, with few criminal code results. State legislatures appear most concerned with preventing genocide and other atrocity crimes through education and awareness. Multiple state civil codes contain commissions, councils, and statutory provisions dedicated to the establishment and function of such programs. State criminal sanctions against genocide specifically, however, are few and far between.

§ 10.6.3 Accountability of U.S. Persons for the Commission of ICC Crimes

U.S. courts, and particularly federal courts, are generally independent from the executive and legislative branches of government. Accountability for both criminal and civil wrongs is generally demanded by the American public and enforced by the courts and legislature. Even sitting U.S. Presidents have been called to account before the courts in limited cases, as indicated by famous decisions in *United States v. Nixon* 418 U.S. 683 (1974) and *Clinton v. Jones*, 520 U.S. 681 (1997). The United States also has a robust military justice system which operates under the UCMJ, with more than 4,000 JAG lawyers, a highly regulated system of courts martial, and a Federal Court of Military Appeals. In most cases, U.S. service members accused of war crimes would be tried by a court-martial under the UCMJ for violations of the laws of war, as codified in the UCMJ.

At the same time, following the attacks of September 11, 2001, and the U.S. military response thereto, credible allegations of serious violations of both the laws of war and human rights were levied against members of U.S. military forces, CIA officials, and even private military contractors. These have been well-documented, including by a 6,000-page U.S. Senate report on torture issued on December 9, 2014, much of which is classified, which has given rise to the concern that at least some of the allegations could, if proven, constitute ICC crimes.

There have been only a handful of criminal prosecutions brought with respect to any of these allegations, and those brought only involved low-ranking individuals. The U.S. government has generally not pursued accountability for the commission of ICC crimes by U.S. persons and has generally opposed civil suits seeking redress by invoking immunities, the state secrets doctrines, or other legal procedures. This has been true not only of the Bush, Obama, and Trump Administrations, but also the Biden Administration, all of which have repeatedly and successfully invoked the State Secrets privilege in cases involving allegations of detainee mistreatment. *See, e.g.*, U.S. v. Zubaydah, 595 U.S. 195 (2022).

V. CONCLUSION

The United States has a complicated relationship with the ICC. With a vigorous system of federal and state criminal justice, and a robust system of military justice, the United States is more than capable of prosecuting ICC crimes effectively. However, there are legal gaps in coverage, particularly regarding crimes against humanity, that could prevent U.S. courts from exercising criminal jurisdiction over U.S. and foreign nationals accused of committing ICC crimes abroad.

The United States is broadly supportive of efforts to combat impunity for the commission of ICC crimes abroad when it is the U.S. national interest to do so, as demonstrated by strong bipartisan support for investigations relating to Russia's invasion of Ukraine in February 2022. In addition, the Darfur, Sudan referral suggests that civil society coalitions can trigger U.S. support for the Court in specific situations. U.S. courts often cite the Rome Statute as evidence of customary international law, and U.S. public opinion favors U.S. support for the Court. This suggests that the Court's influence may be greater than the formal legal relationship between itself and the United States suggests. The Biden administration, like the Clinton and Obama administrations before it, see the ICC as a useful tool with which the United States can constructively engage even if it does not join. This has been particularly true, and even represents a bipartisan consensus, as regards the conflict in Ukraine. That said, it is likely that the United States will have an uneasy relationship with the International Criminal Court for some time.

Selected Sources and Additional Reading

FANNY BENEDETTI, KARINE BONNEAU & JOHN WASHBURN, NEGOTIATING THE INTERNATIONAL CRIMINAL COURT (2013).

DAVID BOSCO, ROUGH JUSTICE: THE INTERNATIONAL CRIMINAL COURT IN A WORLD OF POWER POLITICS (2014).

SAMANTHA POWER, "A PROBLEM FROM HELL:" AMERICA AND THE AGE OF GENOCIDE (2002).

DAVID J. SCHEFFER, ALL THE MISSING SOULS 28 (2012).

THE UNITED STATES AND THE INTERNATIONAL CRIMINAL COURT (Sarah Sewall & Carl Kaysen, eds., 2000).

Jack Goldsmith, *The Self-Defeating International Criminal Court,* 70 U. CHI. L. REV. 89 (2003).

Jason Ralph, *International society, the International Criminal Court and American foreign policy,* 31 REV. INT'L. STUD. 27 (2005).

Leila Nadya Sadat, *Summer in Rome, Spring in The Hague, Winter in Washington? U.S. Policy towards the International Criminal Court*, 21 WIS. INT'L. L.J. 557 (2003).

Leila Nadya Sadat & S. Richard Carden, *The New International Criminal Court, An Uneasy Resolution*, 88 GEO. L.J. 381 (2000).

President Bill Clinton, A Commitment to Human Dignity, Democracy, and Peace, *in* 1 ISSUES OF

DEMOCRACY: CONFRONTING HUMAN RIGHTS VIOLATIONS 10, 12–13 (1996).

Am. Soc'y of Int'l L. Int'l Crim. Ct. Task Force, *Pol'y Op. for U.S. Engagement with the Int'l Cri. Ct. Rep.* (2021), https://www.asil.org/asil-icc-task-force.

Justin Cole, *11 Takeaways from Senate Hearing on Expanding War Crimes Act and a Crimes Against Humanity Statute,* JUST SEC., Oct. 3, 2022, https://www.justsecurity.org/83339/11-takeaways-from-senate-hearing-on-expanding-war-crimes-act-and-a-crimes-against-humanity-statute/.

Floriane Lavaud, Ashika Singh, and Isabelle Glimcher, *The American Servicemembers' Protection Act and the Dodd Amendment: Shaping United States Engagement with the ICC (Part II)*, JUST SEC. (Feb. 14, 2023), https://www.justsecurity.org/85121/the-american-servicemembers-protection-act-and-the-dodd-amendment-shaping-united-states-engagement-with-the-icc-part-ii/.

Is A U.N. International Criminal Court in the U.S. National Interest?: Hearing Before the S. Subcomm. on Int'l Relations & the S. Comm. on Foreign Relations, 105th Cong. 10, 12–15 (1998) (statement of David J. Scheffer, Ambassador at-Large for War Crimes Issues, Head of the U.S. Delegation for the U.N. Diplomatic Conference on the Establishment of a Permanent International Criminal Court, U.S. Department of State).

OFFICE OF THE PROSECUTOR, INT'L CRIM. CT., SITUATION IN IRAQ/UK: FINAL REPORT (Dec. 9, 2020), https://www.icc-cpi.int/sites/default/files/items Documents/201209-otp-final-report-iraq-uk-eng.pdf.

OFFICE OF MGMT. & BUDGET, EXEC. OFFICE OF THE PRESIDENT, US CONTRIBUTIONS TO THE UNITED NATIONS SYSTEM 3, FISCAL YEAR 2010 (2011).

Exec. Order No. 13928, 85 Fed. Reg. 36139 (2020).

Barbara Crossette, *Helms Vows to Make War on U.N. Court*, N.Y. TIMES (Mar. 27, 1998), http://www.nytimes.com/1998/03/27/world/helms-vows-to-make-war-on-un-court.html.

Paul R. Williams, Alexandra Koch & Lilian Waldock, *U.S. Strategic Interests in Contributing to the ICC Trust Fund for Victims (Part I)*, JUST SEC. (Feb. 13, 2023), https://www.justsecurity.org/85112/u-s-strategic-interests-in-contributing-to-the-icc-trust-fund-for-victims-part-i/.

Statement on the Rome Treaty on the International Criminal Court (Dec. 31, 2000), 37 WEEKLY COMP. PRES. DOC. 4 (Jan. 8, 2001).

The White House, *National Security Strategy of the United States of America* (May 27, 2010), https://obamawhitehouse.archives.gov/sites/default/files/rss_viewer/national_security_strategy.pdf.

Genocide Convention Implementation Act of 1987, as amended 2007, 18 U.S.C. §§ 1091–1093.

War Crimes Act of 1996, as amended, 18 U.S.C. § 2441.

Justice for Victims of War Crimes Act, 18 U.S.C. § 2441.

Child Soldiers Accountability Act of 2008, 18 U.S.C. §§ 2442, 3300.

Foreign Relations Authorization Act, Fiscal Years 1994 and 1995 § 706, 18 U.S.C. §§ 2340–2340B.

Violence Against Women Act Reauthorization Act of 2022, 34 U.S.C. § 12291(a)(16).

INDEX

References are to Pages